America's
TEST KITCHEN

ALSO BY THE EDITORS AT AMERICA'S TEST KITCHEN

The America's Test Kitchen Family Cookbook
The Best of America's Test Kitchen 2007

THE BEST RECIPE SERIES:
The Best 30-Minute Recipe
The Best Light Recipe
The Cook's Illustrated Guide to Grilling & Barbecue
Best American Side Dishes
The New Best Recipe
Cover & Bake
Steaks, Chops, Roasts, & Ribs
Baking Illustrated
Restaurant Favorites at Home
Perfect Vegetables
Italian Classics
The Best American Classics
The Best Soups & Stews

Cooking at Home with America's Test Kitchen
America's Test Kitchen Live!
Inside America's Test Kitchen
Here in America's Test Kitchen
The America's Test Kitchen Cookbook

To see a full listing of all our books
or to order them, visit us at
http://www.cooksillustrated.com
http://www.americastestkitchen.com
or call 800-611-0759

834
KITCHEN
QUICK TIPS

TECHNIQUES AND SHORTCUTS
FOR THE CURIOUS COOK

BY THE EDITORS OF
COOK'S ILLUSTRATED

ILLUSTRATIONS BY JOHN BURGOYNE

America's Test Kitchen
17 Station Street
Brookline, Massachusetts 02445

Library of Congress Cataloging-in-Publication Data
The Editors of Cook's Illustrated

834 Kitchen Quick Tips
Techniques and Shortcuts for the Curious Cook
1st Edition

ISBN-13: 978-1-933615-10-3
ISBN-10: 1-933615-10-9 (paperback): $16.95 US/$21.50 CAN
I. Cooking. I. Title
2006

Manufactured in the United States of America

10 9 8 7 6 5 4 3 2 1

Distributed by America's Test Kitchen,
17 Station Street, Brookline, Massachusetts 02445

EXECUTIVE EDITOR: Jack Bishop
ASSISTANT EDITOR: Elizabeth Wray Emery
ART DIRECTOR: Carolynn DeCillo
DESIGNER: Joanna Detz
ILLUSTRATOR: John Burgoyne
SENIOR PRODUCTION MANAGER: Jessica Lindheimer Quirk
COPYEDITOR: Cheryl Redmond
PROOFREADER: Jayne Yaffe Kemp
INDEXER: Judith Kip

Contents

Introduction

What is a quick tip? For the editors of *Cook's Illustrated*, it's an easier way of performing a kitchen task and it either saves time or money or improves the quality of the outcome. The tip may call for an odd appliance such as a hair dryer (for smoothing chocolate frosting), a surprising ingredient such as miniature marshmallows (placed on the ends of toothpicks to hold plastic wrap above a frosted cake), or a common kitchen tool such as an egg slicer, which can be used to slice mushrooms.

These tips are the best picks from thousands of techniques and shortcuts submitted by our readers over the past eleven years. You will find practical tricks for peeling tomatoes, mincing garlic, and organizing your pantry along with truly original ideas for getting the lumps out of polenta (use an immersion blender), knowing when your steamer is out of water (add marbles to the bottom of the pot), and toasting pine nuts without burning them (use a popcorn popper).

You will also find two of my favorite tips: use a coffeemaker to melt chocolate and store natural peanut butter upside down so the oil doesn't separate and float to the top.

If you like this book or have a quick tip of your own, please visit our website at www.cooksillustrated.com. Here you can submit a tip, subscribe to the magazine, or ask a question on our bulletin board.

All the best,
Christopher Kimball
FOUNDER AND EDITOR
Cook's Illustrated and *Cook's Country*
HOST, *America's Test Kitchen*

Welcome to America's Test Kitchen

This book has been tested, written, and edited by the folks at America's Test Kitchen, a very real 2,500-square-foot kitchen located just outside of Boston. It is the home of *Cook's Illustrated* magazine and *Cook's Country* magazine and is the Monday through Friday destination for more than two dozen test cooks, editors, food scientists, tasters, and cookware specialists. Our mission is to test recipes over and over again until we understand how and why they work and until we arrive at the "best" version.

We start the process of testing a recipe with a complete lack of conviction, which means that we accept no claim, no theory, no technique, and no recipe at face value. We simply assemble as many variations as possible, test a half dozen of the most promising, and taste the results blind. We then construct our own hybrid recipe and continue to test it, varying ingredients, techniques, and cooking times until we reach a consensus. The result, we hope, is the best version of a particular recipe, but we realize that only you can be the final judge of our success (or failure). As we like to say in the test kitchen, "We make the mistakes, so you don't have to." All of this would not be possible without a belief that good cooking, much like good music, is indeed based on a foundation of objective technique. Some people like spicy foods and others don't, but there is a right way to sauté, there is a best way to cook a pot roast, and there are measurable scientific principles involved in producing perfectly beaten, stable egg whites. This is our ultimate goal: to investigate the fundamental principles of cooking so that you become a better cook. It is as simple as that.

You can watch us work (in our actual test kitchen) by tuning in to America's Test Kitchen (www.americastestkitchen.com) on public television or by subscribing to *Cook's Illustrated* magazine (www.cooksillustrated.com) or to *Cook's Country* magazine (www.cookscountry.com), which are each published every other month. We welcome you into our kitchen, where you can stand by our side as we test our way to the "best" recipes in America.

Almond Paste | SOFTENING

Almond paste is expensive and seldom used, which means
that leftovers often sit around and harden. When faced with
hard-as-a-rock almond paste, try this softening method.

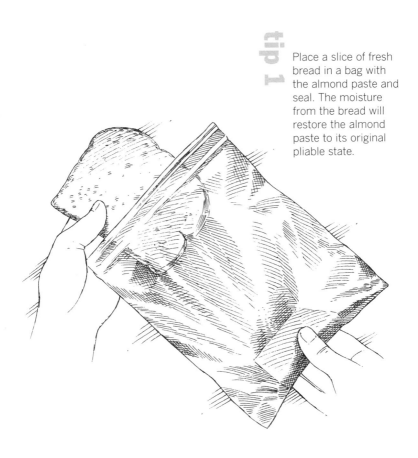

tip 1

Place a slice of fresh
bread in a bag with
the almond paste and
seal. The moisture
from the bread will
restore the almond
paste to its original
pliable state.

Aluminum Foil | MAKING EXTRA-WIDE SHEETS

When you need to cover an especially large item with foil, follow this procedure to fashion a double-width sheet.

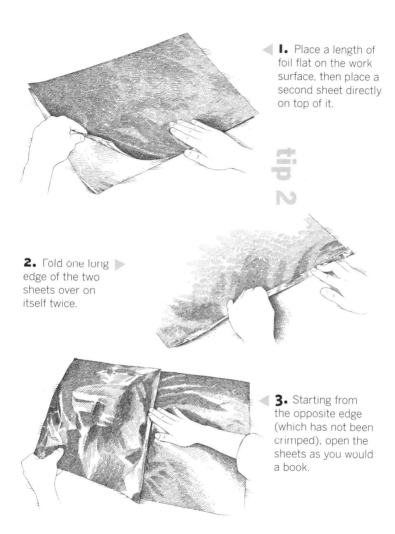

1. Place a length of foil flat on the work surface, then place a second sheet directly on top of it.

2. Fold one long edge of the two sheets over on itself twice.

3. Starting from the opposite edge (which has not been crimped), open the sheets as you would a book.

Aluminum Foil | TAMING WILD SHEETS

Sheets of aluminum foil sometimes seem to have minds of their own, crinkling and folding in every direction but the one you want. Here's a way to tame a wild sheet of foil.

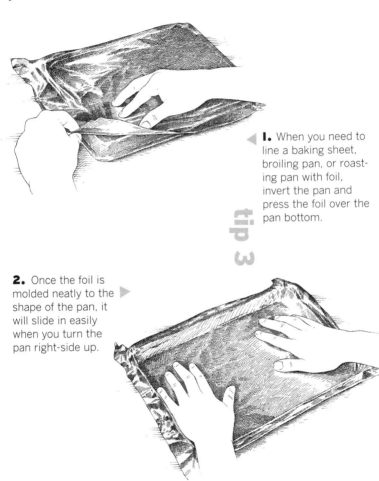

1. When you need to line a baking sheet, broiling pan, or roasting pan with foil, invert the pan and press the foil over the pan bottom.

2. Once the foil is molded neatly to the shape of the pan, it will slide in easily when you turn the pan right-side up.

tip 3

Anchovies | MINCING

Anchovies often stick to the side of a chef's knife, making it hard to cut them into small bits. Here are two better ways to mince anchovies.

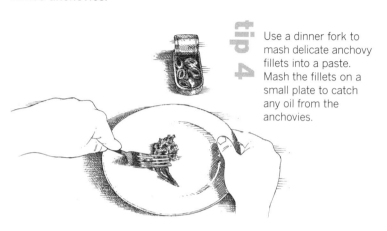

tip 4

Use a dinner fork to mash delicate anchovy fillets into a paste. Mash the fillets on a small plate to catch any oil from the anchovies.

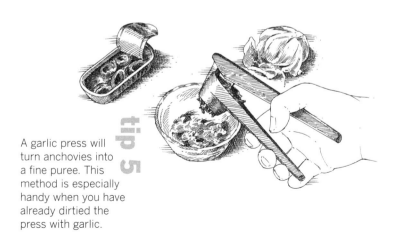

tip 5

A garlic press will turn anchovies into a fine puree. This method is especially handy when you have already dirtied the press with garlic.

Apples | BAKING

Many apples lose their shape when baked. Among common varieties, we find that Golden Delicious apples bake up best. Other good choices include Baldwin, Cortland, Ida Red, and Northern Spy.

I. To allow steam to escape and to keep the apples from bursting in the oven, remove a strip of skin around each apple's stem with a vegetable peeler. Leave the rest of the skin on the apple. We find that the skin helps the apple retain its shape in the oven.

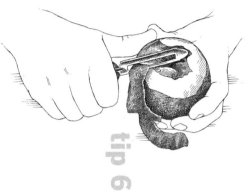

tip 6

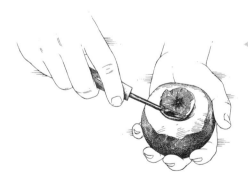

2. Removing the inedible core gives you a chance to stuff a baked apple with brown sugar, nuts, or raisins. The easiest way to core a whole apple is with a melon baller. Just be careful not to puncture the blossom end or the filling may leak out from the bottom of the apple.

Apples and Pears | EASY CORING

Many cooks like to use fresh-picked pears or apples in crisps, cakes, and the like. Coring the fruit can be accomplished quickly and easily with kitchen tools commonly found in the utensil drawer.

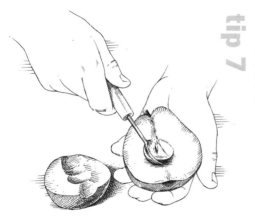

A melon baller is just the right size and shape to carve out the core cleanly and easily.

Alternatively, a sturdy rounded metal ½ teaspoon measure will core just as well.

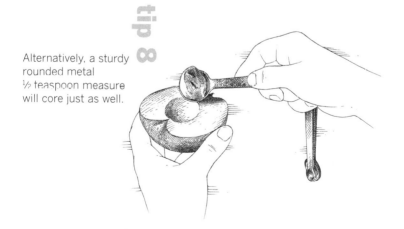

Aprons | APRON SUBSTITUTE

Holiday baking sprees are lots of fun but can leave your clothes streaked with flour, butter, and chocolate.

tip 9

Protect your clothing with the homey equivalent of a professional chef's jacket: Wear a large old shirt to get extra coverage (more than an apron provides). It's smart to roll up the sleeves if they are baggy.

Artichokes | STEAMING

Whole, trimmed artichokes should remain upright when steamed so that the leaves on one side don't cook faster than the leaves on the other side. And it is imperative that the artichokes don't tip over. Here's an easy way to steady artichokes as they steam.

tip 10

Cut very thick slices (about 1½ inches) from an onion and remove the outer three or four rings from each slice. Set the onion rings on the bottom of the pan, and place one artichoke on each ring. In addition to steadying the artichoke, the onion lifts the stem end off the bottom of the pot and keeps it from overcooking. You can use the band from a canning jar lid in the same fashion.

8

Asparagus | TRIMMING THE TOUGH ENDS

The tough, woody part of the stem will break off in just the right place—without cutting—if you hold the spear the right way.

tip 11

With one hand, hold the asparagus about halfway down the spear; with the thumb and index finger of the other hand, hold the spear about an inch up from the bottom. Bend the spear until it snaps.

Avocados | TESTING FOR RIPENESS

We find that Hass avocados (the variety with dark, pebbly skin) are creamier and more flavorful than large, smooth-skinned varieties. Squeeze the avocado to judge ripeness. The flesh should yield to moderate pressure.

A soft avocado is sometimes bruised rather than truly ripe. To be sure, flick the small stem of the avocado. If it comes off easily and you can see green underneath it, the avocado is ripe. If the stem does not come off or if you see brown underneath it, the avocado is not ripe.

tip 12

Avocados | PITTING

Digging out the pit with a spoon can mar the flesh and is generally a messy proposition. This method solves the problem.

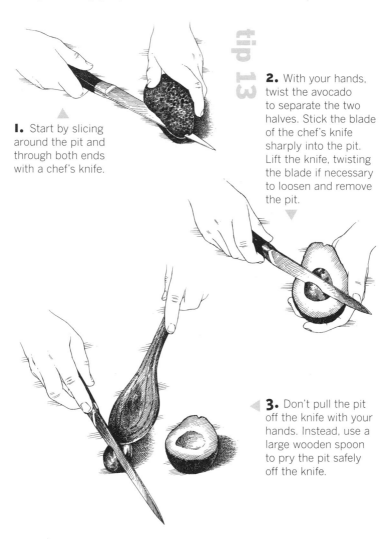

tip 13

I. Start by slicing around the pit and through both ends with a chef's knife.

2. With your hands, twist the avocado to separate the two halves. Stick the blade of the chef's knife sharply into the pit. Lift the knife, twisting the blade if necessary to loosen and remove the pit.

3. Don't pull the pit off the knife with your hands. Instead, use a large wooden spoon to pry the pit safely off the knife.

Avocados | SLICING

A

Once an avocado has been pitted, you may want to remove neat slices, especially for salads.

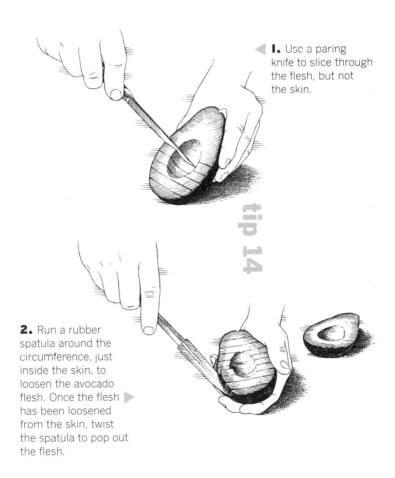

1. Use a paring knife to slice through the flesh, but not the skin.

2. Run a rubber spatula around the circumference, just inside the skin, to loosen the avocado flesh. Once the flesh has been loosened from the skin, twist the spatula to pop out the flesh.

Bacon | BETTER OVEN-FRIED BACON

Here's a way to add flavor to oven-fried bacon.

For another flavor dimension, make maple-glazed bacon. When the bacon has reached a nice golden brown shade and is almost done, pour off most of the grease and drizzle maple syrup over each strip. Return the tray to the oven and continue cooking for 2 to 3 minutes, or until the maple syrup begins to bubble.

Bacon | SEPARATING PIECES

There's an easy way to separate strips of bacon stuck together in a shrink-wrapped package.

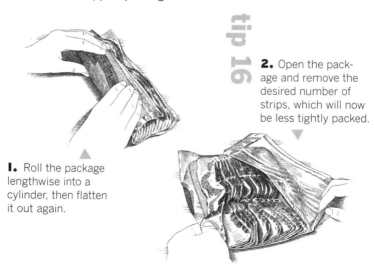

2. Open the package and remove the desired number of strips, which will now be less tightly packed.

I. Roll the package lengthwise into a cylinder, then flatten it out again.

Bacon | STORING

Many people eat bacon less often than they used to and in smaller amounts, and it can be difficult to use up a pound, once opened, before it becomes rancid. Freezing is the best way to preserve bacon, but if frozen in the original package it's impossible to later remove just a few slices at a time.

To solve this dilemma, roll up the bacon in tight cylinders, each with two to four slices of bacon. Place the cylinders in a zipper-lock bag and place the bag flat in the freezer. (Once the slices are frozen, the bag can be stored as you like.) When bacon is needed, simply pull out the desired number of slices and defrost.

tip 17

Bacon Drippings | SAVING FOR ANOTHER USE

Bacon grease lends a prized flavor to many dishes, especially Southern ones. Instead of keeping a bulky jar in the refrigerator, we like to store bacon drippings in the freezer.

1. Collect the drippings in a bowl and melt them in the microwave. Let the solids settle at the bottom of the bowl. Pour the fat through a fine-mesh sieve, keeping the solids in the bowl. (The solids can burn when the fat is reheated and are best discarded.)

2. Pour the strained fat into an ice cube tray and freeze. When frozen, pop out the cubes and transfer them to a zipper-lock bag to prevent freezer burn. Each cube will be approximately 1 heaping tablespoon.

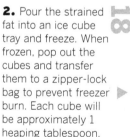

tip 18

Bacon Grease | REMOVAL

Here are a couple of ways to make cleanup easier after frying (or oven frying) bacon, and avoid making your sink and wash-cloth greasy.

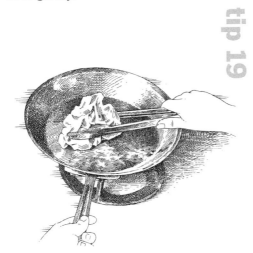

After pouring off the bacon grease, crumple up a wad of paper towels, grab it with tongs, and use it to swab the extra grease from the pan. You might need a couple of wads depending on how much grease is in the pan.

If oven-frying bacon, line the baking sheet with wide foil (18 inches), covering the entire surface, including the sides. Cook and drain the bacon as the recipe instructs, and allow the baking sheet and any remaining grease to cool completely. Cleanup is easy: Just roll up the soiled foil and discard.

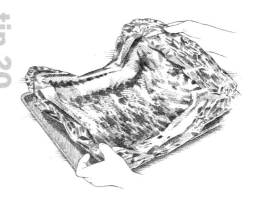

Bagels | SHAPING A STIFF DOUGH INTO RINGS

It can be difficult to shape stiff dough, especially for bagels, into rings. Rather than trying to roll the dough into ropes and attach the ends (which may not stick together), try this method.

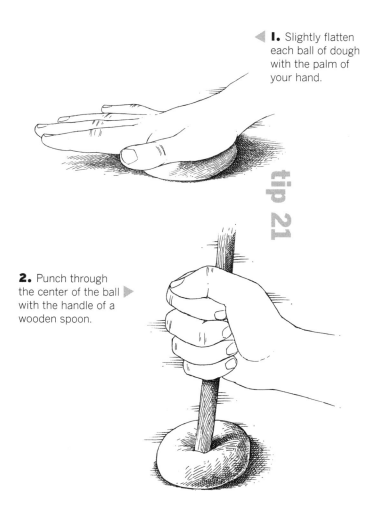

1. Slightly flatten each ball of dough with the palm of your hand.

2. Punch through the center of the ball with the handle of a wooden spoon.

3. Holding the spoon by the handle, twirl it gently to enlarge the dough ring to the ▷ desired size.

4. Stretch the hole with your fingers as you place the dough ring on a baking sheet.

Bakeware | KEEPING TRACK OF SIZE

Manufacturers' indications of size on baking pans are often either illegible or nonexistent, leaving the user to guess if it's the right one.

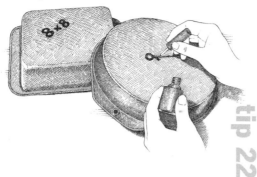

Use ovensafe metal paint (available at hardware stores) to mark pan bottoms, noting dimensions or capacity.

tip 22

Baking | NO MORE GREASY HANDS

Using shortening or butter to grease a pan can be a messy affair. Keep hands clean inside a plastic sandwich bag.

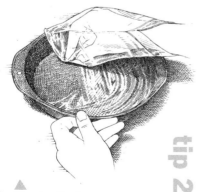

2. When finished, remove the bag by turning it inside out and neatly discarding it. No more messy paper towels!

▼

I. Wearing the bag like a glove, grease the pan.

tip 23

Baking | NEATER DUSTING WITH POWDERED SUGAR

When a small item like a cookie or a piece of cake calls for a dusting with powdered sugar, don't pull out the sifter.

Fill a mesh tea-ball strainer with a quick scoop into the sugar. It is much neater and easier to use than a sifter and won't create a cloud of sugar.

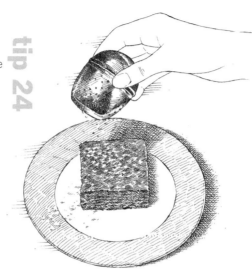

Baking | KEEPING PARCHMENT IN PLACE

Spooning soft cookie dough onto a baking sheet layered with parchment can be a frustrating task, as the parchment has a propensity to curl up and become unruly.

Grab four refrigerator magnets and place one over each corner of the parchment. Make sure to return the magnets to the fridge before baking the cookies.

tip 25

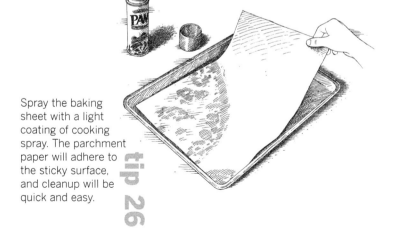

Spray the baking sheet with a light coating of cooking spray. The parchment paper will adhere to the sticky surface, and cleanup will be quick and easy.

tip 26

Baking | CREATING A FLATTER COUNTERTOP

Tiled countertops may look attractive, but they are not especially practical when it comes to baking.

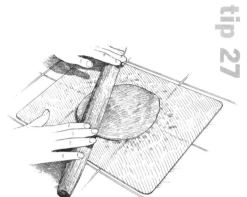

tip 27

To avoid rumpled rolled cookie or pie dough (not to mention a floury mess between the cracks of the tile), place a flexible cutting board over the bumpy tile countertop to create a smoother surface.

Baking | MEASURING AHEAD OF TIME

During the holidays, many bakers find themselves making multiple batches of cookies, cakes, and quick breads. Here's a way to save some time during a baking marathon.

tip 28

Measure out and label the ingredients for each recipe ahead of time, storing the dry ingredients in zipper-lock bags on the counter and wet ingredients in plastic containers in the refrigerator. When it's time to bake, everything is ready to be mixed.

Baking | KEEPING TRACK OF DRY INGREDIENTS

When a recipe calls for a number of dry ingredients to be added simultaneously (such as baking powder, baking soda, salt, and spices), it's easy to lose track of what's been added to the bowl, especially if you get interrupted.

tip 29

Place the measured ingredients in separate mounds on a sheet of parchment or waxed paper. This way you can see not only what, but also how much, you have measured.

tip 30

Imagine that your mixing bowl is the face of a clock. If you've added 3 cups of flour and encounter a distraction, place a spoon at the 3 o'clock position on the bowl.

tip 31

Alternatively, place a long-handled measuring cup on the counter with the handle pointing at 3 o'clock.

Baking | MEASURING LIQUIDS

Holding a cup may jostle or tilt the liquid and can destroy the accuracy of the measurements that might make all the difference when baking.

tip 32

To avoid possible mis-measurements, pour liquids into clear measuring cups set on the counter and lean down to read them at eye level.

Baking | MESS-FREE BAKER'S COATING

Accomplished and novice bakers alike know that the traditional method of greasing and flouring cake pans can be a bit of a nuisance. Save yourself some work by using this all-in-one baker's coating.

Mix 2 parts shortening with 1 part flour and brush this paste lightly onto the cake pans. Store any remaining mixture at room temperature in a plastic resealable container, so you'll have the coating on hand when the need arises.

tip 33

Baking Powder | TESTING FOR FRESHNESS

Baking powder will lose its leavening ability with time. If the can is not marked with an expiration date, we suggest writing the date the can was opened on a piece of masking tape. Affix the tape to the bottom of the can. After six months, baking powder will begin to weaken, and after a year it should be discarded. If you have any doubts about the strength of your baking powder, use this test.

Mix 2 teaspoons baking powder with 1 cup hot tap water. If there's an immediate reaction of fizzing and foaming (right), the baking powder can be used. If the reaction is at all delayed or weak (left), throw the baking powder away and buy a fresh can.

tip 34

Bananas | SAVING OVERRIPE FRUIT FOR BREAD

Rather than throwing away one or two overripe bananas, save them until you have enough fruit to make banana bread.

Place overripe bananas in a zipper-lock bag and freeze them. As necessary, add more bananas to the bag. When you are ready to make bread, thaw the bananas on the counter until softened.

tip 35

Barbecue Sauce | APPLYING WITH A SQUEEZE BOTTLE

Instead of brushing barbecue sauce onto foods and dirtying both the brush and bowl, recycle a pull-top water bottle by filling it with sauce and keeping it in the refrigerator until needed.

tip 36

When the chicken, pork chop, or other meat is almost done, squirt on a little sauce, taking care not to let the bottle touch the food. Wipe the bottle clean and store it in the refrigerator until needed again.

Basil | RELEASING FLAVORFUL OILS

It's easy to make pesto in a food processor or blender, but the fast grinding action of the blades doesn't create the richest-tasting sauce. For the fullest flavor in pesto and other sauces, we find it best to bruise basil leaves before placing them in a food processor or blender. This trick also works with other soft herbs, especially mint and cilantro.

Place the basil leaves in a zipper-lock bag and bruise with a meat pounder or rolling pin.

tip 37

Beans | SORTING DRIED BEANS WITH EASE

It is important to rinse and pick over dried beans to remove any stones or debris before cooking.

tip 38

To make the task easier, sort dried beans on a large white plate or on a white, rimmed cutting board. The neutral background makes any unwanted matter a cinch to spot and discard.

Bean Sprouts | KEEPING CRISP AND FRESH

Bean sprouts are prized for their crunch. To keep them crisp, try this tip, which also works with peeled jícama slices.

Submerge the sprouts in a container of cold water, then refrigerate the container. The sprouts will stay crisp for up to 5 days.

tip 39

Beef | PREPARING MEAT FOR KEBABS

Top blade and top sirloin are the best cuts for kebabs. Butterflying the cubes before marinating creates more surface area so the marinade can penetrate the meat in a shorter amount of time, resulting in faster, more flavorful kebabs. This method also produces a less chewy kebab that's easier to eat.

tip 40

Cut the meat into large cubes. Cut each cube almost through at the center, making sure to leave the meat attached on one side. The meat is ready to be marinated.

Beef | TYING UP A ROAST

In the oven, the outer layer of meat often pulls away from the rib-eye muscle and overcooks.

To prevent this problem, tie the roast at both ends, running the kitchen twine parallel to the bone.

tip 41

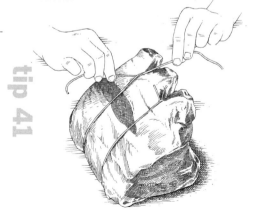

Beef | CHECKING THE INTERNAL TEMPERATURE

Most instant-read thermometers work best when the tip is stuck at least an inch deep into foods. On a thin steak, the tip can go right through the meat if inserted from the top. Use this method for steaks as well as chops.

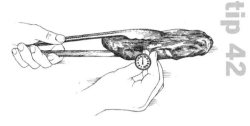

tip 42

For the most accurate reading, hold the steak with a pair of tongs and slide the tip of the thermometer through the side of the steak. Make sure that the shaft is embedded in the meat and not touching any bone.

Beef | GRILLING T-BONE STEAKS EVENLY

T-bone and porterhouse steaks contain portions of the delicate, buttery tenderloin as well as some of the chewier, more flavorful strip, making them especially enjoyable to eat but somewhat challenging to cook. A two-level fire (see tip 409, page 275), with more coals banked to one side than the other, helps even out the rate at which these two muscles cook.

tip 43

When grilling T-bone or porterhouse steaks, keep the tenderloin (the smaller portion to the left of the bone) over the cooler part of the fire. The strip (the larger portion to the right of the bone) should be placed over the hotter part of the fire.

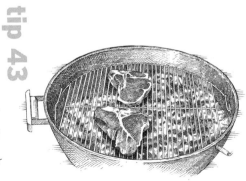

Beef | SLICING T-BONE STEAKS

A thick T-bone or porterhouse steak weighs between 1$\frac{1}{2}$ and 2 pounds, too much for a single serving. Here's how to serve one steak to two people. Once cooked, let the steak rest for 5 minutes so the juices can redistribute themselves evenly throughout the meat.

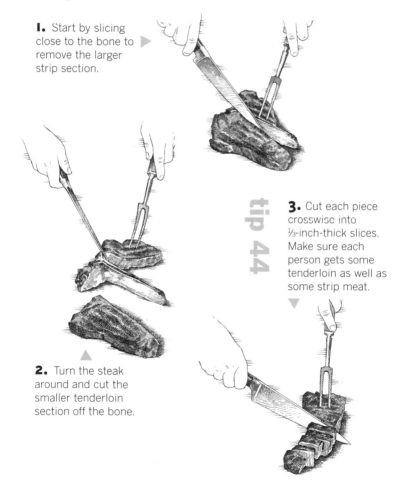

1. Start by slicing close to the bone to remove the larger strip section.

tip 44

3. Cut each piece crosswise into $\frac{1}{3}$-inch-thick slices. Make sure each person gets some tenderloin as well as some strip meat.

2. Turn the steak around and cut the smaller tenderloin section off the bone.

Beef | PREPARING PHILLY STEAK SANDWICH MEAT

It's not necessary to own a meat slicer to make a good Philly steak sandwich. You can cut paper-thin pieces of steak, ready to be thrown onto a hot, oiled griddle, by starting with partially frozen sirloin, blade, or round steaks and using your food processor.

1. Trim the fat from the steaks and cut into 1-inch-wide strips. Freeze the meat until the exterior hardens but the interior remains soft and yields to gentle pressure, 25 to 50 minutes.

2. Once the meat has been partially frozen, place the strips in the feed tube ▶ of a food processor fitted with the slicing disk. Turn on the food processor, and use the plunger to push the meat down into the blade.

tip 45

3. The food processor will shave the meat into small, paper-thin pieces.

Beef | SLICING FLANK STEAK FOR STIR-FRIES

Flank steak is our favorite cut for stir-fries. It has the right balance of tenderness (with some chew) and beef flavor. It must be sliced as thin as possible, so a sharp knife is essential. Freezing the meat for 30 to 60 minutes also helps.

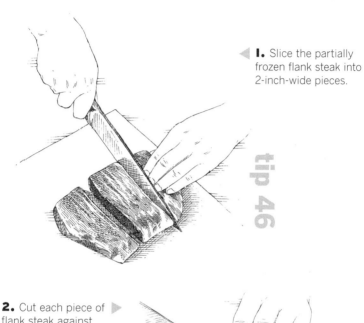

I. Slice the partially frozen flank steak into 2-inch-wide pieces.

tip 46

2. Cut each piece of flank steak against the grain into very thin slices.

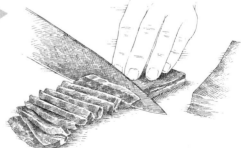

Beef | TYING TENDERLOIN TO ENSURE EVEN COOKING

The tenderloin narrows at one end, called the tip. If roasted or grilled as is, this end will be overcooked by the time the thicker end is done.

1. To prevent over-cooking, fold the last 6 inches of the thin tip end under the roast.

tip 47

2. Tie 12-inch lengths of kitchen twine crosswise along the length of the roast, spacing the ties about 1½ inches apart.

Beef | CUTTING THE SILVER SKIN FROM TENDERLOIN

The tenderloin is covered with a thin, shiny membrane called the silver skin, which can contract in the oven and cause the roast to bow. Rather than trying to peel off this very thin membrane, use this technique to keep it from bowing the meat.

tip 48

Slide a knife under the silver skin and flick the blade upward to cut through the membrane. Do this at five or six spots along the length of the roast.

Beets | REMOVING STAINS

When cut, beets stain everything they touch, including hands and cutting boards.

To help remove these stains, sprinkle the stained area with salt, rinse, and then scrub with soap. The salt crystals help lift the beet juices away.

tip 49

Berries | MIXING GENTLY

When making a fresh fruit salad or tart, it's nearly impossible to avoid crushing fresh berries in a mixing bowl, and it's even more difficult to keep them intact when you're trying to coat them with sugar. Try this method instead.

tip 50

Place the berries in a large plastic bag and add the sugar, if using. Hold the bag closed with one hand, and use the other hand to gently jostle the berries to combine them. If using the berries in a tart, simply empty the bag directly into the pastry shell.

Biscotti | QUICK-DRYING ON A RACK

Traditionally, biscotti dough is baked in a log, then cut into slices and baked a second time. These slices must be flipped halfway through the baking time to dry both sides of each slice. Here's how to streamline this method.

Bake the dough in a log as usual and then cut into slices. Place the slices on a wire cooling rack set on a baking sheet and bake again. The rack elevates the slices, allowing air to circulate all around them and drying both sides at once.

Biscuits | SPLITTING FOR SHORTCAKES

It's important to split biscuits evenly when making shortcakes. A knife sometimes tears the biscuits and isn't necessarily the best tool for the job.

When the biscuits have cooled slightly, look for the crack that naturally forms around the circumference of each biscuit. Gently insert your fingers into the crack and split the biscuit in half.

Biscuits | CUTTING WEDGES

There is no re-patting of biscuits when you use the wedge method—an economical and quick way to get biscuits ready for the oven. And there's no need for a biscuit cutter.

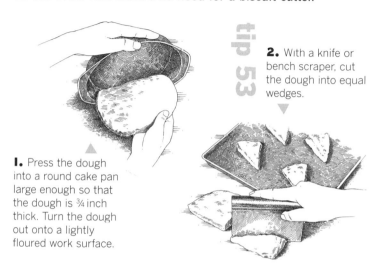

tip 53

2. With a knife or bench scraper, cut the dough into equal wedges.

I. Press the dough into a round cake pan large enough so that the dough is ¾ inch thick. Turn the dough out onto a lightly floured work surface.

Blender | NEATER BLENDING

Oil or melted butter added to dressings or sauces in a whirring blender can splatter back up through the opening in the lid and make a mess.

It's easy to eliminate this problem by placing a small funnel in the opening and pouring the liquid through it slowly and steadily.

tip 54

Blender | CLEANING THE JAR

Washing the blender jar can be a real chore, especially if foods have had time to harden. Get a head start on the cleaning process by following this method.

2. With the top firmly in place, turn the blender on high for 30 seconds. Most of the residue pours right out with the soapy water, and the blender jar need only be rinsed or lightly washed by hand.

I. Fill the dirty blender halfway with hot water and add a couple of drops of liquid dish soap.

tip 55

Blender | CLEANING THE FACE

Nooks, crannies, and crevices on the face of a blender pose a particular cleaning challenge. Here is an idea that makes the chore less cumbersome.

Use a nailbrush to get in between the buttons or around the dials on your blender.

tip 56

Bok Choy | SLICING WHITES AND GREENS

The thick, fleshy white stalks take much longer to cook than the tender, leafy greens. For this reason, you should slice them separately, so the whites can be added to a stir-fry or other dish first.

1. Cut the leafy green portions of the bok choy away from either side of the white stalk.

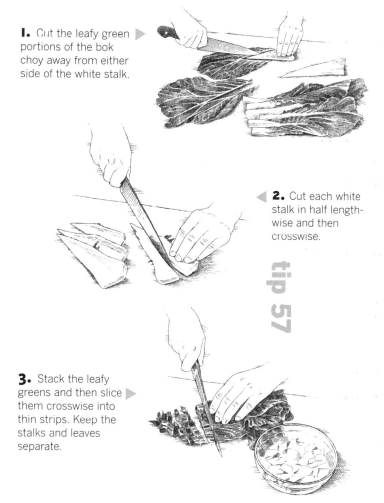

2. Cut each white stalk in half length-wise and then crosswise.

tip 57

3. Stack the leafy greens and then slice them crosswise into thin strips. Keep the stalks and leaves separate.

Bottle Tops | CLEANER SQUEEZE TOPS

Squeeze-bottle tops can get caked with ketchup, mayonnaise, or mustard. Keep yours clean with this simple tip.

tip 58

Wash the tops from empty bottles and store them in a drawer. When the top of a new bottle gets dirty, unscrew it, replace it with a clean one, and throw the dirty top into the dishwasher.

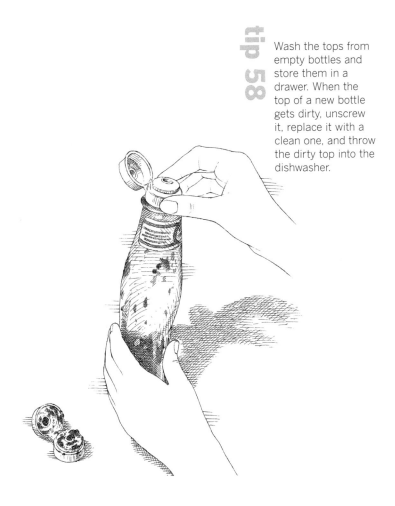

Bread | EASIER SLICING

Slicing a loaf of rustic bread that's been freshly heated in the oven can be a hot and messy proposition: It's hard to get a hold on the bread, and the crumbs tend to spray everywhere.

B

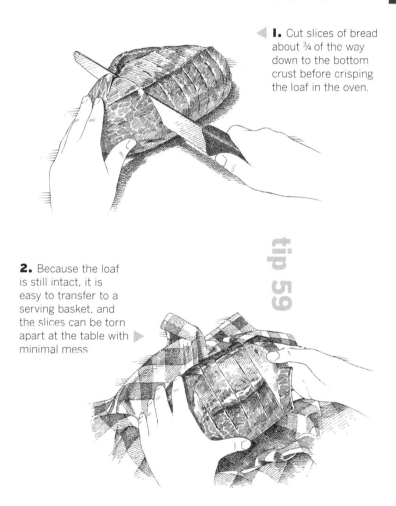

1. Cut slices of bread about ¾ of the way down to the bottom crust before crisping the loaf in the oven.

2. Because the loaf is still intact, it is easy to transfer to a serving basket, and the slices can be torn apart at the table with minimal mess.

tip 59

Bread | PERFECT SLICES FROM CRUSTY LOAVES

Artisan breads have heavy crusts that can be difficult to slice neatly. Often the bread knife fails to cut all the way through the thick bottom crust. The result is that you must yank the slice free from the loaf, possibly tearing it in the process. Here's how to slice a crusty loaf neatly.

tip 60

Turn the loaf on its side and cut through the top and bottom crust simultaneously. The crust on the side of the bread, which is now facing down, is often thinner and easier to slice.

Bread | KEEPING SLICES FRESH

The twist ties that come with loaves of sandwich bread have an uncanny ability to disappear. Don't let your bread grow stale because of a lost tie.

Twist the bread bag shut and fold the excess back on itself, over the remaining bread. This works best after a few slices have been eaten.

tip 61

Bread | FRESHENING STALE LOAVES AND SLICES

We all know that bread goes stale very quickly. Here are two tricks for reviving slightly stale loaves and slices. Neither trick will work with rock-hard, days-old bread.

B

tip 62

Individual slices of stale bread can be freshened on a splatter screen held over a pan of simmering water. The rising steam will soften the bread in a minute or two.

tip 63

Place a stale loaf of bread inside a brown paper bag, seal the bag, and lightly moisten the outside of the bag with some water. Place the bag on a baking sheet in a 350-degree oven for 5 minutes. When you remove the loaf, you will find that it is warm and soft.

Bread | IMPROVISED LOAF PANS

If you own just one loaf pan but need to make two loaves at the same time, try this trick for improvising a second, or even third, pan.

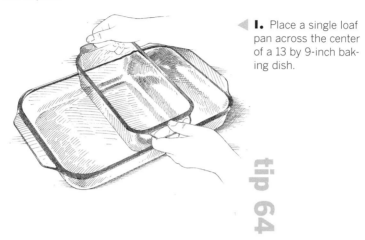

1. Place a single loaf pan across the center of a 13 by 9-inch baking dish.

2. Position one portion of shaped dough on either side of the loaf pan and bake. (Fill the loaf pan with a third portion of dough to bake three loaves.)

tip 64

Bread | JUDGING WHEN DOUGH HAS ENOUGH FLOUR

Many bakers add too much flour to bread dough, which results in dry loaves. Here's an easy test to see if your bread has enough flour.

tip 65

Squeeze the dough gently with your entire hand. Even with especially soft, sticky doughs, your hand will pull away cleanly once the dough has enough flour.

Bread | TRACKING DOUGH RISE

Not every baker owns a dough-rising bucket with markings for tracking the rise of the dough, but any baker with a large, clear container can improvise one with this trick.

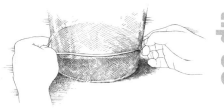

tip 66

2. This reference will make it easy to judge when the dough has doubled in volume.

▼

▲

I. After adding the dough to the container, mark its height by placing a rubber band around the container.

Bread | COVERING THE DOUGH

Once the dough is ready to rise, most recipes suggest putting it into a deep bowl and covering the bowl with a damp kitchen towel. We find that the towel doesn't protect the dough from drafts.

Instead, tightly seal the bowl with plastic wrap, which keeps out drafts and traps moisture so the dough remains supple.

Bread | SPEEDY DOUGH RISING

Making bread is a time-consuming project, and waiting for the dough to rise only adds to the lengthy process. Use a microwavable neck wrap to speed up the process. When wrapped around a bowl of dough, it provides just enough extra heat to cut the rising time in half.

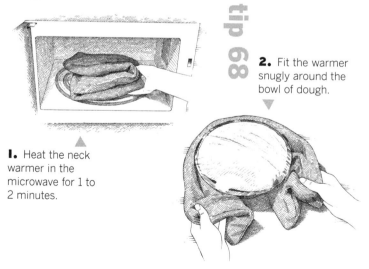

2. Fit the warmer snugly around the bowl of dough.

1. Heat the neck warmer in the microwave for 1 to 2 minutes.

Bread | IMPROVISED PROOFING BOX

Getting bread to rise in a dry climate can be a challenge.

Use your dishwasher to create a humid, draft-free environment in which bread dough can rise. Turn on the dishwasher for about 4 minutes, or long enough for some warm water to fill the bottom. Place the dough to be proofed in a loaf pan or bowl, cover it with plastic wrap, set it on the bottom rack of the dishwasher, and close the door. Make sure to turn off the dishwasher; otherwise the water will start to flow again once you close the door.

tip 69

Bread | FOOLPROOF PROOF BOX

When a chilly or drafty house makes it hard to proof dough for bread or pizza, try one of these clever tricks.

1. Place a coffee mug filled with ½ cup water in the microwave. Run the microwave on high power for about 1 minute.

2. Open the microwave, push the cup to a back corner, and set the dough inside. Close the door and let the dough rise. (The warmed mug will keep the interior between 80 and 90 degrees for up to 90 minutes.) Remove the dough once it has doubled in size or reached the desired volume in your recipe.

tip 70

tip 71

Place the dough in a lightly oiled food storage container, preferably shallow and with a flat bottom, and then float the container in a large, covered stockpot almost full of warm water (90 to 100 degrees).

Bread | MEASURING BREAD AND PASTRY DOUGHS

Recipes often call for bread dough to be shaped to a specific length or pastry to be rolled to a specific size. Rather than fumbling in drawers with messy hands to find a ruler each time, put this tip to work.

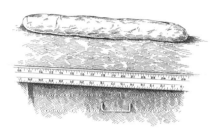

Affix a yardstick to the front of a countertop. It's not obtrusive, and it's always there when you need it. To measure dough, simply line up the ends with markings on the ruler and do the math.

Bread | DRAFT-FREE RISING IN A LOAF PAN

Some doughs should rise right in a loaf pan just before baking. (This is called the second rise.) If your kitchen is drafty, the dough may not rise properly. Here's a defense against a drafty environment.

2. Place this loaf pan into another loaf pan so that the air inside the bag is pushed up, providing room for the dough to expand.

I. After forming the dough and placing it in a loaf pan, slip the pan into an empty plastic bag. Blow air into the bag to inflate it, then seal it securely with a twist tie.

Bread | IMPROMPTU MOLD

Try this trick to keep loaves of bread in their long, narrow shape as they proof without using a mold.

1. Save the cardboard box from a spent roll of parchment paper or extra-wide aluminum foil or plastic wrap. Line the box with a lightly floured kitchen towel and place the shaped loaf inside, seam-side down.

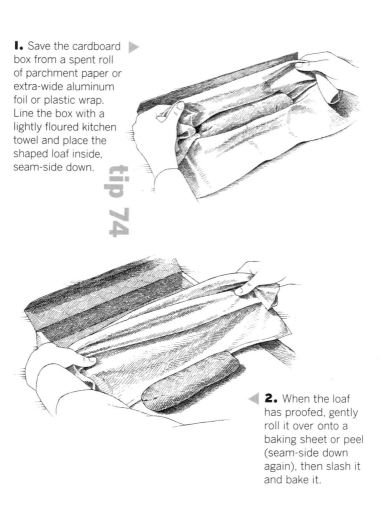

2. When the loaf has proofed, gently roll it over onto a baking sheet or peel (seam-side down again), then slash it and bake it.

Bread | SLASHING A PROOFED LOAF NEATLY

A proofed loaf of bread should be slashed across the top to allow some of the trapped air to escape, but the knife used for this purpose often snags and drags the loaf out of shape.

tip 75

For clean, neat slashes, spray the knife blade lightly with cooking spray before slashing the loaf.

Bread | TAKING THE TEMPERATURE IN A LOAF PAN

Internal temperature is a good way to gauge whether a loaf of bread is done. Don't be tempted to pierce the top crust in the center, which will leave behind a conspicuous hole.

Insert the thermome-ter from the side, just above the edge of the loaf pan, directing it at a downward angle toward the center of the loaf.

tip 76

Bread | QUICK RELEASE FOR QUICK BREADS

Although we use nonstick cooking spray on our loaf pans when making quick breads, we also like to add a layer of parchment for extra assurance.

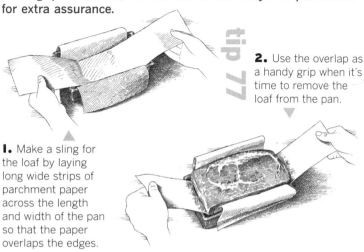

2. Use the overlap as a handy grip when it's time to remove the loaf from the pan.

I. Make a sling for the loaf by laying long wide strips of parchment paper across the length and width of the pan so that the paper overlaps the edges.

Bread Crumbs | MAKING EXTRA

Cooks who plan ahead make more bread crumbs than called for in a recipe and freeze them in a zipper-lock bag. But transferring the crumbs from food processor to bag can be tricky.

Remove the blade from the workbowl, lift the workbowl from its base, and lock the lid in place. Next, invert the whole unit to funnel the crumbs through the feed tube into the bag.

Bread Crumbs |
SLICING OFF THE TOUGH BOTTOM CRUST

Homemade bread crumbs are far superior to commercial dry crumbs. To make your own crumbs, simply grind cubes of stale bread in a food processor until coarsely chopped. There's one hitch: Many loaves of bread have a thick bottom crust that won't break down in a food processor.

To prevent this problem, simply slice off and discard the bottom crust before cutting the bread into large cubes that will fit in the food processor.

tip 79

Breakfast | PERFECT FRIED EGGS

Nothing is worse than cooking a perfect fried egg only to tear it while transferring the egg from the skillet to a plate, but you can easily avoid this mishap.

Apply cooking spray to the spatula, which allows you to gently slide the cooked eggs onto the plate.

tip 80

Breakfast | NEATER EGG SANDWICHES

Fried-egg sandwiches always seem to taste better when made with English muffins or bagels, but it can be tricky to fry a round egg of just the right size—one that won't flop messily over the sides of the sandwich. Use large cookie cutters to make round fried eggs that are a perfect fit for English muffins.

I. Butter one or more 2 ½- to 3-inch round cookie cutters. Melt butter in a nonstick skillet, then place the cutters in the skillet, being sure not to scrape the pan's surface. Pour one egg into each cutter and season with salt and pepper. Cover the pan and cook to the desired doneness.

2. Remove both the egg and the cutter with a spatula. If necessary, run a paring knife around the inside of the cutter to loosen the egg.

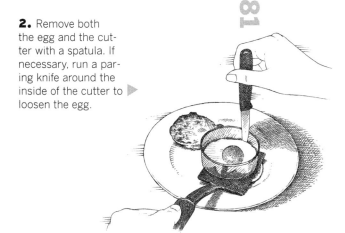

tip 81

Breakfast | "INSTANT" OATMEAL

A quick bowl of hot oatmeal can start the day on a warm note. But those gluey instant packets just don't deliver. Try this clever idea to have the best of both worlds: instant homemade oatmeal.

B

I. Measure the dry 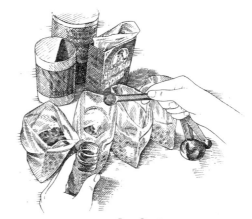 ingredients for one serving of oatmeal into a sandwich-size zipper-lock bag; we like ½ cup quick-cooking (or 1-minute) oats, ¼ teaspoon cinnamon, 1 tablespoon brown sugar, a pinch of salt, and 1 tablespoon dried fruit (raisins, cranberries, or chop-ped apricots, figs, or apples are all good choices). Repeat with as many bags as you like.

tip 82

2. When it's time for breakfast, empty the contents of a bag into a bowl and add ⅔ cup boiling water. Stir, cover with plastic wrap, and let sit for 5 minutes. Uncover and stir again, and your "instant" oatmeal is ready.

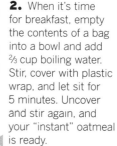

Breakfast | NEATER FRENCH TOAST

No one likes to waste French toast batter by dripping it all over the stovetop while transferring soaked slices of bread from bowl to skillet. Try this clever way to soak up each and every drop.

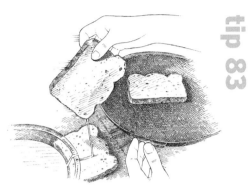

tip 83

Simply place one piece of plain bread between the bowl and the skillet. Once all of the other slices have been added to the skillet, the catch-all slice can be used for the last piece of French toast.

Breakfast | SPEEDY FRENCH TOAST

French toast is usually reserved for weekend mornings because it takes some time to coat each bread slice in a mixture of milk and eggs before frying. Instead of using a shallow dish for dipping bread slices one at a time and then having to flip them, try this timesaver.

tip 84

Put the dipping mixture into a zipper-lock bag and add bread slices. This allows the bread to soak up the liquid with little effort. Even better, all of the pieces are ready for the hot griddle at the same time.

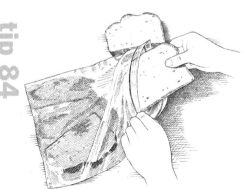

Breakfast | REHEATING FRENCH TOAST

After a big weekend breakfast, there are inevitably a few uneaten pancakes or slices of French toast. No need to throw out leftovers—try this method for reheating them.

1. Layer parchment ▶ paper between the cooked French toast slices or pancakes, wrap portions in plastic wrap and then in foil, and store in the freezer.

tip 85

2. To reheat, unwrap and heat the French toast or pancakes for 10 to 12 minutes on a baking sheet in a 350-degree oven and serve with hot maple syrup. The breakfast treats can also be reheated in a toaster oven.

Breakfast | KEEPING WAFFLES WARM

Many cooks pull their waffle irons out of storage to make holiday breakfasts for company. But most machines can bake only four waffles at a time, and some smaller models make only one at a time. Here's what to do when you're preparing waffles for a crowd.

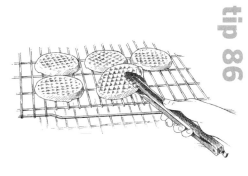

tip 86

Keep waffles warm by placing them in a single layer on an oven rack in a preheated 250-degree oven. The waffles stay crisp, and everyone can be served at the same time. This works much better than stacking waffles on a heated plate or placing them on a baking sheet where they can steam and become soggy.

Breakfast | QUICKER CUTTING

Try this easy technique the next time there are young children waiting impatiently for breakfast.

tip 87

Use a pizza cutter to cut French toast, pancakes, or waffles neatly and quickly into bite-sized pieces.

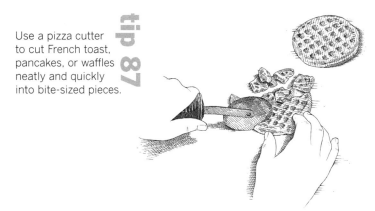

Brining |
IMPROVISING A SECURE COVER
FOR BRINING BUCKETS

It's always a good idea to cover any large container filled with liquid—be it sauce, soup, or a brining solution—to prevent spills. But sometimes the container cover is missing and plastic wrap will not stay in place no matter how hard you press on it. To provide an extra measure of security against spills and splashes, try this trick as a way to secure plastic wrap over the mouths of containers.

I. Tear off a piece of plastic wrap long enough to fit around the mouth of the container, plus about 12 inches. Roll the sheet of plastic lengthwise into a rope. Pull on both ends to make it taut.

tip 88

2. Cover the mouth of the container with a second sheet of plastic wrap, coil the plastic wrap rope tightly around the sheet of plastic at the top of the container, and secure it by tying the ends into a knot.

Broccoli | TWO WAYS TO REMOVE FLORETS

Some heads of broccoli have closely bunched branches that meet the central stalk at roughly the same point. On other heads, the branches are widely spaced. You should adjust the way you remove florets depending on how a head of broccoli is shaped.

Lay a head of broccoli with closely bunched branches on its side, and use a chef's knife to cut off the florets about ½ inch below their heads.

I. When working with ▶ a head of broccoli with widely spaced branches, stand the broccoli upside down and use a chef's knife to trim off the florets close to their heads.

◀ **2.** Break the large florets into bite-sized pieces, snapping them apart where individual clusters meet.

Broth | DEFATTING CANNED BROTH

If you try to skim the blob of fat from canned broth with a spoon, it's likely to break into little pieces, making it difficult to remove. This simple, quick method offers foolproof skimming.

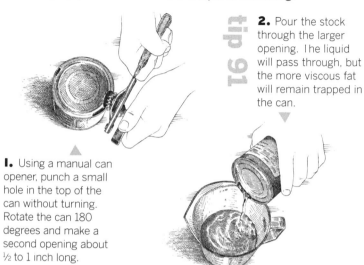

tip 91

2. Pour the stock through the larger opening. The liquid will pass through, but the more viscous fat will remain trapped in the can.

1. Using a manual can opener, punch a small hole in the top of the can without turning. Rotate the can 180 degrees and make a second opening about ½ to 1 inch long.

Brown Sugar | MEASURING

Here's how to measure brown sugar neatly and accurately.

tip 92

Use two nested measuring cups to pack brown sugar. The flat bottom of the smaller cup also helps to obliterate any hard lumps that may have developed in the bag. Fill the correct dry measure with the sugar and use the next smallest cup to pack it down.

Brown Sugar | SOFTENING

There's nothing worse than hardened brown sugar, which is impossible to measure and can't be incorporated into batters. Here's how to bring back its original texture.

tip 93

Place a cup or so of brown sugar in a glass pie plate or bowl, cover with a small piece of waxed paper, and then top with a slice of bread to provide a bit of moisture. Loosely cover the pie plate or bowl with plastic wrap and microwave until softened, about 30 seconds.

Brown Sugar | STORING AND MEASURING

Pouring brown sugar out of its narrow box into a measuring cup can be a messy, frustrating chore. This method will not only make measuring easier, but will help the sugar remain moist.

tip 94

Transfer the brown sugar from the box to a large, heavy-duty zipper-lock bag. A measuring cup will fit inside the bag easily and can be loaded up by pressing the sugar into it through the plastic. No pouring, spilling, or sticky hands.

Brownies | CUTTING NEATLY

Neatly cutting brownies can be tricky because half the crumbs end up sticking to the knife, especially if the brownies are really fudgy.

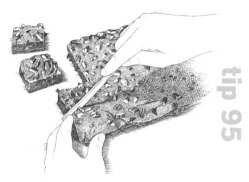

Instead of using a serrated or chef's knife, use a sturdy plastic knife. It glides easily through even the stickiest brownies, picking up no crumbs.

tip 95

Brownies | INDIVIDUAL BROWNIES

Here's a quick way to make easy, no-cut brownies.

Pour the batter into greased muffin tins rather than a baking pan. The treats are perfect for tossing into a lunchbox or for portable snacking. Fill regular muffin tins with brownie batter to a depth of 1 inch, or two-thirds full. Just be sure to adjust the baking time accordingly—one batch of brownies we prepared this way was ready in less than half the normal baking time.

tip 96

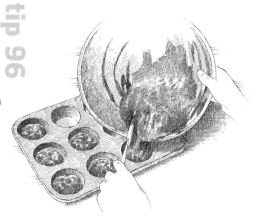

Brownies | EASY REMOVAL FROM PANS

It can be difficult to extract fudgy brownies and bar cookies from baking pans. Parchment paper or aluminum foil helps solves this problem and makes cleanup a breeze.

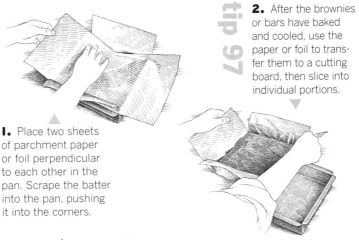

2. After the brownies or bars have baked and cooled, use the paper or foil to transfer them to a cutting board, then slice into individual portions.

tip 97

I. Place two sheets of parchment paper or foil perpendicular to each other in the pan. Scrape the batter into the pan, pushing it into the corners.

Brushes | CLEANING

Basting brushes can be difficult to clean, so they often remain sticky or get smelly. Here's a solution.

Wash the dirty brushes thoroughly with liquid dish soap and very hot water, then rinse well and shake dry. Place the brushes, bristles pointing down, into a cup and fill the cup with coarse salt until the bristles are covered. The salt draws moisture out of the bristles and keeps them dry and fresh between uses.

tip 98

Buns | "GRILLING" INDOORS

Hot dogs taste good any time of year and are even better when eaten on a warm, toasted bun. Throwing the buns on the grill is easy, but when cold weather keeps you from going outdoors, try this alternative.

tip 99

Use a toaster, letting the buns lie on top of the slots, then flipping them over.

Burgers | ACCURATE TEMPERATURE READING

It's hard to get an accurate temperature reading even in the thickest burgers. While we like to hold steaks and chops with tongs and slide an instant-read thermometer through the side (see tip 42, page 28), we find this technique can cause delicate burgers to break apart.

Instead, slide the tip of the thermometer into the burger at the top edge and push it toward the center.

tip 100

Butter | CUTTING INTO FINE DICE

Many recipes call for chilled butter cut into small dice. Although this sounds easy enough, the butter can soften if you start chopping away with abandon. Here's how to handle the task, quickly and efficiently, so the butter doesn't warm up.

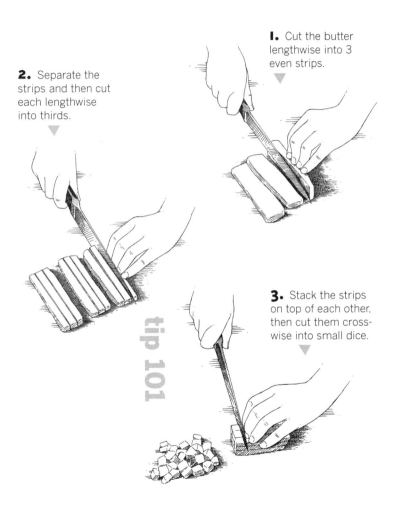

I. Cut the butter lengthwise into 3 even strips.

2. Separate the strips and then cut each lengthwise into thirds.

3. Stack the strips on top of each other, then cut them crosswise into small dice.

tip 101

Butter | DOTTING WITH BUTTER

Recipes often instruct the cook to "dot" the top of casseroles, fruit pies, and other baked desserts with butter for extra richness and browning. But cutting the butter into small pieces and then sprinkling them over the dish with warm hands can be a messy proposition. Try one of these tips instead.

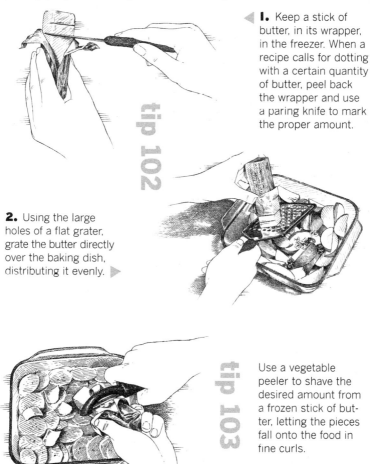

1. Keep a stick of butter, in its wrapper, in the freezer. When a recipe calls for dotting with a certain quantity of butter, peel back the wrapper and use a paring knife to mark the proper amount.

2. Using the large holes of a flat grater, grate the butter directly over the baking dish, distributing it evenly.

Use a vegetable peeler to shave the desired amount from a frozen stick of butter, letting the pieces fall onto the food in fine curls.

Butter | TABLESPOONS AT THE READY

Measured tablespoons of softened butter are at the ready
with this method.

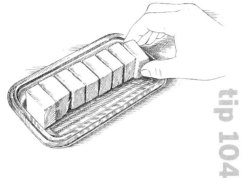

When unwrapping a
new stick of butter,
cut it into tablespoons
(using the markings
on the wrapper as a
guide) before placing
it in the butter dish.
The smaller pieces
will soften faster than
an entire stick, and
there's no last-minute
measuring.

tip 104

Butter | MEASURING GUIDE

When you want to measure out only 1 or 2 tablespoons of butter from the butter dish, it seems silly to pull out a whole fresh
stick just to use the marks on the wrapper as a measuring
guide. Here's an easy solution.

Staple a clean wrap-
per around an index
card and use that to
measure small por-
tions of butter.

tip 105

Butter | MAKING COMPOUND BUTTERS

Use of compound butters (softened butters mixed with chopped herbs, citrus zest, minced ginger or garlic, and other seasonings) is a quick way to add rich flavor to grilled or roasted fish, chicken, chops, or steaks. Once the butter has been shaped, it can be wrapped and frozen for up to three months.

tip 106

2. Roll the butter into a long, narrow cylinder. Transfer the paper-wrapped cylinder to a zipper-lock bag and freeze.

1. Place the compound butter on top of a piece of waxed paper.

3. When you need it, take the butter out of the freezer, unwrap it, and cut off rounds about ½ inch thick. Place the rounds on top of freshly cooked hot foods and let them melt as you carry plates to the table.

Butter | QUICK COMPOUND BUTTER

Compound butter is generally prepared by softening butter, mixing in flavoring ingredients, shaping the mixture into a log, and then rechilling or freezing the butter so that it can be sliced and served as a savory topping for steak, chops, or fish. This method saves time by using a whole stick of salted butter straight from the refrigerator.

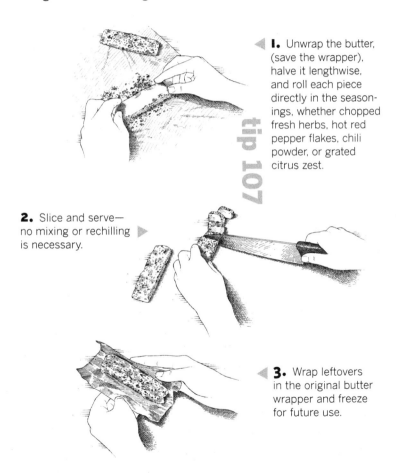

I. Unwrap the butter, (save the wrapper), halve it lengthwise, and roll each piece directly in the seasonings, whether chopped fresh herbs, hot red pepper flakes, chili powder, or grated citrus zest.

2. Slice and serve— no mixing or rechilling is necessary.

3. Wrap leftovers in the original butter wrapper and freeze for future use.

Butter | GRATING INTO FLOUR

Many cooks use their fingertips to cut butter into flour, but the heat from one's hands can cause the butter to melt. We think the food processor is the best tool for cutting butter into flour to make pie pastry or biscuits, but if you don't have a food processor, try this method.

1. Rub a frozen stick of butter against the large holes of a regular box grater over the bowl with the flour.

tip 108

2. Once all the butter has been grated, use a pastry blender or two table knives to work the butter into the flour. Keep cutting in the butter until the pieces are pea-sized.

Butter | QUICKLY CUTTING INTO FLOUR

When a recipe calls for cold butter to be cut into flour, here's a way to do it quickly.

Press the butter through a potato ricer rather than using a pastry cutter. Once the butter has been extruded into the flour, it can be incorporated very quickly to achieve a crumb-like consistency without any danger of overworking the dough.

tip 109

Butter | GAUGING SOFTNESS

To cream butter for cookies or cakes, the butter must be brought to cool room temperature (about 67 degrees) so that it is malleable but not soft. Don't hurry this step. Cold butter can't hold as much air as properly softened butter, and the resulting cakes and cookies may be too dense. If you don't have an instant-read thermometer to take the temperature of butter, use these visual clues.

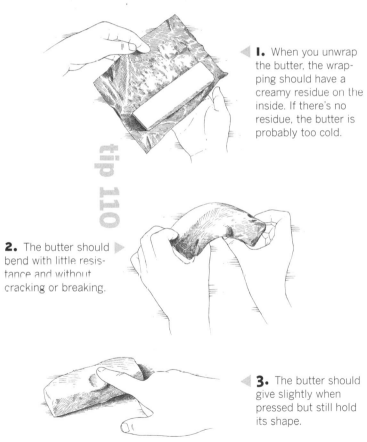

1. When you unwrap the butter, the wrapping should have a creamy residue on the inside. If there's no residue, the butter is probably too cold.

2. The butter should bend with little resistance and without cracking or breaking.

3. The butter should give slightly when pressed but still hold its shape.

tip 110

Butter | SOFTENING IN A HURRY

It can take a long time for a stick of chilled butter to reach the right temperature for creaming. Many cooks are tempted to use the microwave, but this is an imperfect solution because the edges of the butter often begin to melt before the center is really softened. If you are in a hurry, cut the butter into tablespoon-sized pieces. It will be soft enough to use in about 15 minutes.

tip 111

If, despite all your efforts, the butter is still too cool, a quick remedy is to wrap the bowl with a warm, damp towel and continue creaming.

Butter | SOFTENING QUICKLY

Here is another way to soften butter quickly when you don't have time to wait.

tip 112

Place the cold butter in a plastic bag, then use a rolling pin to pound it to the desired consistency in a matter of seconds.

Cabbage | CUTTING THROUGH A BIG HEAD

Because most heads of cabbage are at least the size of your chef's knife, it can be hard to figure out how to cut them.

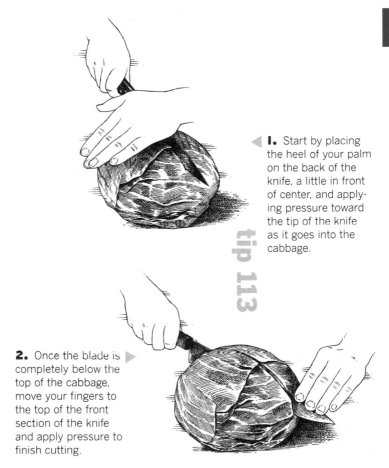

1. Start by placing the heel of your palm on the back of the knife, a little in front of center, and applying pressure toward the tip of the knife as it goes into the cabbage.

tip 113

2. Once the blade is completely below the top of the cabbage, move your fingers to the top of the front section of the knife and apply pressure to finish cutting.

Cabbage | TWO WAYS TO SHRED

For many recipes, including coleslaw, cabbage should be cut into long, thin strips. This process is called shredding. Start by cutting the cabbage into quarters (see tip 113, page 73).

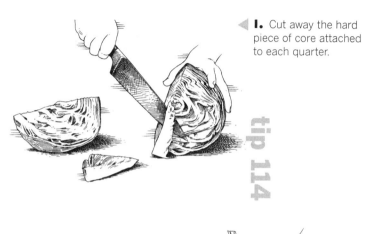

1. Cut away the hard piece of core attached to each quarter.

2. Separate the cored cabbage quarters into stacks of leaves that flatten when pressed lightly.

3. From here you have two choices:

Use a chef's knife to cut each stack diagonally (this ensures long pieces) into thin shreds.

tip 115

tip 116

Or, roll the stacked leaves crosswise to fit them into the feed tube of a food processor fitted with a shredding disk.

Cakes | DIVIDING THE BATTER

It's important to divide cake batter evenly between pans so that the layers are the same height when baked. Eyeballing the amount of batter can be tricky.

tip 117

To ensure that you put equal amounts of batter in each cake pan, use a kitchen scale to measure the weight of each filled pan.

Cakes | FILLING TUBE PANS WITH BATTER

Many bakers know the frustration of spilling batter down the hole in the center of a tube pan. Here's how to keep the batter from running inside the tube, where it can burn and cause a mess.

After the pan has been prepared (greased and/or lined with parchment paper), set a small paper cup over the center tube. You can then scrape the batter into the pan without worrying that some may end up in the tube.

Cakes | LINING THE PAN AND SERVING PLATTER

Most recipes call for lining cake pans with parchment paper to ensure easy removal. It's also a good idea to line a serving plate with parchment paper before decorating the cake so that excess frosting and nuts do not dirty the plate. The paper is removed once you've finished decorating. Here's how to use one piece of parchment to do both jobs.

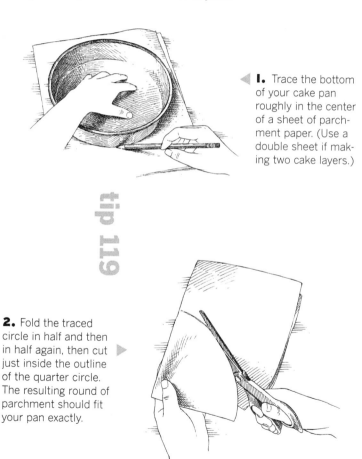

1. Trace the bottom of your cake pan roughly in the center of a sheet of parchment paper. (Use a double sheet if making two cake layers.)

2. Fold the traced circle in half and then in half again, then cut just inside the outline of the quarter circle. The resulting round of parchment should fit your pan exactly.

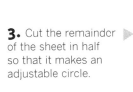

3. Cut the remainder of the sheet in half so that it makes an adjustable circle.

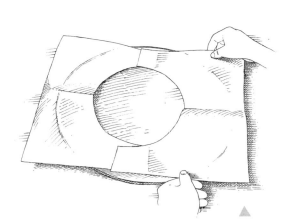

4. This circle will fit perfectly around the cake on a serving plate, keeping the plate rim neat while you frost and decorate.

Cakes | ROTATING DURING BAKING

Most bakers know that cakes need to be rotated during baking to ensure even browning, but a hand clad in a bulky oven mitt can easily mar the surface of a cake. Here's a better method to rotate your cake.

tip 120

Use a pair of kitchen tongs, which easily grasp the lip of the cake pan without touching the surface of the cake.

Cakes | HANDY TESTER

Here's an easy way to ensure you always have something at the ready to test a cake for doneness.

tip 121

Hang a small, clean, unused straw whisk broom near the oven. When you need to test a cake for doneness, simply break off a straw and insert it into the cake.

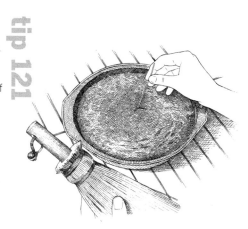

Cakes | TESTING FOR DONENESS

When testing an especially deep or thick cake, such as a Bundt cake, chiffon cake, or angel food cake, a toothpick won't be long enough and a knife will create too big a hole. Here's how to test whether crumbs cling without marring the surface too much.

Stick an uncooked strand of spaghetti or a thin skewer deep into the center of the cake and remove. If the tester is covered with moist batter, the cake needs more time in the oven.

Cakes | EASIER REMOVAL

In a busy household, it's easy to get interrupted while trying to bake in the kitchen, but if you allow a cake to cool too long in the greased pan, it can be difficult to remove.

Carefully run the cake pan over low heat on the stovetop, which will melt the grease that was initially spread on the pan bottom. The cake pops out easily when the pan is flipped over. This technique also works well for loosening stubborn Bavarians, flans, and crème caramels.

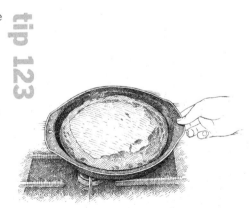

Cakes | UNCRACKING CRACKED CHEESECAKE

Even when every precaution is taken, the occasional cheese-cake will develop unsightly cracks. Not to worry: Here is a simple method for repairing them.

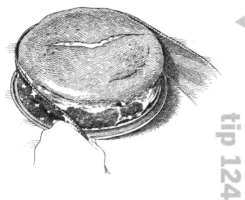

I. Remove the sides of the springform pan while the cheesecake is warm. Wrap a cloth ribbon snugly around the cake, preferably one that covers the sides completely (about 3 inches wide for most pans).

tip 124

2. Secure the ribbon with a binder clip, and leave the ribbon in place until the cake has cooled completely.

Cakes | ALIGNING LAYERS

When you want to make a cake with more than two layers, you will need to split the baked layers in half horizontally. However, if you cut the layers a bit unevenly (which is bound to happen), the cake can lean to one side or the other. Here's a neat trick that helps compensate for less-than-perfect cutting.

C

I. Place one cooled cake layer on top of the other and make a ⅛-inch-deep cut down the side of each cake layer with a serrated knife.

tip 125

2. Split the cake layers and then begin to fill and assemble the cake, realigning the vertical cuts in the side of each layer. By putting the layers back in their original orientation to each other, you will conceal any unevenness in the way you cut them.

Cakes | ANCHORING THE BOTTOM LAYER

Once the cake layers have cooled, it's time to frost them. We find it best to frost a cake on a cardboard round cut slightly larger than the cake layers. The cardboard supports the cake and makes it easy to move around.

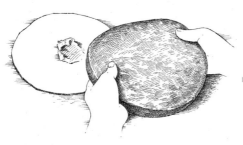

Use a dab of frosting to anchor the cake layer to the cardboard round.

Cakes | PLACING THE TOP LAYER

It can be tricky to lift a top cake layer into place. If you use your hands, the layer may break. Here's a safe way to position the top layer.

Place the layer on a cardboard round or on the removable bottom of a tart pan and then slide the layer into place.

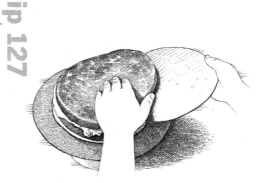

Cakes | EASIER WAY TO FROST A CAKE

Frosting a cake is made much easier when it can be elevated on a cake stand, but many infrequent bakers do not own one. Here are two good substitutes.

Place the cake on a cardboard round, then on an overturned 12-inch pizza pan or similarly sized baking sheet. Set the pizza pan on an upside-down, flat-bottomed metal bowl. The bowl provides height, and the pizza pan can be rotated as needed to ice the cake.

tip 128

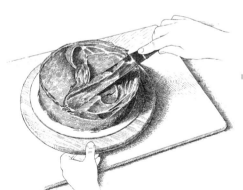

tip 129

A lazy Susan makes an admirable substitute for a rotating cake stand.

Once a cake has been frosted, there are several ways to style the icing.

tip 130
Use the tines of a dinner fork to make wave designs in the icing. Wipe the fork clean intermittently. You can make this pattern on the top of the cake or on the top and sides.

tip 131
Use the back of a large dinner spoon to make swirls on the top and/or sides of the cake.

tip 132
Use the tip of a thin metal icing spatula to stipple the top and/or sides of the cake.

Professionally decorated cakes seem to have a molten, silky look.

To get that same appearance at home, frost as usual and then use a hair dryer to "blow-dry" the frosted surface of the cake. The slight melting of the frosting gives it that smooth, lustrous appearance.

tip 133

C

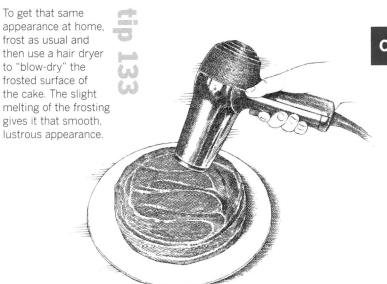

Cakes | MAKING A TWO-TONE PATTERN

Powdered sugar and cocoa powder can be used singly or in combination to give a frosted cake a polished look. When using stencils of any sort, freeze the cake for 15 minutes before decorating. Powdered sugar will gradually dissolve, so apply this fancy decoration just before serving.

2. Remove the lids, grasping them by the lip and lifting straight up. Rearrange them randomly again, then dust with a contrasting color, using confectioners' sugar, cocoa, or very finely ground nuts. Remove the lids carefully.

I. Gather six jar lids, varying in size from small to medium. Place the lids facedown on the surface of the cake in a random arrangement, letting some hang over the edge. Dust the cake with cocoa or confectioners' sugar.

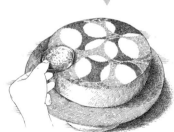

Cakes | FINISHING WITH NUTS

The shape and color of sliced almonds lend them to simple, elegant designs. Here are two tips that can be used singly or in combination.

Arrange sliced almonds in a fleur-de-lis design around the perimeter of the cake. Use four slices to make a flower design in the center of the cake.

tip 135

C

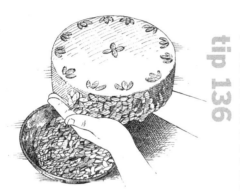

tip 136

To press nuts onto the sides of the cake, lift the cake off the stand or counter and hold it by the cardboard round underneath. Use one hand to hold the cake above a bowl containing nuts; use the other hand to press the nuts into the icing, letting the excess fall back into the bowl. You will need about 1 cup of nuts to cover the sides of a 9-inch layer cake. You can use sliced almonds (as pictured) or chopped pecans or walnuts.

Cakes | APPLYING SPRINKLES

When you want to add your own special touch to freshly frosted cakes or cupcakes, try this easy method.

Press a simply shaped cookie cutter into smooth frosting on a cake or cupcake. Using the cookie cutter outline as a guide, fill the shape with sprinkles, colored sugar, or another confection of a contrasting color. Carefully remove the cookie cutter, leaving behind a fanciful decoration.

tip 137

Cakes | APPLYING CHOCOLATE SHAVINGS

If the chocolate is too hard, it can be difficult to pull off thick shavings. Even if you do cut off nice shavings, warmth from your fingers can cause the pieces to melt as you try to place them on the cake. Here's how to avoid both problems.

tip 138

◀ **1.** Warm a block of bittersweet or semi-sweet chocolate by sweeping a hair dryer over it, taking care not to melt the chocolate. Holding a paring knife at a 45-degree angle against the chocolate, scrape toward you, anchoring the block with your other hand.

2. Pick up the shavings with a toothpick and place them as desired on the frosted ▶ cake.

Cakes | WRITING ON FROSTING

When writing a message on top of a frosted cake, it's easiest to use chocolate on a light-colored frosting.

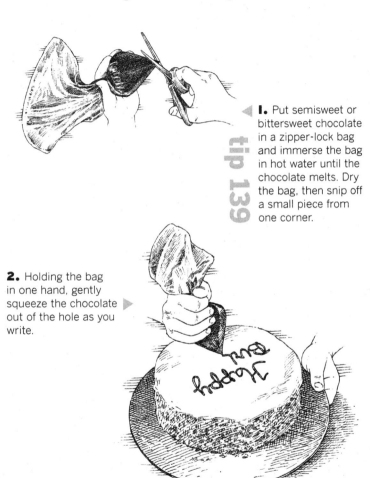

tip 139

1. Put semisweet or bittersweet chocolate in a zipper-lock bag and immerse the bag in hot water until the chocolate melts. Dry the bag, then snip off a small piece from one corner.

2. Holding the bag in one hand, gently squeeze the chocolate out of the hole as you write.

Cakes | REMOVING STENCILS

Using a store-bought stencil (available in most kitchen shops) is an easy way to decorate an unfrosted cake. The problem is removing the stencil without marring the design.

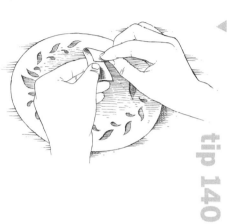

1. Create two handles for the stencil by folding two short lengths of masking tape back on themselves, pinching the middle sections together. Stick the ends of the tape to the top and bottom of the stencil, placing a handle on either side.

2. Place the stencil on the cake and dust with confectioners' sugar or cocoa powder. When you are done, use the tape handles to grasp and lift the stencil straight up and off the cake.

Cakes | DUSTING A FLOURLESS CHOCOLATE CAKE

A flourless chocolate cake is rarely frosted, but it can be dressed up a bit with some confectioners' sugar.

1. Lay strips of paper about ½ inch wide across the top of the cake, then sieve confectioners' sugar over the top.

2. Carefully peel away the paper strips to reveal an attractive striped pattern.

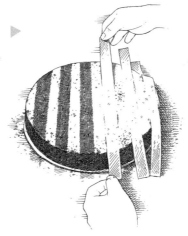

Cakes | IMPROVISING A COVER

A glass cake plate with a footed stand and large domed cover is the ideal place to store a frosted cake. Here's how to keep a cake fresh and safe from kitchen accidents if you don't own a cake plate.

Turn the outside bowl of a large salad spinner upside down and place it over the frosted cake, resting the bowl on the edge of the cake plate.

Cakes | TRANSPORTING A FROSTED CAKE

The common method for keeping plastic wrap from touching a gooey frosting or glaze is to stick the food with toothpicks and place the wrap over the toothpicks. Occasionally, though, the sharp points of the toothpicks puncture the wrap, which can then slide down and stick to the frosting. To keep the wrap securely above the frosting, try this method.

Place a miniature marshmallow over the point of each toothpick. Insert toothpicks into the cake with the marshmallows facing up. Lay the plastic wrap over the marshmallows.

Can Opener | CLEANING

A manual can opener should be cleaned after each use. Running it through the dishwasher accomplishes the task, but usually leaves some rust. Try this quick and easy method instead.

tip 144

Run a folded sheet of paper towel through the opener. The towel does a great job of cleaning both the blade and the gear.

Cappuccino | FOAMING MILK

Here's how to make steamed, frothy milk for coffee without an expensive espresso machine.

tip 145

Place a pan filled with heated milk on a potholder or other protective surface and beat the milk with a handheld electric mixer until the consistency of the milk is foamy and velvety. Milk foamed this way will hold soft peaks, even when spooned into coffee mugs.

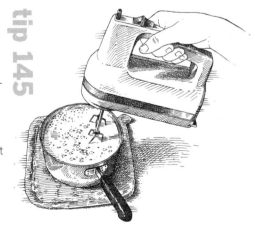

Carrots | CUTTING INTO JULIENNE

The term *julienne,* which usually applies to vegetables, means to cut into long, thin strips. It can be tricky to figure out how to julienne long, thin vegetables such as carrots, zucchini, or parsnips.

1. Start by slicing the vegetables on the bias into rounds about ¼ inch thick and 2 inches long.

tip 146

2. Fan out several rounds and cut them into ¼ inch strips. This shape is sometimes called the "matchstick cut."

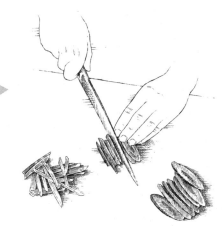

Carving Board |
DOUBLE DUTY FOR MEAT-CARVING BOARDS

The channel around the edge of a meat-carving board is designed to catch juices as you slice, but it is also good for catching other things, as well.

If you cut carrots on a meat-carving board, the channel will catch the slices as they roll and keep them from diving onto the ground.

The channel can also be useful when cutting quantities of small items, such as grapes, cherry tomatoes, hazelnuts, or cranberries, in half. Line up a few inches worth of the items in the channel (keep the row shorter than your knife blade), and carefully cut through the whole row at once. Remove the cut items and repeat until you are finished.

Cauliflower | CUTTING INTO FLORETS

Here's an easy way to cut a head of cauliflower into neat florets. Start by pulling off and discarding the outer leaves.

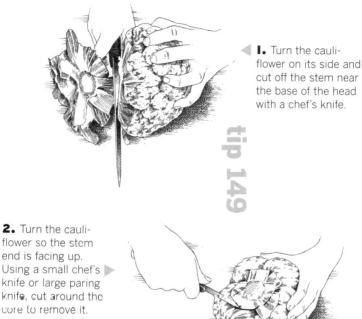

1. Turn the cauliflower on its side and cut off the stem near the base of the head with a chef's knife.

2. Turn the cauliflower so the stem end is facing up. Using a small chef's knife or large paring knife, cut around the core to remove it.

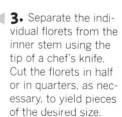

3. Separate the individual florets from the inner stem using the tip of a chef's knife. Cut the florets in half or in quarters, as necessary, to yield pieces of the desired size.

Celery | CHOPPING QUICKLY

Recipes often call for a small amount of chopped celery. Rather than breaking off one or more ribs and ending up with too much, try this method.

tip 150

With a chef's knife, chop the entire bunch across the top. It is easier to get just the amount you need this way, and the whole bunch gets shorter as you use it, so it's easier to store.

Celery Root | REMOVING THE THICK PEEL

Celery root is covered with a thick, hairy skin that can't be removed with a vegetable peeler. Because the round root is too large to hold in your hand, using a paring knife can be tricky. Here's how to cut away the peel safely.

tip 151

Cut off about ½ inch from each end of the celery root so that it can rest flat on a cutting board. To peel, simply cut from top to bottom, rotating the celery root as you remove wide strips of skin.

Cheese | NEATER GRATING

Grating cheese is an easy, but often messy, affair. Here's a neater way to go about it.

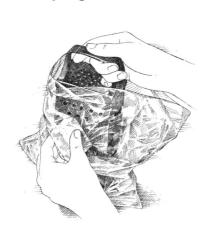

Use a clean plastic bag (such as a large zipper-lock bag or a grocery store shopping bag) to hold both grater and cheese. By placing the bag around the grater and the cheese, you can grate cheese with clean hands and eliminate flyaway bits. Leftover grated cheese is ready for storage in a handy bag.

Cheese | GRATING SMALL AMOUNTS

A Microplane rasp-style grater is our favorite tool for grating small amounts of hard cheese, but not every cook has one.

Use a serrated steak knife to grate Parmesan or Asiago over bowls of pasta or risotto. Hold the cheese in one hand and the small serrated steak knife in the other, then lightly scrape the cheese directly over the food.

Cheese | CUTTING HARD CHEESE SAFELY

Because hard cheese is difficult to cut through, many cooks often place one hand over the top of their chef's knife blade and the other over the handle to put their weight into the cut, but a slip could result in an accident. We advise taking this extra safety measure.

tip 154

Put a folded dish towel between your hand and the blade. This protects your hand and makes the cutting more comfortable.

Cheese | SHAVING PARMESAN

To slice Parmesan paper-thin for salads, use your vegetable peeler.

Run a vegetable peeler over a block of Parmesan. Use a light touch for thin shavings.

tip 155

Cheese | STORING GOAT CHEESE

It can be a bother to rewrap goat cheese every time you remove a small portion. Keep goat cheese at the ready with this convenient storage method.

A covered butter dish works well to keep goat cheese neatly protected and easy to use.

Cheese | SLICING GOAT CHEESE

A knife quickly becomes covered with this soft cheese, making it difficult to cut clean, neat slices. Here's how to avoid a sticky situation.

Slide an 18-inch piece of dental floss under a log of goat cheese. Cross the ends of the floss above the cheese and then pull the floss through the cheese to slice it. Move the floss and cut again to make slices of the desired thickness.

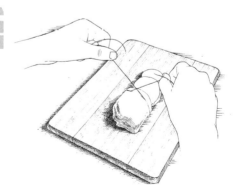

Cheese | SHREDDING IN THE FOOD PROCESSOR

It's easy to shred semisoft cheeses such as mozzarella or cheddar in the food processor—until, of course, a big chunk sticks in the feed tube or gums up the shredding disk. Avoid problem stickiness with this trick.

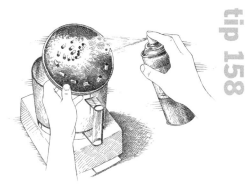

tip 158

Spray the feed tube, disk, and workbowl of the food processor with a light coating of nonstick cooking spray before you begin shredding.

Cheese | SHREDDING SEMISOFT CHEESE NEATLY

Semisoft cheeses such as cheddar or commercial mozzarella can stick to a box grater and cause a real mess. Here's how to keep the holes on the grater from becoming clogged.

Use nonstick cooking spray to lightly coat the coarse side of the box grater, then shred the cheese as usual. The cooking spray will keep cheese from sticking to the surface of the grater.

tip 159

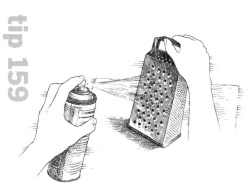

Cheese | SLICING FRESH MOZZARELLA

Fresh mozzarella cheese is quite soft, which makes it difficult to slice neatly with a knife. Here's a neater, faster way to slice fresh mozzarella.

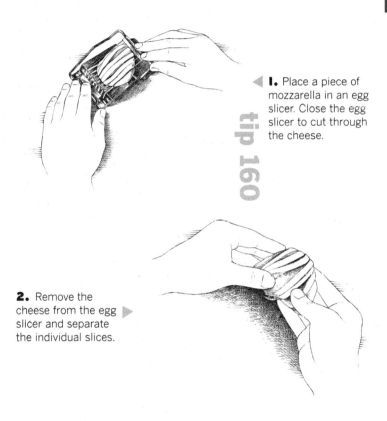

1. Place a piece of mozzarella in an egg slicer. Close the egg slicer to cut through the cheese.

tip 160

2. Remove the cheese from the egg slicer and separate the individual slices.

Cherries | PITTING FIVE WAYS

Cherry pitters work well, but not every cook has one. Here are some techniques you can use to pit cherries without a specialized tool. Always work over a bowl to catch the juices.

tip 161 Push the cherry firmly down onto the pointed, jagged end of a pastry bag tip. Take care not to cut your fingers on the points as they pierce the fruit.

tip 162 Pierce the skin at the stem end with a pair of clean needle-nose pliers. Spread the pliers just enough to grasp the pit, then pull it straight out.

tip 163 Push a drinking straw through the bottom of the cherry, forcing the pit up and out through the stem end.

tip 164

2. Holding the cherry in one hand, stick one end of the S into the stem end of the cherry, hook it around the pit, and flick the pit out.

▼

C

▲

1. Use a paper clip to pit cherries. Unfold one bend of a clean, large metal paper clip to create an elongated S-shape.

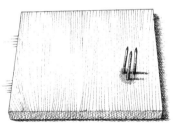

tip 165

2. Gently push the cherry down onto the sharp tips of the nails to extract the pit. Entry and exit "wounds" are minimal.

▼

▲

1. Drive three clean stainless steel nails close together through a piece of clean, thin scrap wood to form a "basket."

Chicken | GETTING A GRIP ON RAW CHICKEN

Raw chicken is slippery, which means that halving whole breasts can be a hazardous job. This method ensures a firm grip.

tip 166

Use a folded wad of paper towels to hold the chicken in place as you cut. You can also use a paper towel to firmly grasp chicken skin when removing it from the meat.

Chicken | CONTAINING RAW CHICKEN

The possibility of raw chicken contaminating any surface it touches is a real concern. It can be especially tricky to avoid cross-contamination when washing and drying raw chicken. The slippery chicken can slide right off a cutting board onto the counter or soak through protective layers of paper towel. Here's a good way to keep the bird contained as you wash and dry it.

Set the raw chicken in a metal colander while washing it, then pat the chicken dry while it's still in the colander. When done, simply transfer the chicken to your cooking vessel. Remember to wash your hands and the colander with hot, soapy water.

tip 167

Chicken | SAFELY SEASONING RAW CHICKEN

Many recipes call for seasoning raw chicken with salt and pepper before it is cooked. Touching other dishes or the pepper mill after you've handled raw chicken is a concern if you want to minimize the chances of cross-contamination.

tip 168

Before handling the chicken, mix the necessary salt and pepper in a small bowl so you can move between the seasoning and chicken without fear of contamination. Discard leftover seasoning mix and wash the bowl.

Chicken | SEASONING WITH LEMON

The flavor of lemon is lovely with poultry, but squeezing a lemon half or pouring lemon juice into the cavity of a bird can result in a messy spill. Here's how to limit the mess and maximize the amount of lemon juice that gets into the bird.

tip 169

Choose a thin-skinned lemon. Cut the lemon in half and turn the halves inside out. It's now easy to rub the cavity evenly and neatly with lemon juice.

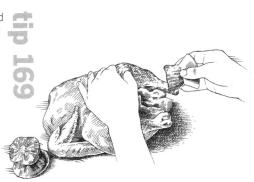

Chicken | MAKESHIFT VERTICAL ROASTER

Roasting a chicken on a vertical roaster cuts cooking time significantly and eliminates the need to turn the bird, but some households may not have one.

A tube pan insert mimics a vertical roaster very well. Just place it in a shallow baking dish and spray it with nonstick cooking spray before putting the chicken onto the tube.

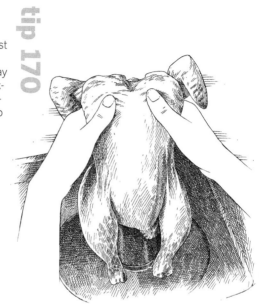

tip 170

Chicken | BUTTERFLYING FOR FASTER COOKING

A whole small chicken takes an hour or more to roast. If you are in a hurry, you can butterfly the chicken (basically, opening up the bird so it forms a single, flat piece of meat) to shave at least 20 minutes off the cooking time. A butterflied chicken can also be grilled or broiled.

tip 171

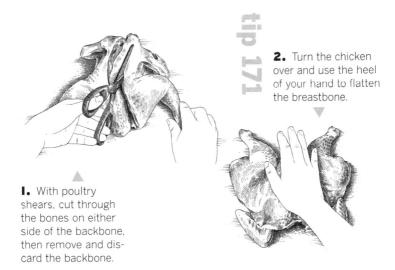

2. Turn the chicken over and use the heel of your hand to flatten the breastbone.

1. With poultry shears, cut through the bones on either side of the backbone, then remove and discard the backbone.

Chicken | GRILLING BUTTERFLIED CHICKEN

Butterflied chicken on the grill cooks faster and more evenly when weighted down.

To weight a butter-flied chicken while it grills, set a rimmed baking sheet on top of the chicken. Put two bricks in the pan to add the necessary weight.

Chicken | SEALING THE CAVITY

Lemon, garlic, and herbs placed inside a chicken as it roasts can add flavor. But these items can fall out when the bird is turned during the cooking process. In the test kitchen we use a wooden skewer to sew the cavity shut.

Holding the two flaps of skin together over the cavity with one hand, thread a long wooden skewer through both flaps about 1 inch down from the top of the cavity. Turn the skewer and rethread back through the flaps about ½ inch below the first stitch. Turn the skewer one last time and make the third stitch. Cut off the excess skewer with shears.

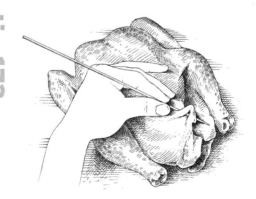

Chicken | MEASURING THE INTERNAL TEMPERATURE

The most accurate way to tell if a chicken is done is to use an instant-read thermometer. Be sure to put the thermometer into the thickest part of the bird and avoid all bones, which can throw off your reading.

C

I. To take the temperature of the thigh, insert the thermometer at an angle into the area between the drumstick and breast. Dark meat should be cooked to 165 or 170 degrees.

tip 174

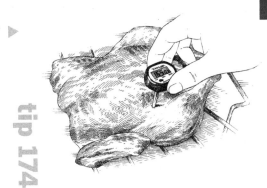

2. To take the temperature of the breast, insert the thermometer from the neck end, holding it parallel to the bird. The breast meat is done at 160 degrees and will begin to dry out at higher temperatures.

Chicken | TRIMMING FAT AND TENDONS FROM CUTLETS

Boneless, skinless chicken cutlets are a great convenience
food. For the best results, take a few minutes to cut away
excess fat and tendons that would be unpleasant to eat.

1. Lay each cutlet
tenderloin-side down
(the tenderloin is that
floppy, thin piece of
meat attached to the
breast) and smooth
the top with your
fingers. Any yellow
fat will slide to the
periphery, where it
can be trimmed with
a knife.

tip 175

2. To remove the
tough white tendon,
turn the cutlet
tenderloin-side up,
then peel back the
thick half of the
tenderloin so it lies
top down on the work
surface. Use the point
of a paring knife to
cut around the tip of
the tendon to expose
it, then scrape the
tendon free with the
knife.

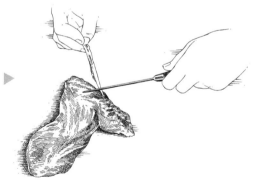

Chicken | CUTTING CUTLETS INTO UNIFORM PIECES

When stir-frying or making pot pies, it's nice to have uniform pieces of chicken breast that will cook at the same rate. Here's how to turn an ungainly cutlet into neat, even strips of meat. It's easiest to slice the cutlet when it has been partially frozen for an hour or so.

C

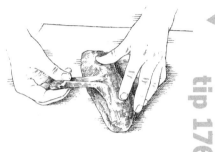

I. Separate the tenderloins (the long, floppy pieces of meat) from the breasts and set them aside.

tip 176

2. Slice the breasts across the grain into long, thin strips. Center pieces need to be cut in half so that they are approximately the same length as end pieces.

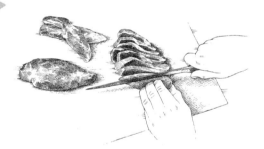

3. Cut the tenderloins on the diagonal to produce pieces the same size as the strips of breast meat.

Chicken | POUNDING CUTLETS

For breaded cutlets, it's important to pound the meat thin. The thicker the cutlet, the more time it needs in the pan, and the more time it spends in the pan, the more likely the breading will burn. The problem is that by the time you get thick cutlets thin enough, they may be so large that they won't fit in a skillet. Here's how to minimize the pounding to produce good-looking cutlets that are thin but not excessively large.

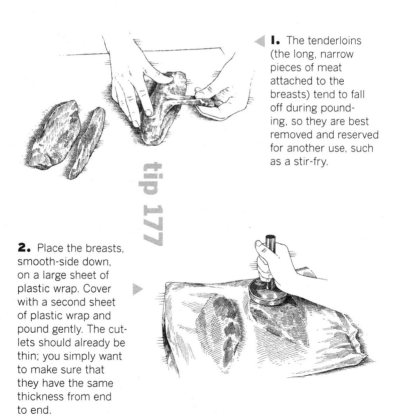

1. The tenderloins (the long, narrow pieces of meat attached to the breasts) tend to fall off during pounding, so they are best removed and reserved for another use, such as a stir-fry.

2. Place the breasts, smooth-side down, on a large sheet of plastic wrap. Cover with a second sheet of plastic wrap and pound gently. The cutlets should already be thin; you simply want to make sure that they have the same thickness from end to end.

Chicken | MAKING CUTLETS

A tortilla press is an infrequently used piece of equipment that tends to gather dust on the kitchen shelf. Give it new life by using it to flatten chicken breasts into cutlets.

C

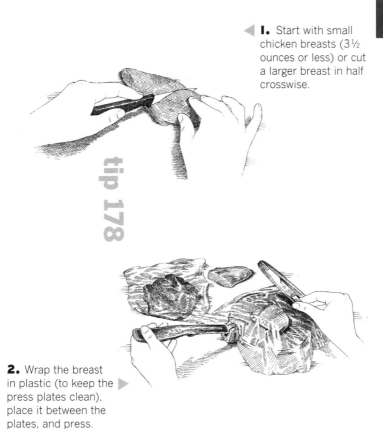

I. Start with small chicken breasts (3½ ounces or less) or cut a larger breast in half crosswise.

tip 178

2. Wrap the breast in plastic (to keep the press plates clean), place it between the plates, and press.

Chicken | MESS-FREE BREADING

Dipping pounded cutlets into a bowl of beaten eggs and then bread crumbs can be messy. Before you know it, your fingers— not the cutlets—are coated with crumbs. This tip works equally well with turkey or veal cutlets, or fish fillets, such as flounder.

1. Use a pair of tongs to dip a cutlet into the bowl with the beaten eggs.

2. Use the tongs to transfer the cutlet to a pie plate filled with bread crumbs. Press the crumbs lightly onto the cutlet with your fingertips to ensure that the crumbs adhere to the surface of the food. Because your fingers never touch the eggs, they should remain dry and crumb-free.

tip 179

Chicken | KEEPING BREADING FIRMLY ATTACHED

It's disappointing when breading comes off cutlets when they are cooked. Here's how to prevent this problem with chicken, veal, or turkey cutlets.

tip 180

Transfer the breaded cutlets to a baking rack set over a baking sheet. Allow the cutlets to dry for 5 minutes. This brief drying time stabilizes the coating so that it won't stick to the pan or fall off.

C

Chicken | SAUTÉING SAFELY

Hot fat can splash hands and arms when cold cutlets are added to a skillet. Here's how to minimize that risk.

tip 181

Lay the cutlet into the pan thick-side first. Hang onto the tapered end until the whole cutlet is in the pan. The tapered ends of the cutlets should be at the edges of the pan where the heat is less intense, so they will cook a bit more slowly than the thick middle portions.

Chicken | SKEWERING MEAT FOR KEBABS

When it comes to kebabs, raw chicken (which is slippery and made more so by the addition of marinade) tends to spin around on the skewer, inhibiting even cooking. Threading the chicken onto two skewers held side by side keeps the chicken stable.

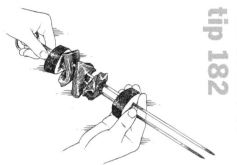

tip 182

Use one hand to hold two skewers about ½ inch apart, then thread boneless chunks of chicken breast or thigh and vegetables, if desired, onto the skewers simultaneously.

Chicken |
SEPARATING THE THIGH FROM THE DRUMSTICK

Whole legs are readily available and inexpensive, but they can be difficult to cook and eat. Here's how to separate them neatly.

tip 183

A thin joint connects the drumstick to the thigh. A line of fat runs right over the joint. Simply turn the leg skin-side down and locate the line of fat. With a large chef's knife, cut down through the fat and the joint that lies below to separate the two pieces.

Chicken | TRIMMING WINGS

Some cooks love inexpensive chicken wings and buy them especially for grilling or roasting. Yet even wing lovers will admit that eating this jointed piece of chicken can be messy. To minimize the mess, we like to separate the three sections of the wing before cooking.

I. With a chef's knife, cut into the skin between the two larger sections of the wing until you hit the joint.

2. Bend back the two sections to pop and break the joint.

tip 184

3. Cut through the skin and flesh to completely separate the two meaty portions. One portion will contain the thin wingtip, which has absolutely no meat. Hack off the wingtip and either discard or save it for stock. The two remaining pieces are small enough to be eaten as finger food and much less awkward to hold.

Chicken | GRILLING BONE-IN BREASTS

Everyone loves grilled bone-in, skin-on breasts. But all too often the exterior burns before the meat in thick breasts is fully cooked. Here's how to make sure the meat near the bone is done without causing the skin to burn. You can use this same trick to finish cooking thick chops.

Once the chicken is nicely browned and nearly done, slide the pieces to a cool part of the grill and cover them with a disposable aluminum roasting pan. The pan traps the heat to create an ovenlike effect on your grill. While the meat continues to cook, the skin won't color any further.

Chiles | SEEDING HOT PEPPERS

Using a knife to remove the seeds and ribs from a hot chile pepper takes a very steady hand. Fortunately, there is a safer and equally effective alternative.

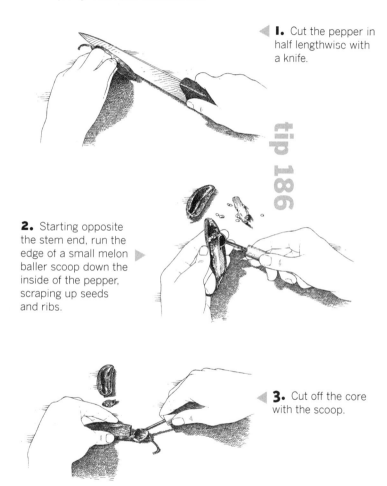

1. Cut the pepper in half lengthwise with a knife.

2. Starting opposite the stem end, run the edge of a small melon baller scoop down the inside of the pepper, scraping up seeds and ribs.

3. Cut off the core with the scoop.

Chiles | SEEDLESS JALAPEÑO RINGS

To make neat rings of jalapeños without the seeds or spicy ribs when garnishing nachos, use a vegetable peeler.

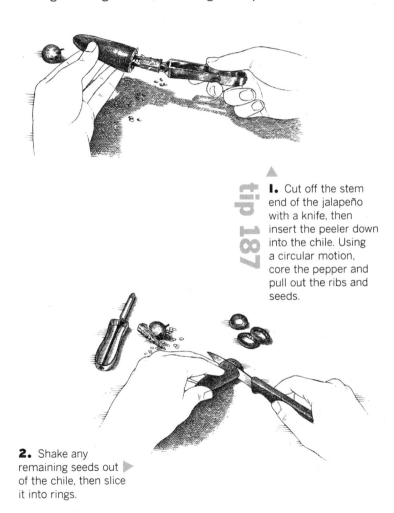

tip 187

1. Cut off the stem end of the jalapeño with a knife, then insert the peeler down into the chile. Using a circular motion, core the pepper and pull out the ribs and seeds.

2. Shake any remaining seeds out of the chile, then slice it into rings.

Chiles | PICKING MORE THAN ONE PEPPER

Running out to the store each time you need a tiny chile pepper can be a pain, but if you buy several at once they may go bad before you have time to use them.

tip 188

Buy large bags of peppers and store them in the freezer. When a chopped or minced pepper is needed for a recipe, take it straight from the freezer to a cutting board.

Chiles | MINCING

Chipotle peppers or pickled jalapeño chiles are a great way to season dips and sauces, but mincing them is tedious work. Here's an easier way.

tip 189

Simply put a small amount of chile into the well of a garlic press and squeeze.

Chiles | TAKING THE STING OUT OF CUTTING CHILES

Chiles add welcome heat to many dishes, but they can also add unwelcome heat to your hands during preparation. Here are two quick and clever ways to protect fingers from the sting of fresh chiles when you don't have gloves.

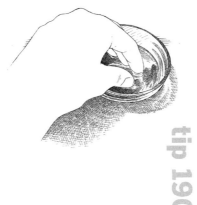

tip 190

1. Coat one hand with oil (not the hand you use to hold the knife).

2. Cut the chiles, making sure to touch them only with your oiled hand. When done, wash your hands with hot soapy water.

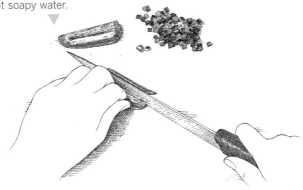

1. Turn a zipper-lock bag inside out to create a glove. It's helpful to secure the bag with a rubber band around your wrist.

C

▼

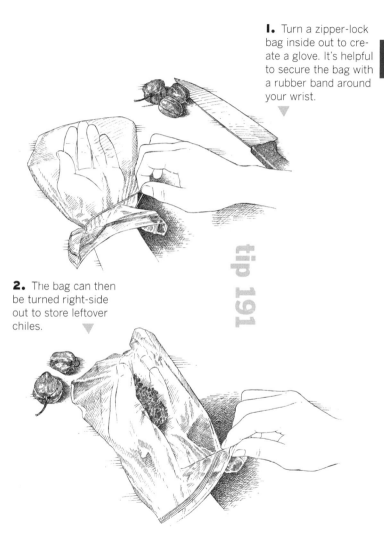

tip 191

2. The bag can then be turned right-side out to store leftover chiles.

▼

Chiles | FREEZING CHIPOTLES IN ADOBO SAUCE

Chipotles (smoked, dried jalapeño chiles) are among our favorite chiles because they are so flavorful. Chipotles are often packed in adobo sauce (a vinegary tomato sauce flavored with garlic) and canned. Because a little bit of chipotle chile goes a long way, it can be difficult to use up an entire can once it has been opened. Rather than letting the remaining chiles go bad in the refrigerator, try this trick. We like to preserve tomato paste in the same fashion.

I. Spoon out the chipotles, each with a couple of teaspoons of adobo sauce, onto different areas of a baking sheet lined with parchment paper or waxed paper. Place the baking sheet in the freezer.

tip 192

2. Once frozen, the chipotles should be transferred to a zipper-lock bag and stored in the freezer. You can remove them, one at a time, as needed. They will keep indefinitely.

Chips | REVIVING STALE CHIPS

Potato chip lovers hate to throw away leftover chips, even if they've gone stale.

Microwaving stale potato or tortilla chips restores their crispness beautifully. Spread 2 cups of chips on a Pyrex pie plate and microwave on high for 1 minute. Place the hot chips on a double layer of paper towels and allow them to come to room temperature before serving.

tip 193

C

Chocolate | MELTING

Here's a great way to melt chocolate without a microwave.

tip 194

Roughly chop the chocolate and place it in a small, heatproof bowl. Cover the top of the bowl with plastic wrap, being careful not to bring the plastic too far down the sides of the bowl. Place the bowl on the burner plate of an electric drip coffee machine, turn on the coffee maker, and let the gentle heat of the burner melt the chocolate without scorching it.

Chocolate | EASIER CHOPPING

A large block of chocolate can be unwieldy, but most home cooks don't own a fancy chocolate fork, which is used to break up blocks of chocolate into more manageable pieces. There's an easy way to improvise one.

Use the sharp two-tined fork from a meat-slicing set and a secured cutting board. Press straight down into the chocolate. The chocolate breaks into neater pieces than when cut by a knife, and a lot less effort is required.

tip 195

Chopsticks | SECURING IN THE DISHWASHER

Chopsticks are useful kitchen utensils, but they can be hard to wash in the dishwasher because they slide through the holes in the silverware bin. Here are two ways to keep them in place.

With a paring knife, cut a small X for each chopstick in the plastic lid from a yogurt container. Slide each chopstick into an X and place the lid in the top rack of the dishwasher.

tip 196

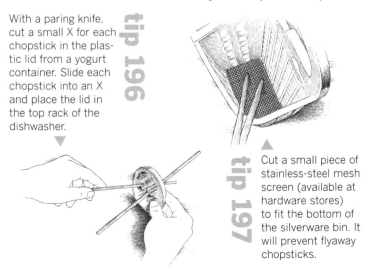

Cut a small piece of stainless-steel mesh screen (available at hardware stores) to fit the bottom of the silverware bin. It will prevent flyaway chopsticks.

tip 197

Cinnamon Rolls | CUTTING FILLED ROLLS

A knife can squish and tear soft yeast doughs, causing the filling to leak out the sides. Here's how to cut the dough for cinnamon rolls quickly and safely.

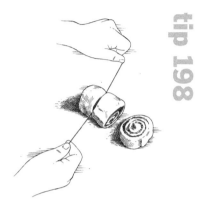

tip 198

Hold a piece of dental floss in each hand and carefully saw through the dough with the floss to separate individual pieces.

Citrus | EASIER CITRUS PRESSING

A citrus press can be a handy tool, but using one to press the juice from several lemons or oranges can be a pain—literally. Here's a way to ease the pressure on your hands.

tip 199

Cut the fruit into quarters rather than halves. Juicing a quarter is not only easier than juicing a half, but it also yields more juice.

Citrus | JUICING

Sometimes you need just a little lemon or lime juice, but not enough to warrant dragging out the juicer.

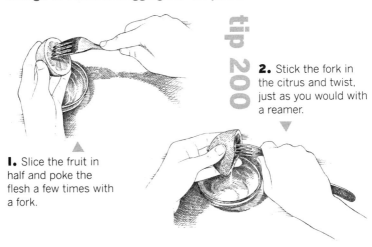

tip 200

2. Stick the fork in the citrus and twist, just as you would with a reamer.

1. Slice the fruit in half and poke the flesh a few times with a fork.

Clams | SCRUBBING

Many recipes instruct the cook to scrub clams and other shell-fish. Don't skip this step; many clams and mussels have bits of sand embedded in the shell that can mar a sauce.

Use a soft brush, sometimes sold in kitchen shops as a vegetable brush, to scrub clams under cold, running water.

tip 201

Clams | STRAINING PRECIOUS LIQUID

Clams (as well as mussels) are often steamed with a little wine and herbs in a covered pot. The cooking liquid is delicious but sometimes gritty. Here's how to remove the grit. (Note that bits of garlic, shallots, and herbs will be lost when the liquid is strained, but their flavors will remain.)

tip 202

Pour the cooking liquid through a sieve lined with a single paper towel and set over a measuring cup.

Cleaning | STOVETOPS

Everyone knows how fat can splatter from a hot skillet. Here's a neat way to sauté and keep the mess under control.

Before you start to cook, lay an over-turned baking sheet across the burners next to the pan. The baking sheet, which is easy to clean, catches most of the grease, leaving the burner plates and stovetop relatively free of fat.

tip 203

Cleaning | SPILLED OIL

Anyone who has ever dropped a bottle of oil on the floor and had it shatter knows how difficult it can be to clean up. Here's how we deal with an oil-slicked floor in our test kitchen.

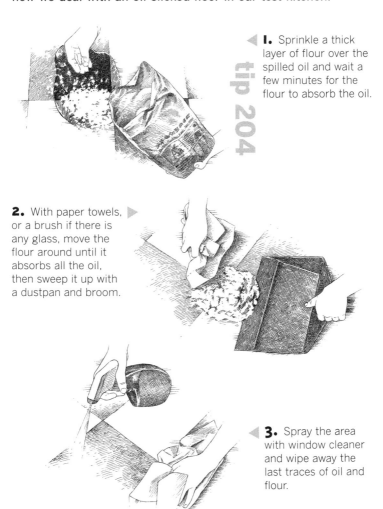

1. Sprinkle a thick layer of flour over the spilled oil and wait a few minutes for the flour to absorb the oil.

tip 204

2. With paper towels, or a brush if there is any glass, move the flour around until it absorbs all the oil, then sweep it up with a dustpan and broom.

3. Spray the area with window cleaner and wipe away the last traces of oil and flour.

Cleaning | UTENSILS AT THE READY

Every cook knows the frustration of having to stop in the middle of meal preparation to wash a utensil, such as a paring knife, which you've dirtied but need to use again. Here's how we like to make cleanup quick and convenient.

tip 205

Fill a large glass or jar with hot, sudsy water. Then, when you dirty a utensil, place it in the glass as soon as you've used it, so that it will need only a quick rinse when you need to reach for it again.

Cleaning | QUICK DRY FOR BAKING UTENSILS

Most home bakers have just one piece of any given type of equipment, such as a strainer or sifter. Of course, these tools must be completely dry before you use them, but waiting for a strainer or sifter to dry fully can be frustrating, and it can't always be accomplished by hand-drying with a dish towel.

tip 206

Because the oven is on anyway, put the utensil in it to dry. Set a timer for about 2 minutes to remind yourself that the utensil is in the oven. Be sure that the utensil doesn't have any plastic parts that can melt. Because the utensil will be quite hot, use a mitt to protect your hand when removing it from the oven.

Cleaning | DRYING DISHES QUICKLY

Many cooks who wash dishes by hand would prefer to wash, dry, and put away the dishes in one fell swoop. Using this method, you can get the dishes dry lickety-split without using a dish towel.

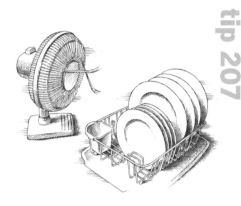

Prop a small table fan level with the dishes in the rack and direct the air flow toward the dishes, which will dry in record time.

Cleaning | KEEPING SCRUB PADS DRY

Steel wool has many great uses, but a wet scrub pad can leave rust all over the countertop.

Store the pad on an unpainted terra cotta planter base. The clay material absorbs any water that drips off the used pad, and the pad stays rust-free.

Cleaning | REMOVING TEA STAINS

Tannin stains build up quickly on ceramics if you brew a fresh pot of tea every morning. Remove stains with one of these methods.

Cut a fresh lemon in quarters and use the fruit as a scrubber, gently squeezing its juice into a stained coffee mug or teapot. For extra cleaning power, first dip the lemon in kosher salt, which acts as an abrasive. Follow with a wash in hot soapy water.

C

Fill the stained teapot, teacup, or any stained piece of ceramic with water and drop in a denture-cleansing tablet. Let it soak for 2 or 3 hours, then wash with dishwashing liquid and hot water. Light stains will disappear, leaving the cup or pot looking as good as new. Heavier stains may need several treatments followed by a scrubbing with hot soapy water.

Cleaning | SMARTER KNIFE CLEANING

Scrub pads do a fine job of removing gunk from knife blades but eventually damage the finish. Here's a good way to keep knives shiny.

Use a wine cork instead. Angling the blade toward the cutting board, simply rub the cork over the knife to remove food residue, then wash the knife in hot, soapy water with a soft sponge.

Cleaning | WINE GLASS BUFFER ZONE

Washing fragile glassware by hand is the best way to stave off breakage—unless it slips from your grasp and crashes down into the sink. Rather than risk broken glasses, take this precautionary measure.

Place rubber shelf liner in the sink for a breakage-free cleaning session.

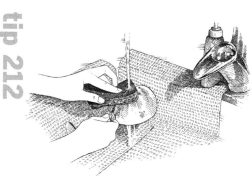

Cleaning |
HANDY DISPENSER FOR DISHWASHING LIQUID

We appreciate the neatness and ease of dispensing hand soap
from a small pump. You can also do the same with dishwashing
liquid. This tip is especially helpful if you buy supersize bottles,
which are usually a bargain but are also ungainly.

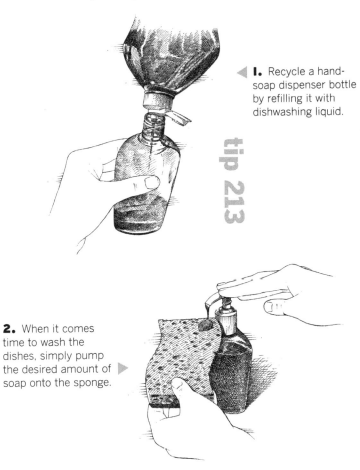

1. Recycle a hand-
soap dispenser bottle
by refilling it with
dishwashing liquid.

tip 213

2. When it comes
time to wash the
dishes, simply pump
the desired amount of
soap onto the sponge.

Cocktails | CHILLING GIBSONS QUICKLY

Here's a novel way to chill a Gibson (a martini garnished with onions instead of olives) without diluting your drink with ice.

Use frozen pearl onions to garnish your Gibson instead of the traditional pickled onions.

tip 214

Cocktails | MAKESHIFT MARTINI SHAKER

Cocktails like martinis and Manhattans should be shaken, not stirred, and not just because James Bond says so. Shaking the cocktail with the ice chills the mixture more thoroughly than simply stirring it. If your bar isn't equipped with a proper cocktail shaker, try this.

A spillproof coffee mug with a screw-on lid makes a fine substitute. Just be sure to place your finger over the sipping hole when you shake. The lid will keep the ice in the "shaker" when you pour.

tip 215

Cocoa | INSTANT HOMEMADE COCOA

Here's a way to make quick individual servings of homemade hot cocoa by making a cocoa "base" to have on hand whenever you're in the mood for a cup of hot chocolate.

To make four servings, whisk together 6 tablespoons unsweetened Dutch-processed cocoa, 5 tablespoons sugar, a pinch of salt, 1 teaspoon vanilla extract, and 1 cup water in a small saucepan. Heat the mixture over low heat for 2 minutes, stirring frequently. Cool to room temperature, then store in the refrigerator in an airtight container for up to three weeks. Multiply the recipe as needed.

When the mood strikes for a nice hot cup of cocoa, simply add 3 to 4 tablespoons of the cocoa base to 8 ounces of hot milk and stir.

Coffee | EFFICIENT GRINDING

Many inexpensive blade-type grinders grind coffee beans unevenly, producing some powder as well as some larger pieces of bean. Here's how to even out the grind.

With your hand over the hopper, lift the whole unit off the counter and shake it gently as it grinds. (The motion is akin to blending a martini in a cocktail shaker.) By moving the beans around, you help the machine grind more evenly.

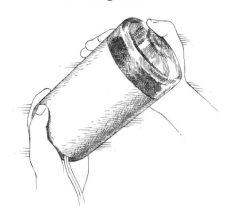

Coffee | STABILIZING FILTERS

When using a manual drip coffee maker, the grounds can spill down into the pot if the paper filter folds over on itself when the water is poured into it. To avoid this problem, try this simple method.

Barely dampen the paper filter with water and press it against the sides of the plastic cone. When you add the coffee and pour the water, the filter will adhere to the cone.

Coffee | SOUNDPROOF GRINDER

Nothing is better than waking up to the smell of fresh-brewed coffee, but no one likes to be jolted from sleep by the loud whirring of the coffee grinder. Here's a way to muffle the noise.

Place an oven mitt over the grinder before turning it on.

tip 219

Coffee | HOMEMADE FLAVORED COFFEE

If you enjoy flavored coffee but only have regular coffee on hand, try making your own.

For 10 cups of coffee, place ½ teaspoon ground cinnamon, ⅛ to ¼ teaspoon cardamom, or ½ teaspoon allspice in the filter of a drip-style coffee maker along with the ground coffee. Brew the coffee as you normally would and enjoy a subtly scented drink.

tip 220

Coffee | PUDDLE-FREE COFFEE MAKING

The poorly designed spouts of most modern coffee carafes make it difficult to pour water into the coffee-maker reservoir without splashing the countertop. Avoid a wet mess and save a step in the process with this easy trick.

tip 221

Fill the reservoir directly from the sink using the spray hose.

Coffee | HEATING MILK FOR COFFEE

If you like your coffee with milk—but also like it piping hot—don't pour cold milk into your cup for a tepid drink.

1. Measure the desired amount of milk into the empty carafe of an electric coffee maker before brewing.

tip 222

2. As the hot coffee drips in, the warming plate of the coffee maker heats the milk, resulting in a pot of steaming hot coffee with milk.

Coffeecakes | DRIZZLING WITH WHITE ICING

The lines of white icing that adorn many coffeecakes are nothing more than sifted confectioners' sugar thinned with a little milk and flavored with a splash of vanilla. Here's how to drizzle the icing over a cooled coffeecake in nice thin lines. Use this tip to decorate molasses spice cookies, too.

tip 223

Dip a large dinner spoon into the bowl with the icing. Quickly move the spoon back and forth over the coffeecake, letting the icing fall in thin ribbons from the end of the spoon. Keep dipping the spoon back into the bowl of icing until the coffeecake is amply iced.

Colander | IMPROVISING WITH A STEAMER BASKET

If you are short on colanders, you might try this handy substitute.

tip 224

Use a steamer basket to drain vegetables, pasta, and the like. Just be sure to pour slowly and carefully because the sides are not as high as the sides of a regular colander.

Cookbooks | PRESERVING

When the pages of a favorite cookbook get soiled or moist from wayward recipe ingredients, use this trick to keep them from sticking together.

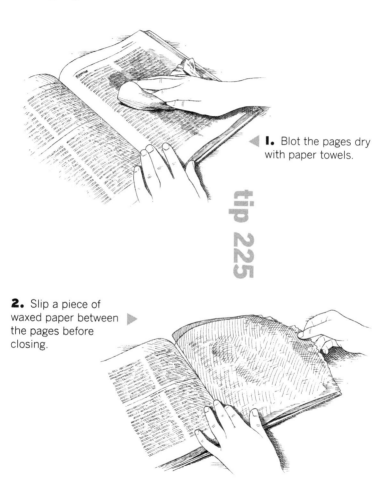

1. Blot the pages dry with paper towels.

tip 225

2. Slip a piece of waxed paper between the pages before closing.

Rolling dough to a specific thickness can be tricky, and, if initially rolled too thin, the dough can toughen with rerolling. This method also works for pie dough.

C

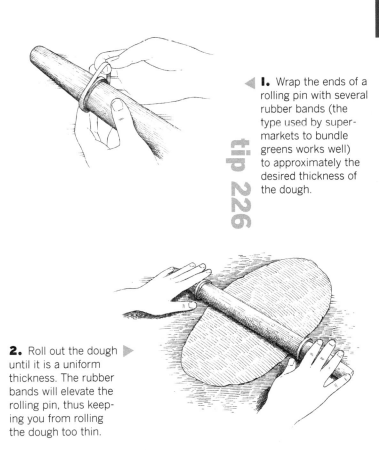

tip 226

1. Wrap the ends of a rolling pin with several rubber bands (the type used by super-markets to bundle greens works well) to approximately the desired thickness of the dough.

2. Roll out the dough until it is a uniform thickness. The rubber bands will elevate the rolling pin, thus keeping you from rolling the dough too thin.

Cookies |
MARKING PEANUT BUTTER COOKIES
WITH HALF THE WORK

Using a fork to make a crosshatch pattern on the tops of
peanut butter cookies is usually a two-step process.

tip 227

To cut the work in
half, mark the cook-
ies in one swipe with
a perforated potato
masher.

Cookies | DISTRIBUTING GOODIES EVENLY IN DOUGH

The last few cookies from a batch of chocolate chip cookies
never seem to have as many chips as the first few. The same
thing often happens with nuts and raisins. Here's how to avoid
this common problem.

Reserve some of the
chips, nuts, or other
goodies and mix them
into the dough after
about half of it has
been scooped out
for cookies. This way,
the last of the cook-
ies will have as much
good stuff as the first
batch.

tip 228

Cookies | MAKING EVEN-SIZED BALLS OF DOUGH

For the best-looking cookies, it is important to start with balls of dough that are all the same size. Many recipes suggest rolling the dough into balls of a specific diameter, but it's difficult to measure the balls with a ruler set on the counter. Here's how to get an accurate measurement.

C

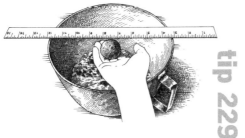

tip 229

Set the ruler on top of the bowl. Rather than placing the ball of dough on top of the ruler (where it's hard to measure the equator), bring the ball up along the side of the ruler.

Cookies | MEASURING OUT STICKY DOUGH

Some cookie dough can be so sticky that your hands become a mess in no time. Here's a way to get equal-sized balls of dough without soiling your hands.

Use a small ice cream scoop to measure out the dough. Dip the scoop into cold water between scoopings to ensure that the dough releases easily every time.

tip 230

Cookies | SHAPING THUMBPRINTS

The best thumbprints have a deep, round indentation to hold the dollop of jam or chocolate securely. Your thumb can be used to make a deep indentation, but for perfectly round ones, try this.

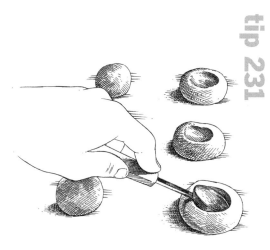

tip 231

Press the back side of a melon baller into dough balls before baking. The end of a wooden honey dipper is also well suited to this task.

Cookies | SHAPING SUGAR COOKIES

Sugar cookies should have an even thickness from side to side and they must be lightly coated with granulated sugar. Here's how to accomplish both goals with one motion.

1. Roll a piece of dough between your palms into a ball (about 1½ table-spoons of dough formed into a ball about 1½ inches in diameter). Roll the ball of dough in a bowl filled with granulated sugar.

tip 232

2. Choose a drinking glass that measures about 2 inches across its bottom. Butter the bottom of the glass and dip it into a bowl of sugar. Use the glass to flatten the dough balls, dip-ping the glass back into the sugar after shaping every other cookie.

Cookies | FREEZING DOUGH

Keeping frozen dough on hand means you can bake just as many, or as few, cookies as you like without first having to whip up a batch of dough. Most cookie doughs can withstand a month or so in the freezer.

Form the dough into balls and arrange them on a baking sheet lined with parchment paper or waxed paper. Place the baking sheet in the freezer. When the balls of dough are frozen, place them in a zipper-lock bag or small airtight container. When you want to make cookies, remove as many balls as you like and bake as directed, increasing the baking time by a minute or two.

tip 233

Cookies | SLICING ICEBOX COOKIES

Logs of dough stored in the freezer are great to have on hand, but we've noticed that the dough can soften by the time you get to the end, making it difficult to cut neat slices. Here's how to prevent this problem.

I. Remove the dough log from the freezer and cut it into pieces no more than 3 inches long. Place all but one piece of dough back in the freezer.

tip 234

2. Using a very sharp chef's knife, slice the piece of dough left out. To prevent one side of the log from flattening due to the pressure you put on it, roll the dough one-eighth of a turn after every slice. Once this first piece of dough has been completely sliced, retrieve the next piece from the freezer and slice in the same manner.

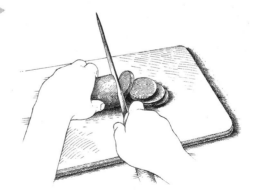

Cookies | KEEPING THEM SEPARATE AS THEY BAKE

Many types of cookies can spread into one another on the cookie sheet as they bake, resulting in odd shapes and soft edges. To keep the cookies separate, try this method of arranging the dough balls.

tip 235

Instead of placing the dough balls in neat rows of three or four so that all the cookies line up, alternate the rows. For example, three cookies in the first row, two in the second, three in the third, two in the fourth, and so on.

Cookies | ROTATING BAKING SHEETS

Often when you have two sheets of cookies in the oven at once, the recipe will direct you to reverse them from front to back and top to bottom. In the bustle of a busy kitchen, however, it can be a challenge to keep track of the direction of the pans.

Line the baking sheets with parchment paper and mark the front edge of the paper, indicating which pans start on the top and the bottom. This marking will help you keep track of which edge goes where when you reverse the pans' positions.

tip 236

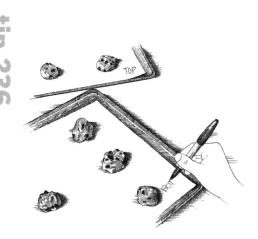

TOP

Cookies | REUSING THE SAME BAKING SHEET

Baking batch after batch of cookies can be a frustrating exercise, especially when you have only one baking sheet. No one wants to scrub the same baking sheet many times, but dough balls must be placed on a clean surface. Here's how to work quickly and efficiently with just one sheet.

1. Load up a sheet of parchment paper with balls of dough, slide the paper onto the baking sheet, and place the cookies in the oven.

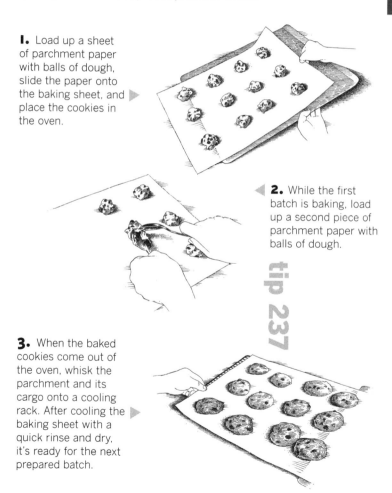

2. While the first batch is baking, load up a second piece of parchment paper with balls of dough.

tip 237

3. When the baked cookies come out of the oven, whisk the parchment and its cargo onto a cooling rack. After cooling the baking sheet with a quick rinse and dry, it's ready for the next prepared batch.

Lifting lace cookies off the pan and shaping them before they harden and become brittle requires exact timing. The method we use makes it easy to lift the cookies while still hot. It also eliminates the need to move the hot cookies off the baking sheet with a spatula, a process that often results in torn or bunched-up cookies.

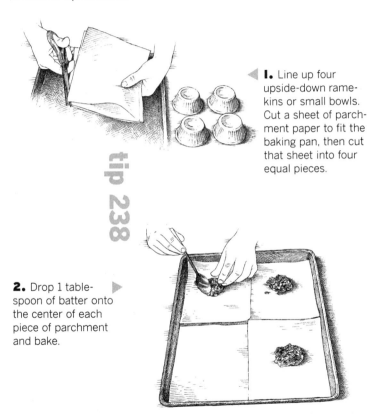

I. Line up four upside-down ramekins or small bowls. Cut a sheet of parchment paper to fit the baking pan, then cut that sheet into four equal pieces.

tip 238

2. Drop 1 tablespoon of batter onto the center of each piece of parchment and bake.

3. When the cookies come out of the oven, remove one of the parchment squares from the sheet to a plate to cool, leaving the others on the hot pan to keep them warm and pliable. Cool the cookie ▶ on the plate to the right consistency for molding (30 to 60 seconds).

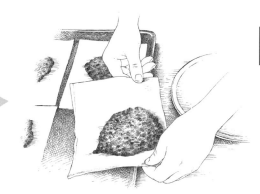

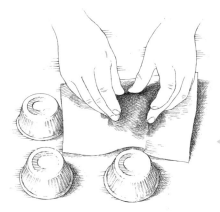

◀ **4.** Lift the parchment square, turn the cookie over, and place it on the bottom of the ramekin or bowl to shape it. Lift the parchment from the cookie. Repeat steps 3 and 4 with the other cookies. Cool the cookies before lifting them off the ramekins or bowls.

C

Cookies | RESCUING BURNT COOKIES

When baking lots of cookies, as for the holidays, it's inevitable that some of the cookies will end up overbrowned or even burnt in some spots. This cookie-saving tip works well with lightly singed cookies, but not thoroughly burnt ones.

tip 239

Gently grate the burnt layer off the bottoms with a Microplane grater.

Cookies | SUGARING CRESCENT COOKIES

Almond crescents as well as Mexican wedding cakes should have a thick, even coating of confectioners' sugar. Many recipes suggest sugaring the cookies as soon as they come out of the oven. Although the coating adheres well to warm cookies, the sugar often tastes pasty because it has melted a bit. Here's how to ensure that the coating is thick but never pasty.

tip 240

Once the cookies have cooled, roll them in a bowl of confectioners' sugar and shake off the excess. Don't worry if the coating is spotty in places; just go ahead and store the cookies in an airtight container. When ready to serve, roll the cookies in sugar again to cover any bare spots.

Cookies | MAKING YOUR OWN COLORED SUGAR

Colored sugar makes a fine decoration for holiday cookies. However, many stores carry just one or two colors, and you often end up with leftover sugar. Here's how to customize your colors and make only as much as you need.

tip 241

I. Sprinkle about ½ cup granulated sugar evenly over the bottom of a pie plate or metal bowl. Add about five drops of food coloring and mix thoroughly.

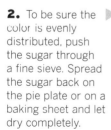

2. To be sure the color is evenly distributed, push the sugar through a fine sieve. Spread the sugar back on the pie plate or on a baking sheet and let dry completely.

Cookies | ORGANIZING DECORATIONS

During the holiday season you may be decorating cookies several times. Here's a good way to organize your favorite decorations. If you bake with children, you'll also appreciate this neat way to organize colored sugar, sprinkles, and such.

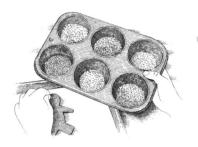

tip 242

Place a different decoration in each cup of a muffin tin, which is easy to move around the kitchen and store for next time.

Cookies | YOGURT CONTAINERS FOR DECORATING

Empty plastic yogurt containers make great storage for cookie-decorating supplies such as colored sugars and sprinkles. Take this idea one step further by turning them into shakers.

tip 243

2. Replace the lids and invert the containers to sprinkle decorations onto frosted cookies.

▼

1. Punch holes in the lids with a paper hole-punch.

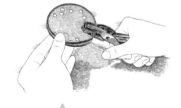

Cookies | EASY DRYING FOR FROSTED COOKIES

A box or tin of colorful frosted cookies makes a nice gift to friends and neighbors, especially around the holidays. But before the cookies can be wrapped, the frosting has to dry thoroughly, and it can be a real challenge to find enough space to spread out a few dozen cookies in a cramped kitchen.

1. Coat the rim of a small paper cup with frosting and invert on the middle of a paper plate. Arrange as many drying cookies around the cup as will fit comfortably on the plate. Dab the exposed rim of the cup bottom with frosting, then make another plate in the same manner and stack it on top of the first.

tip 244

2. Repeat until you have a stack of four or five cookie-laden plates.

Cookies | KEEPING FRESH

Decorative cookie jars, like those made from ceramic, are convenient and attractive but not airtight, allowing fresh-baked cookies to go stale quickly. This method preserves the cookies' freshness and allows you to keep the pretty jar.

tip 245

Line the inside of the jar with a large zipper-lock bag, place the cookies in the bag, and seal tightly.

Cookies | FRESHNESS INSURANCE

We stand by the old method of reviving soft cookies that have begun to harden by placing a small piece of bread in the cookie jar with them. Here's how to take this trick one step further.

When storing cookies in a zipper-lock bag to bring to a picnic or any other event, add a small piece of bread to each bag to make sure that the cookies will be soft and fresh the next day.

tip 246

Cooking Fat | EASY DISPOSAL

Excess fat from cooked bacon, sausage, or ground meat can clog kitchen sink pipes. Here's an easy way to get rid of this fat.

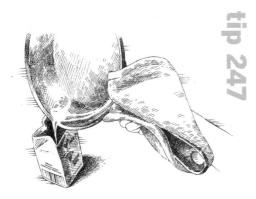

Wash out empty heavy-duty cardboard containers from half-and-half or heavy cream and save them under the sink. When you have some hot bacon or other fat to throw away, pull out one of the stored cartons and pour. Once the fat has cooled, close the carton and dispose of it.

Cooking Spray | NO-MESS SPRAYING

Many cooks have had to clean up the oily film on their counter or workspace which results from using an aerosol nonstick cooking spray. Here's how to avoid this problem.

Open the dishwasher door, place the item to be greased right on the door, and spray away. Any excess or overspray will be cleaned off the door the next time you run the dishwasher.

Cookware | SCRATCHLESS STEAMING

Rather than scratching a saucepan's nonstick surface with the metal legs of a steamer insert, protect it with parchment paper.

1. Cut a piece of parchment paper to fit the inside of your saucepan. Fill with 1 inch of water.

tip 249

2. Place the steamer insert on top of the parchment. Bring to a simmer and steam your food, being careful not to let all the water evaporate.

Cookware | KEEPING PAN HANDLES COOL

Over gas heat, skillets with hollow handles often heat up enough to require potholders. If you own such a skillet, we recommend this simple solution.

tip 250

Stuff the handle with aluminum foil. The foil interrupts the heat flow from the burner up through the handle, keeping it cool enough to be grabbed without a potholder.

C

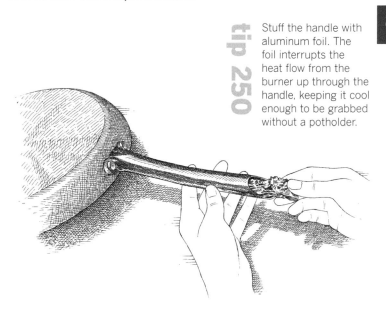

Cookware | PROTECTING NONSTICK PANS

The surfaces on nonstick pans can chip or scratch easily, especially if you stack pans in a cabinet. Here are several ways to store them efficiently and safely.

tip 251

Place a doubled sheet of paper towel or bubble wrap between each pan as you nest the pans in a stack.

tip 252

Use small pieces of cardboard, cut from cardboard sheets such as those placed in laundered shirts.

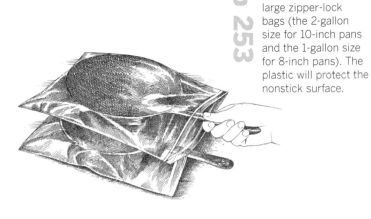

Before stacking the pans, slide them into large zipper-lock bags (the 2-gallon size for 10-inch pans and the 1-gallon size for 8-inch pans). The plastic will protect the nonstick surface.

tip 253

C

Place cheap paper plates between the pans as you stack them. The plates' round shape helps them stay in place, and they last for ages.

tip 254

Cookware | KEEPING TRACK OF POT LIDS

Most cooks throw all their lids into one drawer, making it hard to match the right lid with the right pan. Here are a few ways to keep your lids organized.

tip 255

If you store your pans in a drawer, install a slender expansion curtain rod in the front. Stand the lids up straight against the rod, which will keep the lids in sight and in reach.

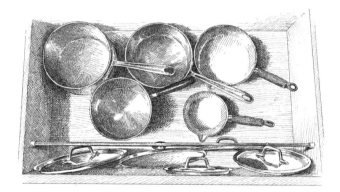

If you store your pans in a cabinet, set an adjustable V-rack for roasting to the widest setting, then stand the lids up in the slots between the wires of the rack.

tip 256

C

tip 257

If you hang your pans from hooks, slide the loop handle of the lid right onto the handle of its matching pan, then hang the pan from the hook.

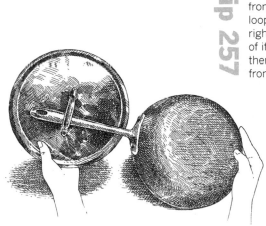

Cookware | LIFTING HOT LIDS

Rather than burning your fingers or searching for a potholder every time you want to lift a lid off a pot on the stove, try this tip.

tip 258

Before cooking, wedge a wine cork under the handle of the lid. The cork stays cool when the lid gets hot, giving you something safe to grab onto when lifting the lid.

Cookware | CLEANING POTS AND PANS

Pans containing baked-on coatings of burned cheese or sauce from a macaroni and cheese, lasagna, or fondue dish pose a formidable cleaning task.

tip 259

Cover the burned-on mess with dishwashing soap and a small amount of boiling water. Allow it to rest overnight. The next morning the mess washes away with ease.

Cookware | CLEANING COPPER

Copper cookware looks great but is notorious for tarnishing quickly. Commercial copper polish requires some scrubbing and costs a lot of money. Here's a way to save money and work.

With a paper towel, smear a thin layer of ketchup over the tarnished surface. Wait 5 minutes, then wipe and rinse off the ketchup. The acidity in the ketchup lifts the tarnish away.

tip 260

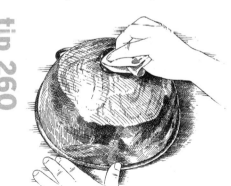

Cooling Rack | IMPROVISING SUBSTITUTES

During holiday baking marathons, cooks may find themselves with a shortage of cooling racks. Here are some clever alternatives.

tip 261

If you have a freshly baked cake, pie, or other confection, set the hot pan on an overturned muffin tin. The muffin tin will also support a cake after it's been turned out of its pan.

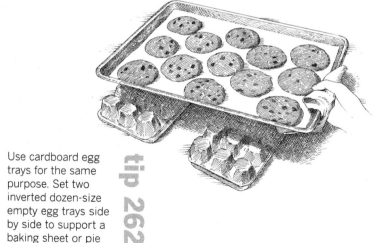

tip 262

Use cardboard egg trays for the same purpose. Set two inverted dozen-size empty egg trays side by side to support a baking sheet or pie plate.

Place canning-jar rings on the countertop. The elevation of the rings allows for just enough air circulation.

Place four dinner knives on a countertop, alternating the direction of the blades and spacing them more than an inch apart. The knives will provide a stable, elevated surface.

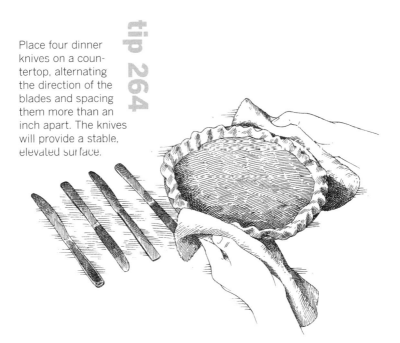

C

Corn | HUSKING MADE EASIER

Husking corn is no one's favorite job, but here's a way to make it much easier.

1. With the husk still attached, cut off both ends of an ear of corn (a serrated knife works best).

2. Roll the ear on the counter, and the husk comes right off. Finish by removing any remaining threads of silk.

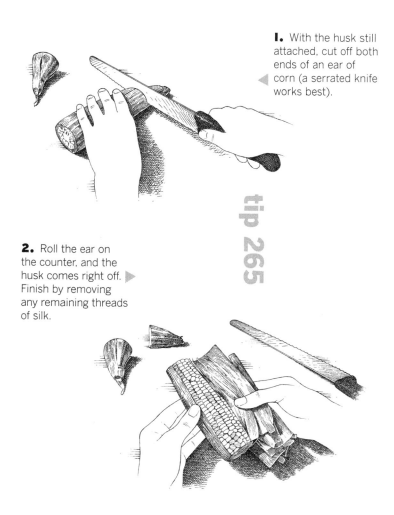

tip 265

Corn | CUT-CORN CORRAL

No one likes to chase fresh corn kernels all over the counter when cutting them off the cob. Here's an easy way to corral them.

tip 266

Line a rimmed baking sheet with a clean kitchen towel. Center a whole or half cob on the cloth-covered sheet and cut away. The fabric will catch the kernels as they fall and keep them from jumping every which way.

Corn | CORN-HOLDER CADDY

While corn holders make eating corn on the cob a neater proposition, finding them in a drawer chock-full of other kitchen tools is neither easy nor safe (many a cook has pricked a finger when so engaged).

To avoid having to empty the entire drawer to find the corn holders, stick them into either end of a cork.

tip 267

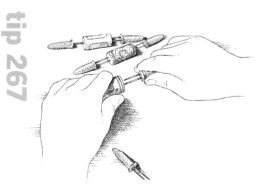

Corn |
LIFTING CORN ON THE COB FROM BOILING WATER

Without a pair of tongs, removing corn on the cob from a pot of boiling water can be quite a challenge.

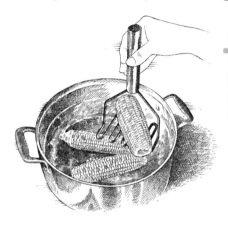

tip 268

Use a potato masher, which both cradles and drains the corn beautifully.

Corn | DRAINING HOT BOILED CORN

Hot boiled corncobs are awkward to drain in a conventional colander.

tip 269

Drain hot boiled corn in a clean dish rack, which can easily accommodate the bulky cobs.

Corn | REMOVING KERNELS

Cutting the kernels from long ears of corn can be tricky.
Tapered ears wobble on cutting boards, and kernels can go
flying around the kitchen. Here's a way to work safely and
more neatly.

tip 270

Cut the ear in half
crosswise and then
stand the half ears
on their cut surfaces,
which are flat and
stable.

C

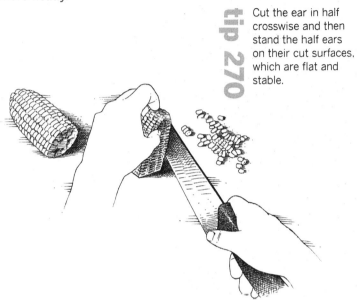

Corn | BUTTERING CORN AND BREAD TOGETHER

Using a knife to butter an ear of corn can be messy and frustrating, as the melting butter slides off the knife and down the ear. Here's an easier way to butter corn.

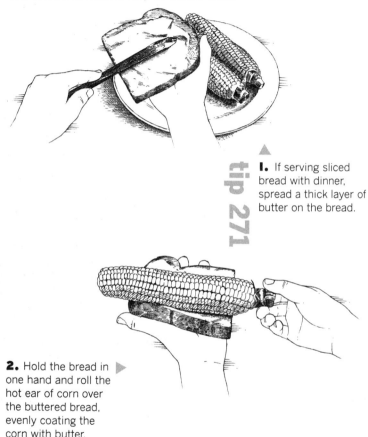

1. If serving sliced bread with dinner, spread a thick layer of butter on the bread.

tip 271

2. Hold the bread in one hand and roll the hot ear of corn over the buttered bread, evenly coating the corn with butter.

Corn | PREPARING FOR GRILLING

Adding flavor from the grill is a nice but tricky thing to do with fresh corn. Husked ears tend to burn, and unhusked ears steam on the grill, failing to pick up that great smoky flavor. Here's how to keep corn from burning while still infusing it with grilled flavor.

C

1. Before grilling, remove all but the innermost layer of husk.

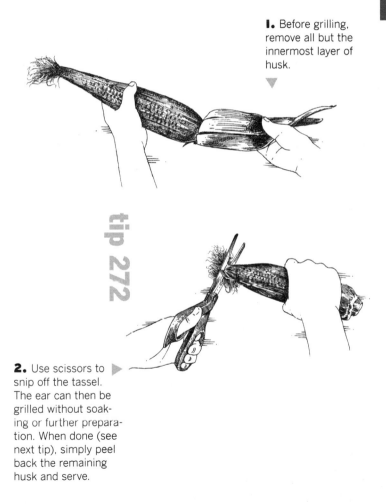

tip 272

2. Use scissors to snip off the tassel. The ear can then be grilled without soaking or further preparation. When done (see next tip), simply peel back the remaining husk and serve.

Corn | KNOWING WHEN GRILLED CORN IS DONE

Most cooks know how long they like to cook corn in water. But timing can be tricky when grilling corn because fires vary in intensity. If you prepare corn according to the method outlined in the previous tip, there's a visual clue you can use to judge when the corn is tender.

tip 273

As soon as the husk picks up the dark silhouette of kernels and begins to pull away from the tip of the ear, the corn is ready to come off the grill.

Corn | CORN ON THE KEBAB

If you like to grill pieces of corn on the cob kebab-style, you know how difficult it can be to poke the skewer, especially one made from bamboo, through the thick center of the cob. Here's a way to streamline the process.

After cutting the cob into chunks, run a corkscrew through each piece, which will make it easy to run a skewer in. The coiled hole helps ensure a snug fit.

tip 274

Corn | MILKING

Releasing the milk from corn kernels yields its sweet flavor for use in creamed corn, corn pudding, fritters, and chowder. Milking corn needn't be a time-consuming, cumbersome process.

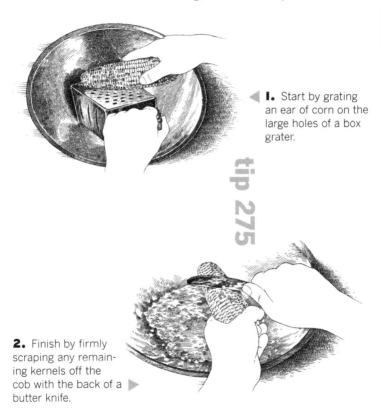

1. Start by grating an ear of corn on the large holes of a box grater.

tip 275

2. Finish by firmly scraping any remaining kernels off the cob with the back of a ▶ butter knife.

Cornish Hens |
PRICKING SKIN TO PREVENT BALLOONING

Cornish hens can build up juices beneath the skin during cooking, causing the skin to balloon. Here's how to prevent this unsightly occurrence.

tip 276

Before cooking, carefully prick the skin (but not the meat) on the breast and leg with the tip of a knife.

Countertop | PROTECTING

On some types of countertops, such as old-fashioned Formica, you run the risk of damaging the surface by setting a hot pan down.

tip 277

Purchase an attractive 12 by 12-inch tile and position it next to your stovetop to use as a trivet. This way, pots coming off of a burner can go onto the trivet, leaving the burner free for another pot.

Crabs | CLEANING SOFT-SHELL CRABS

Although your fishmonger will probably offer to clean soft-shell crabs for you, for optimum freshness you should clean the crabs yourself, right before cooking.

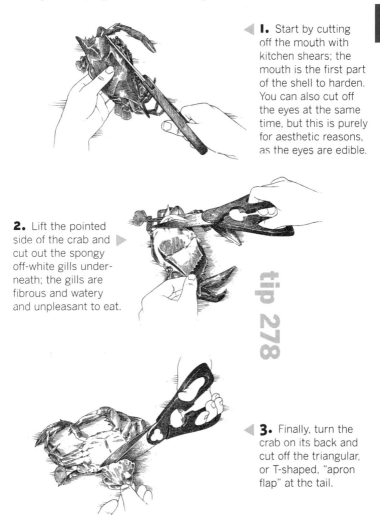

C

I. Start by cutting off the mouth with kitchen shears; the mouth is the first part of the shell to harden. You can also cut off the eyes at the same time, but this is purely for aesthetic reasons, as the eyes are edible.

2. Lift the pointed side of the crab and cut out the spongy off-white gills underneath; the gills are fibrous and watery and unpleasant to eat.

tip 278

3. Finally, turn the crab on its back and cut off the triangular, or T-shaped, "apron flap" at the tail.

Cream | CHILLING THE BOWL

For the best results, you should chill a bowl before whipping cream in it. For many cooks, the freezer is either too small or too full to accommodate a large bowl. Here are a couple of ways to accomplish this task.

1. At least 15 minutes before whipping the cream, fill the bowl with ice cubes and cold water, place the whisk in the ice water (it helps to chill this tool as well), and put the bowl into the refrigerator.

2. When ready to whip the cream, dump out the ice water, dry the bowl and whisk, and add the cream. The bowl will stay cold as you work, and the cream whips up beautifully.

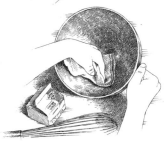

If there's no room in your refrigerator to fit the bowl, fill a zipper-lock bag with ice cubes and place it in the bowl. A bag filled with 20 ice cubes chills a 12-inch stainless steel bowl in about 5 minutes. Alternatively, toss in a couple of frozen freezer packs—they will turn the bowl icy cold in about 10 minutes.

Cream |
JUDGING WHEN CREAM IS PROPERLY WHIPPED

Many recipes instruct the cook to whip cream to either soft or stiff peaks. Here are easy ways to tell when you should stop beating.

tip 281

Cream whipped to soft peaks will droop slightly from the ends of the beaters.

Cream whipped to stiff peaks will cling tightly to the ends of the beaters and hold its shape.

tip 282

Cucumbers | SEEDING

In many recipes, the watery seeds are removed from cucumbers. Here's an easy way to accomplish this task.

tip 283

Halve the cucumber (already peeled if desired) lengthwise. Run a small spoon inside each cucumber half to scoop out the seeds and surrounding liquid.

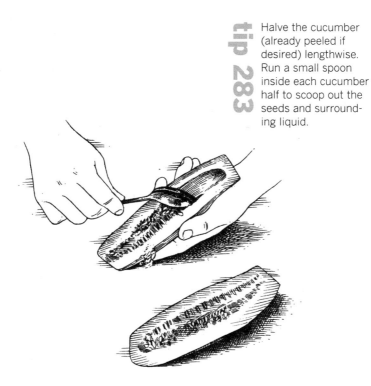

Cucumbers | WEIGHTING

Even when seeded, cucumbers can give off a lot of liquid and make dressings too watery. For this reason, we think it's a good idea to salt and weight cucumbers before dressing them.

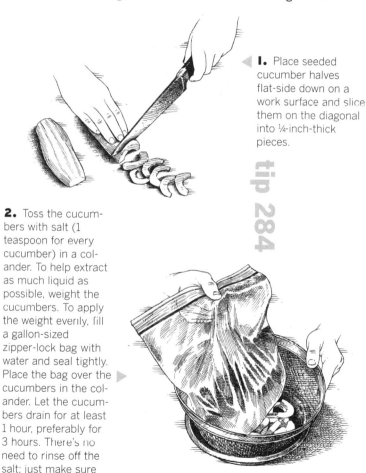

1. Place seeded cucumber halves flat-side down on a work surface and slice them on the diagonal into ¼-inch-thick pieces.

tip 284

2. Toss the cucumbers with salt (1 teaspoon for every cucumber) in a colander. To help extract as much liquid as possible, weight the cucumbers. To apply the weight evenly, fill a gallon-sized zipper-lock bag with water and seal tightly. Place the bag over the cucumbers in the colander. Let the cucumbers drain for at least 1 hour, preferably for 3 hours. There's no need to rinse off the salt; just make sure not to add salt to the dressing.

Cupcakes | SAFE TRANSPORT

One accidental bump can mean disaster for a frosted cupcake (or any other delicate pastry) that you are transporting. Here's an easy way to give cupcakes a little extra protection with the use of an inverted pint-sized deli container.

tip 285

Place the container lid bottom-side up on the work surface (the groove that seals the container should be facing up) and put the cupcake on it. Invert the container, slip it over the cupcake and down onto the lid, and seal it shut, thus creating a safe shell around the cupcake.

Cupcakes | WRAPPING NEATLY

Cupcake aficionados know how messy frosted ones can be when packed into a lunch bag or box, even when plastic wrap is used. Here's a way to keep the delicate frosting intact.

Cut the cupcake in half horizontally and flip the top half upside down so that the icing is in the middle, making a little layer cake. Wrap the cupcake (or piece of frosted sheet cake) in plastic wrap or a plastic bag, and the cupcake is good to go.

tip 286

Custard | SMOOTH CUSTARD SHORTCUT

When making the custard for cream pies, we recommend removing the chalaza—a small cord attached to the yolk of an egg—to ensure a silky-smooth texture. This can be done by grasping the slippery cord with your fingers, but some cooks have difficulty with this technique.

C

Try using a grapefruit spoon instead (a strawberry huller also works well).

Custard | EASY REMOVAL FROM WATER BATH

Baked custards, like pots de crème and crème brûlée, are cooked in a water bath to ensure slow, even cooking, making it hard to remove the ramekins without burning fingers or marring the surface of the custard with a potholder.

Slip rubber bands around the tips of a pair of tongs. The rubber provides a sure grip for easy removal, and there's no danger of burning fingers.

Cutting Board | KEEPING STABLE

Chefs use a no-skid mat beneath a cutting board to keep it from slipping all over the counter. If you don't own a mat, try one of these tips.

tip 289

Lay a damp sheet of paper towel on the counter, then put the cutting board on top. The damp paper towel holds the board in place and can be used to wipe down the counter. When you are done, throw the soiled towel out.

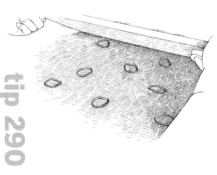

tip 290

Sprinkle a handful of rubber bands on the counter and place your cutting board on top, thereby preventing any slipping or sliding while you chop. If the bands get contaminated with juices from meat or poultry, just throw them out.

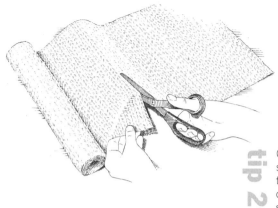

tip 291

Cut leftover nonskid shelf liner into pieces that fit under your cutting boards, thus stopping them from slipping and sliding. When the makeshift mats are not in use, just roll them up and store them neatly in a kitchen drawer.

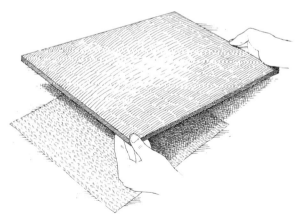

Cutting Mat | CLEVER USES FOR FLEXIBLE MATS

Flexible cutting mats make great chopping surfaces, but they have more unusual uses as well.

tip 292

Cut mats to fit the bottoms of the vegetable bins and deli drawers in your refrigerator. This makes cleaning the bins a breeze—simply lift out the mat and wipe it off.

tip 293

Set heavy countertop appliances, such as standing mixers and food processors, on flexible cutting mats. Store the appliances on top of the mats at the back of the kitchen counter. When you want to use one, just grasp the edge of a mat to slide it forward.

tip 294

To avoid cracking just-sliced cake layers, slide a cutting mat between the layers and use it to gently ease the top layer off the bottom.

tip 295

Recipes often advise pounding cutlets between sheets of plastic wrap, parchment, or waxed paper, all of which can easily rip or tear. Flexible cutting mats serve the same purpose admirably, but they won't rip. And their sturdiness allows you to pound the meat into thinner, more uniform cutlets.

Cutting Mat | BREADBOX CUTTING MAT

It can be a hassle to pull out and dirty a large cutting board every time you want freshly sliced bread. Instead, keep a custom-made plastic cutting mat right in the breadbox. Not only is it conveniently located, but it also needs little maintenance—just a quick wipe to clean off crumbs.

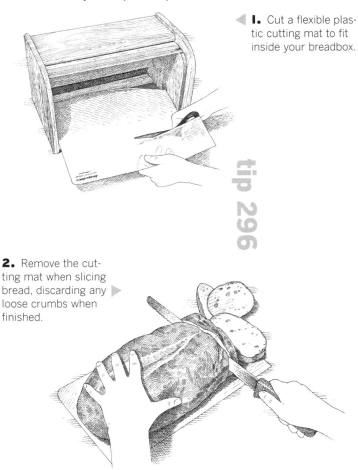

1. Cut a flexible plastic cutting mat to fit inside your breadbox.

tip 296

2. Remove the cutting mat when slicing bread, discarding any loose crumbs when finished.

Dishwasher | SECURING SMALL ITEMS

It's easy for small kitchen utensils such as cake testers, trussing needles, pastry tips, and measuring spoons to fall through
the slots in the dishwasher silverware container. Try this handy
tip to keep them in place.

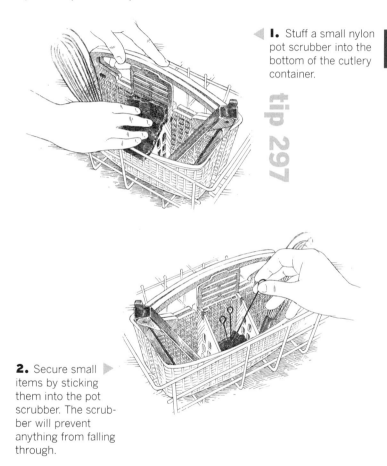

1. Stuff a small nylon pot scrubber into the bottom of the cutlery container.

D

tip 297

2. Secure small items by sticking them into the pot scrubber. The scrubber will prevent anything from falling through.

Dishwasher | UNLOADING SILVERWARE SIMPLIFIED

A little extra care in loading silverware into the dishwasher can make unloading go faster.

tip 298

When loading the dishwasher, separate the silverware by type. At unloading time, simply grab each bunch of silverware and store.

Drinks | FLAVORING SUMMER DRINKS

Here's an easy way to create inventive summer drinks at a moment's notice.

tip 299

Stir scoops of frozen juice concentrate into pitchers of iced tea to taste. Lemonade, limeade, and orange juice concentrates are the best choices.

Duck | PREPARING FOR GRILLING

Duck breast is great grilled, but its abundant fat can be a problem, causing flare-ups that result in charred and ruined meat. Removing the skin entirely can cause the meat to dry out. Here's an easy compromise.

I. With a sharp chef's knife, trim any overhanging skin and fat from around each breast half. Slide your fingers under the remaining skin along the length of the breast to loosen. Turn the breast half on its side and slice off some of the skin and fat so that only a strip of skin (1½ to 2 inches) remains in the center of each breast half.

tip 300

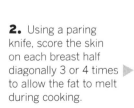

2. Using a paring knife, score the skin on each breast half diagonally 3 or 4 times to allow the fat to melt during cooking.

Dumplings | NO-STICK STEAMING

Steamed dumplings often stick to the steamer and tear as you try to remove them. Here's how to prevent this from happening.

tip 301

Line the steamer basket with sturdy lettuce leaves and then place the dumplings on top of the lettuce. This trick can be used with any steamed pastry item.

Eggplant | SLICING FOR GRILLING

Eggplant is often sliced lengthwise for grilling. The outer pieces are covered with skin and won't get those nice grill marks on both sides unless you use this tip, which also works with zucchini.

tip 302

Use a sharp knife to remove the peel from the outer eggplant slices. Besides creating more attractive grill marks, we find that the flesh cooks better when directly exposed to the heat of the grill.

Eggs | KEEPING IN PLACE

Before tossing out that empty egg carton, make it work double duty as a container to keep the eggs from rolling off the counter and as a receptacle for the empty shells.

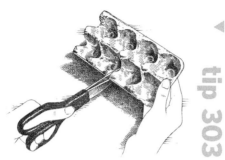

1. Trim the top and the flap from the carton, then cut the base into three sections, each able to hold up to four eggs.

E

2. While measuring the other ingredients of a recipe, safely store the eggs in one section and return the spent shells to the container as you use them.

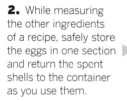

When only one or two eggs need to be corralled, simply nest the egg inside a thick rubber band.

Eggs | A BETTER WAY TO CRACK

Cracking an egg on the side of a mixing bowl is common kitchen practice. This method is just as simple and perhaps more reliable.

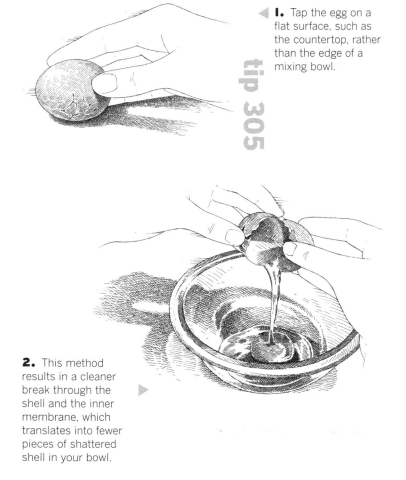

1. Tap the egg on a flat surface, such as the countertop, rather than the edge of a mixing bowl.

tip 305

2. This method results in a cleaner break through the shell and the inner membrane, which translates into fewer pieces of shattered shell in your bowl.

Eggs | SEPARATING

Some cooks find it awkward to crack an egg perfectly down the middle and then juggle the yolk between the shell halves to release all of the white.

tip 306

Wrap a rubber band around the handle of a large slotted spoon. Set the spoon over a small bowl by resting the tip of the spoon and the rubber band on opposite edges of the bowl. Crack each egg over the spoon, and watch the whites slip through the holes into the bowl while the yolk stays in the spoon.

E

Eggs | BEATING THE WHITES

A standing mixer is the best tool for whipping egg whites, but the speed of the mixer means that eggs can go from properly whipped to overwhipped in seconds. Here's an easy way to keep from overbeating egg whites. Use the same technique when whipping cream in a standing mixer.

Just before the whites reach the proper consistency, turn off the mixer. Detach the whisk attachment and remove the bowl from the mixer. Use the whisk attachment to make the last few strokes by hand. Be sure to scrape along the bottom of the bowl.

tip 307

Eggs | FOLDING IN BEATEN WHITES

Recipes for everything from cakes to soufflés call for beaten egg whites, which are usually folded into the batter just before it is baked. If you mix in the whites too vigorously, the cake or soufflé may not rise. If you don't incorporate them thoroughly, you may be left with eggy patches after baking. Here's the best way to fold beaten egg whites into a batter. Start by vigorously stirring a portion of the beaten whites (most recipes will call for a quarter or third of the whites) into the batter. This amount lightens the texture of the batter so the rest of the whites can be folded in more gently.

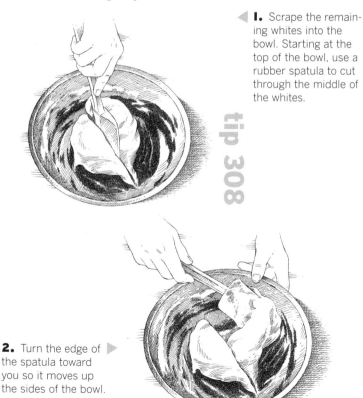

I. Scrape the remaining whites into the bowl. Starting at the top of the bowl, use a rubber spatula to cut through the middle of the whites.

tip 308

2. Turn the edge of the spatula toward you so it moves up the sides of the bowl.

3. Continue this motion, going full circle, until the spatula is back at the center of the bowl again. ▷

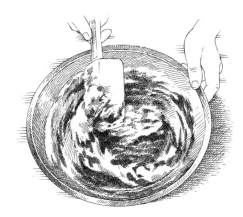

◁ **4.** Follow this procedure four more times, turning the bowl a quarter turn each time. Finally, use the spatula to scrape around the entire circumference of the bowl.

E

Eggs | PEELING EGGSHELLS—FAST

When making recipes such as egg salad or deviled eggs, which call for several hard-cooked eggs, loosening and removing the shells can be a time-consuming process, but there is a quick way to get the job done.

1. After draining the hot water from the pot used to cook the eggs, shake the pot back and forth to crack the shells.

tip 309

2. Add enough ice water to cover the eggs and let cool. The water seeps under the broken shells, allowing them to be slipped off without a struggle.

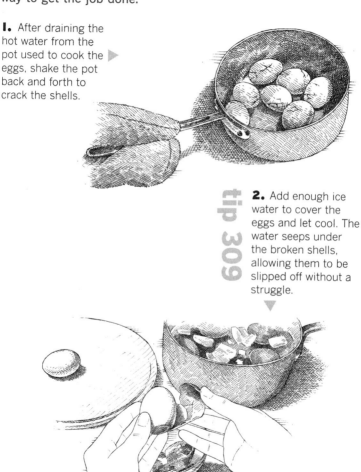

Eggs | FLUFFY FILLINGS FOR DEVILED EGGS

A pasty, heavy texture in the yolk filling is the downfall of many deviled eggs. Here are two ways to keep the filling light and fluffy.

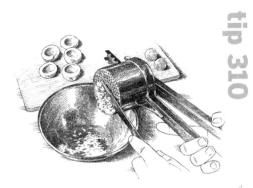

tip 310

If making many deviled eggs at one time, press the yolks gently through a potato ricer and use a knife to shave the extruded yolk off the bottom of the ricer and into a bowl. The yolks come out smooth, light, and airy.

E

tip 311

When making smaller batches, grate the yolks using the drum of a Mouli grater. Don't apply too much pressure on the hopper, and the yolks will emerge light and fluffy.

Eggs | USING A PLASTIC BAG TO FILL DEVILED EGGS

Once the yolks have been riced or grated and then seasoned, the filling is ready to be piped back into the empty egg halves. A pastry bag fitted with a star tip is the ideal tool for the job. Here's what to do if you don't have one.

tip 312

Spoon the yolk mixture into a plastic bag. Snip a small piece from one bottom corner of the bag, then gently squeeze the filling through the hole into the egg halves.

Eggs |
KEEPING DEVILED EGGS STABLE FOR TRANSPORT

Preparing beautiful deviled eggs requires care, so it goes without saying that you want them to arrive at your destination looking as perfect as they did in your kitchen. Here's how to keep the eggs upright if you want to transport them.

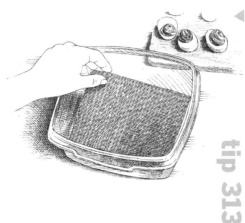

1. Cut a clean piece of rubberized shelf or drawer liner (available at hardware stores) to the size of the dish that will hold the eggs. Make sure to choose a dish with relatively high sides—a square plastic storage container with a lid is perfect.

tip 313

2. Place the fitted liner on the bottom of the container, then stock it with enough eggs to fill it in a single layer. The liner keeps the eggs from sliding when the container is moved.

Eggs | GETTING EGGS INTO A SKILLET

Fried eggs cook so quickly that seconds can make the difference between a runny yolk and one that has set. If you add the eggs one at a time to a hot pan, the first egg will be done well before the last. Adding all the eggs at exactly the same time means that all the eggs will be done at the same time.

Crack two eggs into each of two small bowls. When the pan is ready, slide the eggs from both bowls into the skillet from opposite sides.

Eggs | LIFTING HARD-COOKED EGGS SAFELY

We don't like to use a slotted spoon to transfer hard-cooked eggs from the pot, because a poorly timed nudge, shift in balance, or unsteady hand could send the eggs flying off the spoon and onto the floor.

A pasta server's deep bowl is the ideal size for cradling eggs securely.

Eggs | IDENTIFYING HARD-COOKED EGGS
IN THE REFRIGERATOR

Sometimes it can be difficult to tell which eggs in your refrigerator are raw and which ones are hard-cooked. Here's a simple
trick to keep them straight. This works only with white eggs.

Add a little balsamic
vinegar to the cooking
water along with the
eggs. This dark brown
vinegar tints the
eggshells so you can
distinguish them from
bright white raw eggs.

E

Eggs | CUBING HARD-COOKED EGGS PERFECTLY

For egg salad and other dishes, it's nice to have perfect cubes. Hard-cooked eggs are slippery and oddly shaped, so many cooks end up with uneven pieces or, worse, pieces that are slightly mashed. Here's a neat trick that's fast and foolproof.

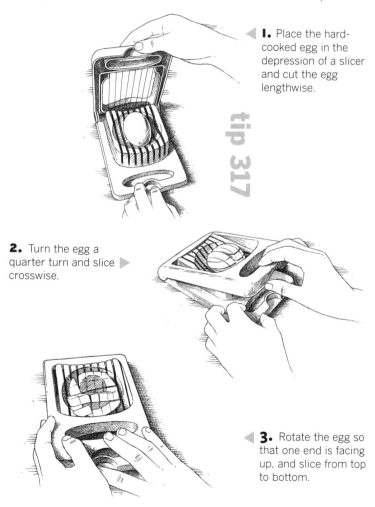

1. Place the hard-cooked egg in the depression of a slicer and cut the egg lengthwise.

2. Turn the egg a quarter turn and slice crosswise.

3. Rotate the egg so that one end is facing up, and slice from top to bottom.

tip 317

Eggs | CRUMBLING HARD-COOKED EGGS

For garnishes and salads, it is best to use very fine pieces of hard-cooked egg. Chopping the egg can be tricky and usually results in fairly large pieces. Here's a better option.

tip 318

Press the egg through a mesh sieve to yield fine, even pieces.

E

Eggs | POACHING FOUR AT ONCE

As with frying (see tip 314, page 208), it is important to get all the eggs into the pan at the same time when poaching them. Because there's water in the pan, you must use a slightly different method.

Crack each egg into a small cup with a handle. When the water is ready, lower the lips of each cup into the water at the same time and then tip the eggs into the pan.

tip 319

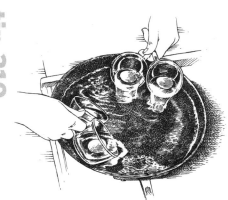

Eggs | FOLDING OMELETS

Omelets are somewhat delicate and when filled can be especially difficult to fold, then remove from the pan without ripping open. Try this quick and easy way to transfer and fold the omelet simultaneously—minus the rips and tears.

I. Be sure that the handle of the nonstick pan is facing you, and when the egg is just set and still moist on the surface, immediately fill the omelet by sprinkling the warmed filling onto the left side of the omelet or, if you're left-handed, the right side.

2. Tip the pan slightly and slide the filled half of the omelet onto a warm plate. With a slight turn of the wrist, slightly invert the pan so the other side of the omelet folds over the filling.

tip 320

Endive | PREPARING FOR THE GRILL

The bitter flavor of endive softens somewhat when grilled, but keeping the leaves intact and cooking evenly can be a challenge.

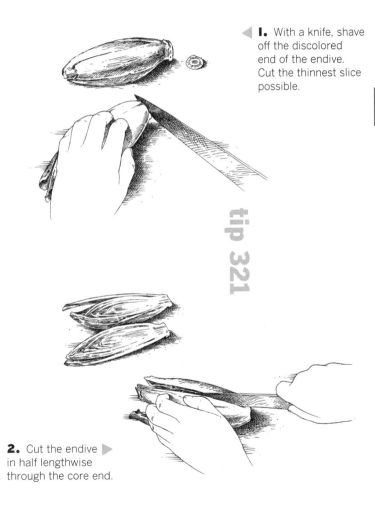

1. With a knife, shave off the discolored end of the endive. Cut the thinnest slice possible.

2. Cut the endive in half lengthwise through the core end.

Entertaining | KEEPING BEVERAGES CHILLED

Refrigerator space for chilling beverages is often at a premium when you're throwing a party. Press another household appliance into action to solve the problem.

tip 322

Use your washing machine as an ice-box. Fill the washer's basket with ice cubes, then nestle in the cans and bottles. When it's time for more cold drinks, they're at the ready. When the party is over and the ice has melted, simply run the washer's spin cycle to drain the water.

Entertaining |
TRANSPORTING FRAGILE PASTRIES AND HORS D'OEUVRES

Individual, bite-sized tartlets are a great dessert to bring to a party, but the delicate shells can easily break and are difficult to transport.

Pack the tartlets in a cardboard egg carton that has been lined with plastic wrap.

tip 323

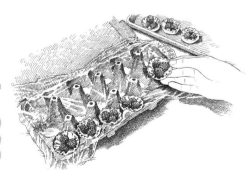

Entertaining | DRIER DINNER GUESTS

Refilling guests' glasses with cold beverages usually means contending with dribbles from the pitcher. Here's a unique solution.

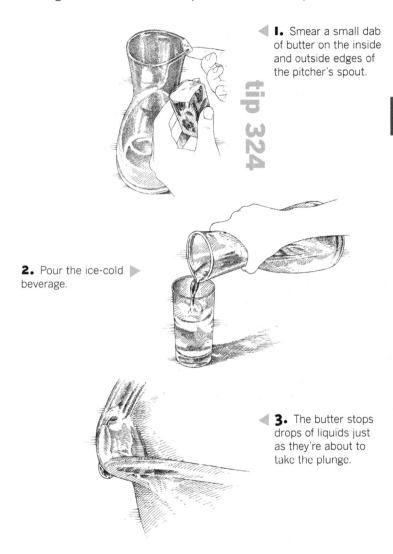

1. Smear a small dab of butter on the inside and outside edges of the pitcher's spout.

tip 324

E

2. Pour the ice-cold beverage.

3. The butter stops drops of liquids just as they're about to take the plunge.

Entertaining | IMPROMPTU ICE BUCKET

If you're down to last-minute preparations for a holiday cocktail party and find yourself without an ice bucket, here's a clever alternative.

tip 325

A frozen ice cream maker canister makes an excellent ice bucket that will keep ice cubes frozen for several hours. To protect furniture in case any condensation forms on the outside of the canister, place it on a plate or tray.

Entertaining | FINISHING RECIPES FOR A PARTY

When entertaining, it's sometimes a challenge to stay organized and finish dishes that have been started ahead of time once guests arrive. To eliminate the need to pull out the recipes themselves in the rush of finishing a dish and getting dinner on the table, try this tip (which also allows friends to help out easily).

tip 326

Write the remaining recipe instructions on a label or piece of masking tape and stick it to the container holding the dish to be finished. For instance, for lasagna, the note might read: "Bake covered for 15 minutes at 375, remove foil, bake 25 minutes longer."

Entertaining | ENGINEERING CRUDITÉS

Height is an important visual element in an appealing crudité presentation. Even with an assortment as simple as cherry tomatoes and carrot and celery sticks, try using the following two tricks to create a little extra height in your displays.

tip 327 To elevate a small bowl full of bite-sized items such as cherry tomatoes or trimmed broccoli florets, overturn a small glass or ceramic bowl to use as a stand for the bowl holding the tomatoes. Put a small piece of folded plastic wrap between the two to keep the top bowl from sliding off the bottom one.

E

Give celery and carrot sticks extra lift (and freshness) by standing them up in glasses or cups with a few ice cubes in the bottom.

tip 328

Entertaining | EDIBLE TOOTHPICKS

Any number of hors d'oeuvres—including small meatballs, crab cakes, marinated mushrooms, and bits of semisoft cheese—are served with toothpick skewers. We like this innovative alternative that avoids the problem of used toothpick disposal.

tip 329

In place of wooden toothpicks, spear each hors d'oeuvre with a slender pretzel stick, which can be eaten right along with the tasty tidbit it has just skewered.

Entertaining | SAUCE BOWL STABILIZER

Many hors d'oeuvres—from crudités to shrimp cocktail to chips and salsa—involve small bowls of dipping sauce that can slide all over the platter, disrupting the carefully arranged tidbits (especially if the platter is being transported to a different location). Add some stability to your next platter.

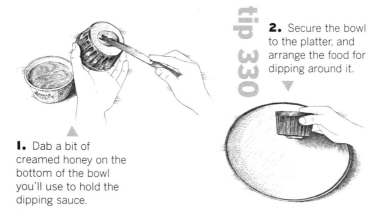

tip 330

2. Secure the bowl to the platter, and arrange the food for dipping around it.

1. Dab a bit of creamed honey on the bottom of the bowl you'll use to hold the dipping sauce.

Extracts | ADDING TINY AMOUNTS

It is difficult to measure small amounts of extracts and food colorings. A baby medicine dropper lets you measure and disperse minute amounts evenly over a batter or icing.

Slowly squeeze the liquid from the medicine dropper into the bowl, letting drops fall in various spots on the surface of the batter.

tip 331

E

Fat Separator | MAKESHIFT FAT SEPARATOR

Here's a novel way to remove fat from pan drippings before making a sauce or gravy.

I. Pour the pan drippings into a paper coffee cup and place the cup in the freezer. Once the fat has separated and begun to solidify on top, after about 10 minutes, poke a hole through to the bottom of the cup with the tip of a skewer.

tip 332

2. Let the defatted drippings run out through the hole until the fat reaches the bottom of the cup.

Fennel | PREPARING

The bulb is the part of this odd-looking vegetable that is used in most recipes. Here's how to trim the stalks and remove the tough core from the bulb.

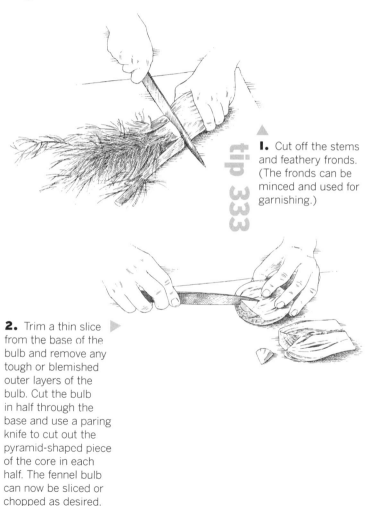

tip 333

1. Cut off the stems and feathery fronds. (The fronds can be minced and used for garnishing.)

2. Trim a thin slice from the base of the bulb and remove any tough or blemished outer layers of the bulb. Cut the bulb in half through the base and use a paring knife to cut out the pyramid-shaped piece of the core in each half. The fennel bulb can now be sliced or chopped as desired.

Fennel Seeds | CHOPPING NEATLY

Small, hard seeds like fennel and cumin are seemingly impossible to chop because they scatter all over the counter when you bear down on them. Here's how to overcome this problem.

tip 334

2. The seeds can now be chopped with a chef's knife and will not fly all over the kitchen.

1. Place the measured seeds in a small pile on a cutting board. Pour just enough water or oil on the seeds to moisten them.

Fish | KEEPING EXTRA-FRESH

Fresh fish and shellfish are best purchased and served on the same day. If fish must be stored, even briefly, it is best kept on ice, but this creates a messy container of melting ice.

Place a layer of sealed frozen ice bricks (the kind used in picnic coolers) along the bottom of the meat drawer in the refrigerator. Place the wrapped fish on top of the ice bricks. For firm-fleshed fish and shellfish, place additional ice bricks on top. Replace melted ice bricks with fully frozen bricks as necessary.

tip 335

Fish | PREPARING BONED HALIBUT STEAKS

It's not difficult to cut a whole halibut steak into 4 boneless portions. Use the long bone running down the center of the fish as a guide.

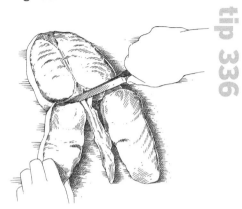

tip 336

Run a knife along the sides of the long bone running down the center of the fish, then follow the line of the thin membrane that crosses the bone, separating it from the flesh.

Fish | SKINNING FILLETS

Removing the skin from fillets can be a tricky job. Here's how to make this task easier.

tip 337

Starting at the thin end of the fillet, slide a knife between the skin and flesh until you can grab hold of the skin with a paper towel. Use this "handle" to help steady the skin as you continue to cut the flesh away from it.

Fish | COOKING THIN FILLETS

Many fillets taper down to a thin end, which is prone to over-cooking. Here's an easy way to ensure even cooking throughout the fillet.

tip 338
Fold the thin tail piece over so that the fillet is now an even thickness from end to end. Once the tail has been folded, place the fish in a hot skillet, folded-side up.

Fish | GRILLING WHOLE FISH

A whole grilled fish is apt to dry out if overcooked. But how do you check the flesh without tearing through the skin? We find that this method not only allows us to peek into the flesh but also promotes even cooking.

tip 339
Once a fish is scaled and gutted, use a sharp knife to make shallow diagonal slashes every 2 inches along both sides of the fish from top to bottom, beginning just behind the dorsal fin.

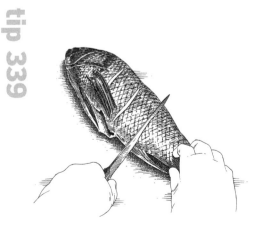

Fish | FILLETING WHOLE FISH

Filleting a whole cooked fish is not difficult. A few cuts with a sharp knife and a metal spatula do the trick.

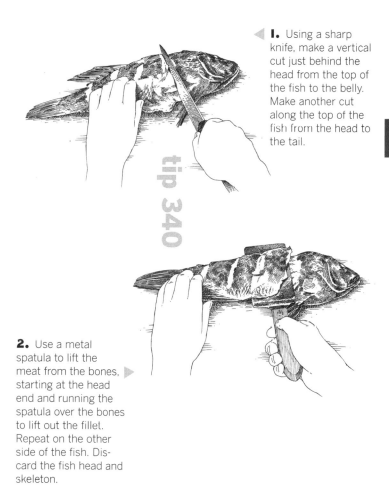

1. Using a sharp knife, make a vertical cut just behind the head from the top of the fish to the belly. Make another cut along the top of the fish from the head to the tail.

2. Use a metal spatula to lift the meat from the bones, starting at the head end and running the spatula over the bones to lift out the fillet. Repeat on the other side of the fish. Discard the fish head and skeleton.

Fish | EASY TRANSFER

Grilling a large fillet or a whole fish can prove a challenge when it comes to turning the fish or removing it from the grill without having it fall apart. Here are two solutions to this problem.

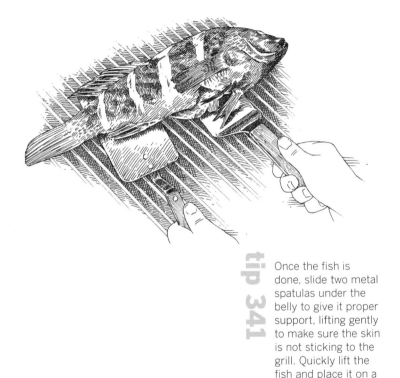

tip 341

Once the fish is done, slide two metal spatulas under the belly to give it proper support, lifting gently to make sure the skin is not sticking to the grill. Quickly lift the fish and place it on a nearby platter.

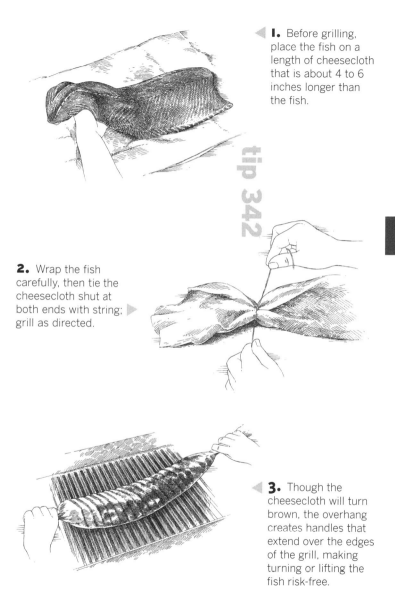

1. Before grilling, place the fish on a length of cheesecloth that is about 4 to 6 inches longer than the fish.

tip 342

F

2. Wrap the fish carefully, then tie the cheesecloth shut at both ends with string; grill as directed.

3. Though the cheesecloth will turn brown, the overhang creates handles that extend over the edges of the grill, making turning or lifting the fish risk-free.

Flame Tamer | MAKING A FOIL RING

A flame tamer is a metal disk that can be used as a buffer between a burner and a pot to maintain a gentle, low level of heat. A flame tamer is especially useful when trying to cook a stew, soup, or sauce at the barest simmer for a long time. Aluminum foil can be fashioned into a thick, slightly flattened ring and placed right on top of a gas burner.

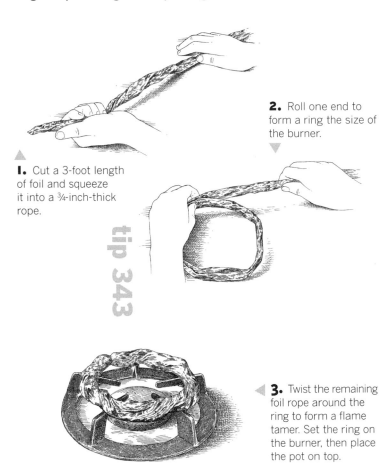

2. Roll one end to form a ring the size of the burner.

1. Cut a 3-foot length of foil and squeeze it into a ¾-inch-thick rope.

tip 343

3. Twist the remaining foil rope around the ring to form a flame tamer. Set the ring on the burner, then place the pot on top.

Flour | WEIGHING

Many bakers weigh out their flour in a bowl or on a piece of parchment paper, but we really like this idea, especially when you are measuring a large quantity.

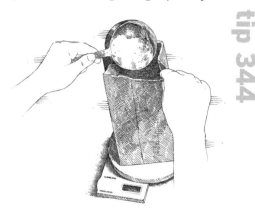

tip 344

Use a brown paper lunch bag to hold the flour. The bag stands open on the scale, is deep enough to hold a lot with no overflow, and pours neatly.

Flour | STORING IN A WIDE-MOUTHED CONTAINER

This is how we store flours, as well as sugar, in our test kitchen. This tip speeds up the measuring process and keeps our counters clean.

tip 345

Place flours in wide-mouthed plastic containers with airtight lids. When you need to measure flour, simply dip the cup into the flour and then sweep the overflow back into the container with a butter knife or icing spatula.

Flour | SUMMER STORAGE

Those who live in humid climates probably know firsthand that flour absorbs moisture from the air, which in turn adds weight when you weigh it out for a recipe. Try these storage methods to ensure accurate weight measurements.

tip 346

Store the flour in its bag in the freezer. This method also eliminates the possibility of bug infestation.

If you're short on freezer space, store the flour in your microwave oven. When you need to use the microwave, just remove the flour and replace it when you're finished.

tip 347

Flour | STORING AND MEASURING BOXED FLOUR

Bakers who make cakes infrequently may not have a covered storage container, especially for cake flour. This storage idea not only keeps flour fresh, it makes measuring the flour a less messy chore.

Transfer the flour from the box to a large, heavy-duty zipper-lock bag. Seal the bag, then store it in the original box. When you need some flour, simply lift the bag out of the box and dip the measuring cup right in.

Flour | NO-FUSS DUSTING

Hauling out a large container can be a nuisance when all you have to do is dust a cake pan or work surface with some flour. Use this tip for confectioners' sugar as well.

Set a funnel in an empty glass salt shaker and scoop a little flour into the funnel. When the shaker has been filled, seal it and store it in the pantry. These small shakers are easy to reach and do an excellent job of lightly coating a surface with flour.

Flour | SIFTER COASTER

When sifting flour into a bowl, it's likely that some of the flour will end up making a dusty mess of your countertop. Here's a way to cut back on the mess.

Overturn your flour canister lid to use as a "coaster" for your sifter. When finished, simply empty the flour from the lid back into the canister.

Flour | ADDING IN INCREMENTS

Many food processor bread recipes call for adding flour in small increments. It can be a real pain to unlock the lid and add flour several times.

Before adding any flour, we shape a doubled piece of parchment or waxed paper into a funnel and then slide it into the feed tube of the food processor. Flour can now be added as needed to the funnel, and it will flow slowly, evenly, and steadily into the workbowl.

Flour | COATING CUTTERS

Recipes for biscuits and cookies often call for dipping the cutter in flour between cuttings. Here's how we do this in our test kitchen, without dirtying an extra bowl.

Fill the cup measure (which is already dirty from measuring flour for the cookies or biscuits) with more flour. As you work, simply dip the cutter into the measuring cup, which is the perfect shape and size.

F

Focaccia | DIMPLING THE DOUGH

Unlike pizza, focaccia is topped not by a sauce but with olive oil and herbs or other small pieces of topping. Without a sauce to anchor the toppings, they are likely to slip off the cooked focaccia. This method keeps them in place.

After the second rise, wet two fingers and use them to make indentations at regular intervals across the dough. The dimples should be deep enough to hold pieces of topping.

Food Processor | EASIER CLEANUP

Some food processor lids have nonremovable sliding feed tubes that don't get completely clean in the dishwasher because the pieces stick together.

Pull up the top portion of the lid and insert a chopstick between the tube and the lid to separate the pieces. Soapy water can now flow through the pieces, and the entire lid emerges from the dishwasher perfectly clean.

tip 354

Food Processor | KEEPING THE LID CLEAN

Everyone knows that food processors save time in the kitchen, but cleaning them can be a real chore. Here's a neat way to keep the lid clean and thus cut down on washing time.

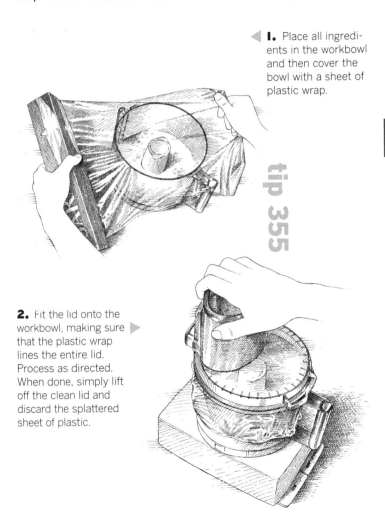

1. Place all ingredients in the workbowl and then cover the bowl with a sheet of plastic wrap.

2. Fit the lid onto the workbowl, making sure that the plastic wrap lines the entire lid. Process as directed. When done, simply lift off the clean lid and discard the splattered sheet of plastic.

tip 355

F

Food Processor |
POURING LIQUIDS FROM THE WORKBOWL

Pouring liquids from the workbowl can be tricky. You don't want to remove the blade (and get your hands dirty), but if you don't the blade will fall out. Here's how to keep the blade safely in the workbowl as you pour.

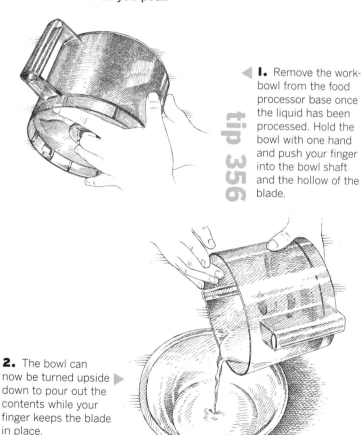

1. Remove the workbowl from the food processor base once the liquid has been processed. Hold the bowl with one hand and push your finger into the bowl shaft and the hollow of the blade.

tip 356

2. The bowl can now be turned upside down to pour out the contents while your finger keeps the blade in place.

Food Processor | CLEANING THE WORKBOWL

The easiest way to clean bowls is to soak them with water before washing. However, the hole in the center of a food processor workbowl makes this impossible to do. Here's a way to plug up that hole.

tip 357

I. Remove the bowl cover and blade. Set an empty 35mm film canister upside down over the hole in the workbowl.

2. Now you can fill the bowl with warm, soapy water and allow it to soak.

Freezer | PORTION CONTROL

Put coffee filters to unusual but effective use with items destined for the freezer.

Place them between pancakes, pork chops, meat patties, and other items while stacking them for storage in the freezer. You can then easily remove individual portions without having to defrost the entire supply.

tip 358

Freezer | "REBAGGING" FROZEN PRODUCE

Savvy cooks often keep bags of frozen fruit and vegetables on hand in case they need something in a pinch. Here's the best way to store the leftovers from a large bag.

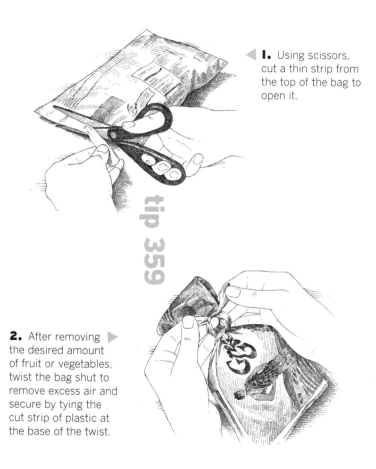

1. Using scissors, cut a thin strip from the top of the bag to open it.

2. After removing the desired amount of fruit or vegetables, twist the bag shut to remove excess air and secure by tying the cut strip of plastic at the base of the twist.

Freezer | FREEZING SMALLER PORTIONS

For cooks feeding small families, or perhaps just one person, freezing in small batches is a must. Here's a good way to freeze in small batches using large, freezer-safe plastic bags. Use this technique with chicken cutlets, steaks, or ground meats.

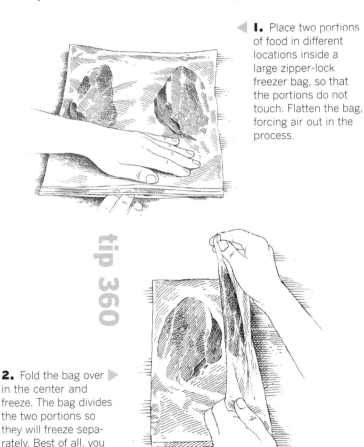

1. Place two portions of food in different locations inside a large zipper-lock freezer bag, so that the portions do not touch. Flatten the bag, forcing air out in the process.

tip 360

F

2. Fold the bag over in the center and freeze. The bag divides the two portions so they will freeze separately. Best of all, you now have the choice of using one or both frozen portions.

Freezer | KEEPING TRACK OF FROZEN FOODS

Most cooks have put something in the freezer only to forget about it completely, then thrown away the freezer-burned mystery parcel months later. Here's an easy way to keep track of what's in your freezer.

tip 361

Every time you put something in the freezer, add the name of the food and the date to a list clipped to the freezer door. The list is a constant reminder and will inspire you to use up those frozen goodies.

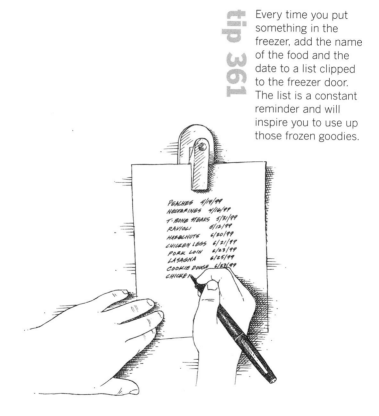

Freezer | FREEING UP CONTAINERS

Plastic food storage containers are at a premium in many kitchens. Unfortunately, many of these containers end up in the freezer for months. Here's how to liberate the containers from the freezer.

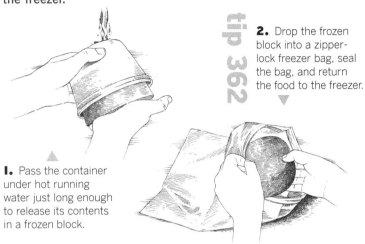

2. Drop the frozen block into a zipper-lock freezer bag, seal the bag, and return the food to the freezer.

I. Pass the container under hot running water just long enough to release its contents in a frozen block.

F

Fruit | CHOPPING DRIED FRUIT

Dried fruit, especially dates, very often sticks to the knife when you try to chop it. Here's how to avoid this problem.

Coat the knife blade with a thin film of nonstick cooking spray just before you begin chopping. The fruit slides right off the slick blade.

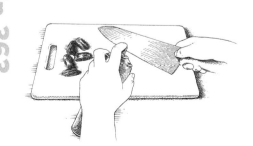

Funnel | QUICK HOMEMADE FUNNEL

Without a funnel, filling a pepper mill or adding spices to jars or a food processor feed tube can be a messy prospect. Make your own with a paper cone-style coffee filter.

1. Cut off the bottom ¼ inch of the filter.

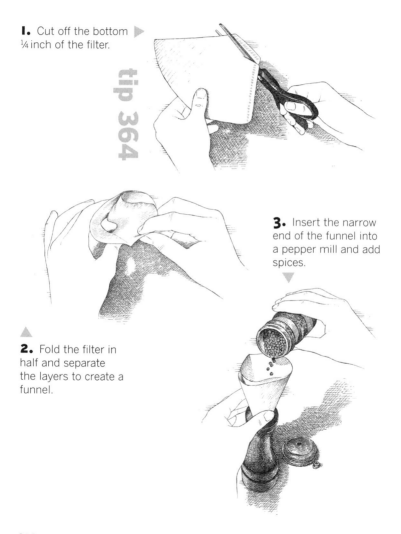

3. Insert the narrow end of the funnel into a pepper mill and add spices.

2. Fold the filter in half and separate the layers to create a funnel.

Garbage | TRASH BAGS

Here's a way to make changing the trash bag in your garbage can just a little bit easier.

tip 365

Store the container of trash bags in the bottom of the trash can; when a full bag is removed, all you have to do is reach down and grab a fresh bag to replace it.

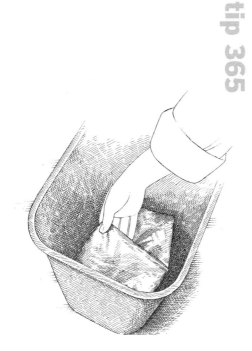

G

Garbage | SECURING KITCHEN GARBAGE BAGS

Most kitchen garbage bags tend to slip down inside the trash can, inviting an unpleasant mess to clean up later. Here are a couple of ways to keep them in place.

Secure the bags to the receptacle with a lightweight bungee cord. Just make sure you don't throw out the cord along with the trash when you change the bag!

tip 366

If you recycle plastic shopping bags, using them to line small trash cans (about 12 inches tall), you know they have an annoying habit of sliding to the bottom of the can. To solve this problem, attach small adhesive coat hooks upside down on either side of the can, about 4 inches from the top. To secure the bag, simply slip the bag handles around the hooks.

tip 367

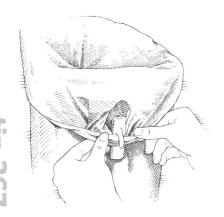

Garbage | HANDY DISPOSAL

When prepping vegetables or other items for a recipe, it can be difficult to keep the work area clean without making multiple trips to the garbage can.

Put a supermarket plastic bag in one half of the sink when preparing recipes. When you are finished putting scraps in the bag, seal it to eliminate odors, then toss it into the garbage can.

tip 368

G

Garbage Disposal | FRESHENING

Unpleasant odors sometime collect in the disposal.

Rather than discard the remnants of zested citrus peels, grind leftover pieces of lemon, lime, orange, and grapefruit rind in the kitchen sink disposal. The strong scent of the fruit helps to mask unpleasant ones.

tip 369

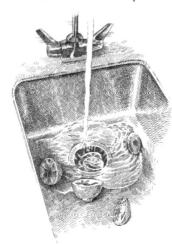

Garbage Disposal | MAKESHIFT FUNNEL TRAP

Cooks who have a garbage disposal often peel and pare vegetables and fruits right over the sink. Of course, this likely means they have at some point also dropped the item they were paring into the disposal's wide drain hole. Take this precaution next time.

Position a small funnel in the drain hole. The funnel, with a diameter just slightly larger than that of the drain opening, catches the desirable pieces of food.

tip 370

Garlic | NO MORE STICKY GARLIC

Home cooks often shy away from hand-mincing garlic because it can be sticky stuff. But if a recipe leaves you no alternative, try this helpful tip.

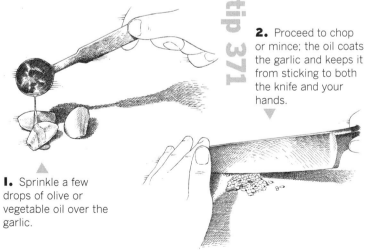

tip 371

2. Proceed to chop or mince; the oil coats the garlic and keeps it from sticking to both the knife and your hands.

1. Sprinkle a few drops of olive or vegetable oil over the garlic.

Garlic | EASY PUREED GARLIC

A Microplane grater is an ideal tool for grating nutmeg, citrus zest, and hard cheese, but it has other uses as well.

A Microplane grater will also produce finely pureed garlic, shallot, or onion. For recipes such as Caesar salad or aioli, peel a clove of garlic and grate it on the Microplane before adding it to the recipe.

G

Garlic | NO-FUSS FLAVOR BOOST

Here's a no-fuss way to add the flavor of garlic to a soup, stew, or other such dish.

Rub the papery outer layer of skin off an intact head of garlic, cut about ½ inch off the top to expose the flesh of the cloves, and throw the whole head into the soup pot. When the soup is done, remove the garlic head and either discard it or squeeze the softened garlic into the soup to further flavor and thicken it.

Garlic | DRY-TOASTING

Here's a simple way to tame that harsh garlic flavor and also loosen the skins for easy peeling. For garlic with a creamier texture (akin to roasted garlic), increase the toasting time to 15 minutes.

tip 374

2. When cooled, the once-clingy skins peel off readily. The garlic can now be sliced, chopped, or minced and used as you normally would.

1. Place unpeeled garlic cloves in a dry skillet over medium-high heat. Toast, shaking the pan occasionally, until the skins are golden brown, about 5 minutes. Set aside to cool.

Garlic | ROASTED GARLIC PASTE

Roasted garlic cloves are great for spreading on bread or stirring into soups and stews for extra flavor, but it can take some time and patience to extrude the roasted cloves from their papery skins. Here's a way to streamline the process.

After dry-toasting individual garlic cloves on the stovetop, pass the unpeeled cloves through a garlic press. This creates a perfectly smooth paste, and the garlic paper is easily removed from the press.

tip 375

Garlic | SAFE PEELING

One effective method for peeling garlic is to crush the cloves using the broad side of a knife blade. While this method is perfectly safe if you treat the knife blade with care, some may prefer skipping the knife altogether.

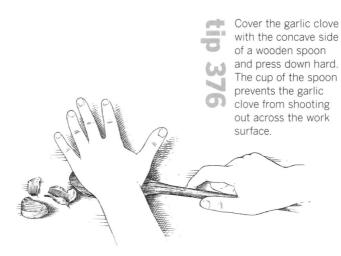

tip 376

Cover the garlic clove with the concave side of a wooden spoon and press down hard. The cup of the spoon prevents the garlic clove from shooting out across the work surface.

G

Alternatively, whack the clove with the bottom of a can. The weight of the contents helps crush the clove, and the lip at the bottom of the can keeps the clove neatly in place on the work surface.

tip 377

Garlic | EASY PEELING

An old-fashioned rubber jar opener can be used instead of a cannoli-style rubber garlic peeler.

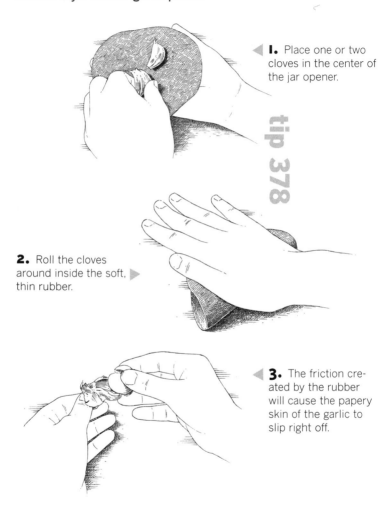

1. Place one or two cloves in the center of the jar opener.

2. Roll the cloves around inside the soft, thin rubber.

3. The friction created by the rubber will cause the papery skin of the garlic to slip right off.

Garlic | CLEANING A PRESS

Dirty garlic presses are notoriously challenging to clean.
Here's an easy way to accomplish this task and recycle an
old toothbrush.

Once the bristles are
worn, clean the tooth-
brush well and keep it
in a handy spot in the
kitchen to clean bits
of garlic from a press.
A toothbrush can
also be used to clean
tight or hard-to-reach
spots in other kitchen
utensils.

tip 379

Garlic | MAKING A SMALL AMOUNT OF PUREE

If you just need a dab of pureed garlic for a vinaigrette, try this
handy technique.

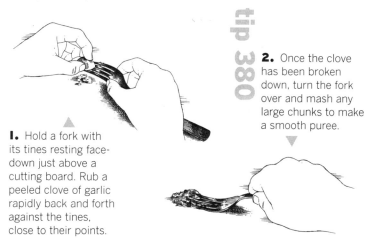

tip 380

2. Once the clove
has been broken
down, turn the fork
over and mash any
large chunks to make
a smooth puree.

I. Hold a fork with
its tines resting face-
down just above a
cutting board. Rub a
peeled clove of garlic
rapidly back and forth
against the tines,
close to their points.

Garlic | MINCING TO A PASTE

Here's how to produce very fine, smooth bits of garlic without a garlic press. If possible, use kosher or coarse salt; the larger crystals do a better job of breaking down the garlic than fine table salt.

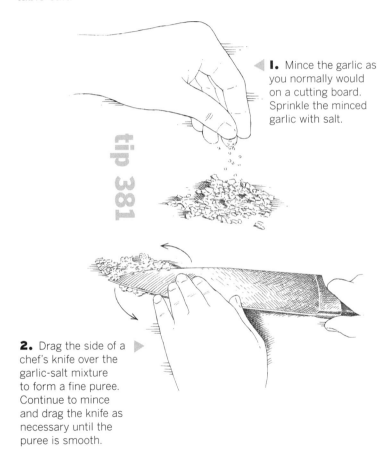

1. Mince the garlic as you normally would on a cutting board. Sprinkle the minced garlic with salt.

2. Drag the side of a chef's knife over the garlic-salt mixture to form a fine puree. Continue to mince and drag the knife as necessary until the puree is smooth.

Garnishes | USING CHOPSTICKS AS A GUIDE

Eating Chinese food isn't the only use for wooden chopsticks. Try putting them to work as a guide when cutting decorative strawberry fans to use as a garnish.

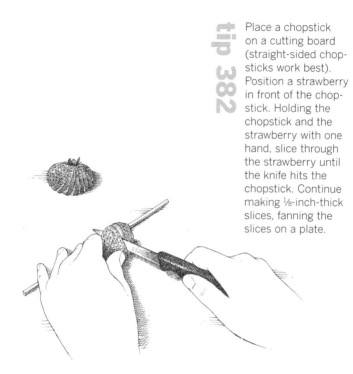

tip 382

Place a chopstick on a cutting board (straight-sided chopsticks work best). Position a strawberry in front of the chopstick. Holding the chopstick and the strawberry with one hand, slice through the strawberry until the knife hits the chopstick. Continue making ⅛-inch-thick slices, fanning the slices on a plate.

G

Ginger | SAVING FRESH GINGER

Fresh ginger is often sold in large pieces that may not be used up in one recipe, usually leaving the rest to go to waste. Here are a couple of easy ways to extend its shelf life.

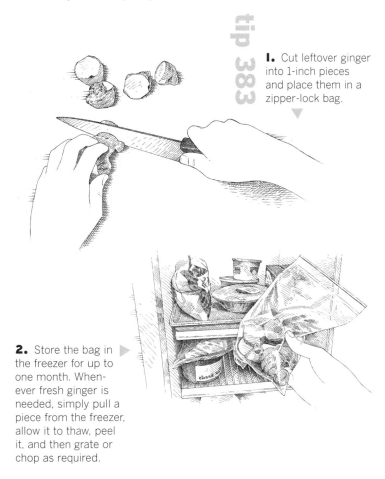

tip 383

1. Cut leftover ginger into 1-inch pieces and place them in a zipper-lock bag.

2. Store the bag in the freezer for up to one month. Whenever fresh ginger is needed, simply pull a piece from the freezer, allow it to thaw, peel it, and then grate or chop as required.

1. Peel and cut the ginger into 1-inch pieces and place in a canning or other ▶ glass jar.

tip 384

G

2. Fill the jar with sherry, cover with an airtight lid, and store in the refrigerator for up to six months. This technique not only preserves the ginger but gives you ginger-flavored sherry to use in Asian recipes.

Ginger | PEELING

Because of its knobby shape, ginger can be difficult to peel, especially with a knife. Try this method to reduce waste.

tip 385

Use the bowl of a teaspoon to scrape off the knotty skin from a knob of ginger. The spoon moves easily around curves in the ginger, so you remove just the skin.

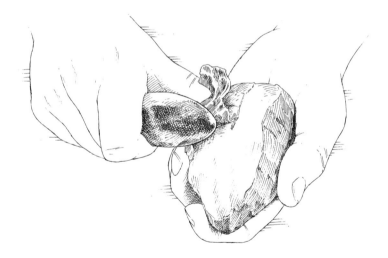

Ginger | JUICING

To produce large amounts of ginger juice for dressings or sauces, you must wrap grated ginger in cheesecloth and squeeze. If you need just a teaspoon or two of ginger juice, try this method.

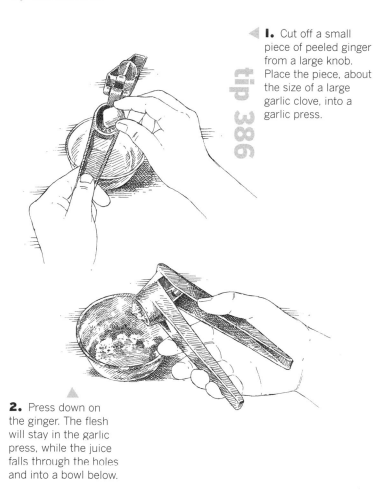

1. Cut off a small piece of peeled ginger from a large knob. Place the piece, about the size of a large garlic clove, into a garlic press.

tip 386

G

2. Press down on the ginger. The flesh will stay in the garlic press, while the juice falls through the holes and into a bowl below.

Ginger | MINCING

Ginger is highly fibrous, which makes it tricky to mince.
A sharp knife is a must. This technique works best.

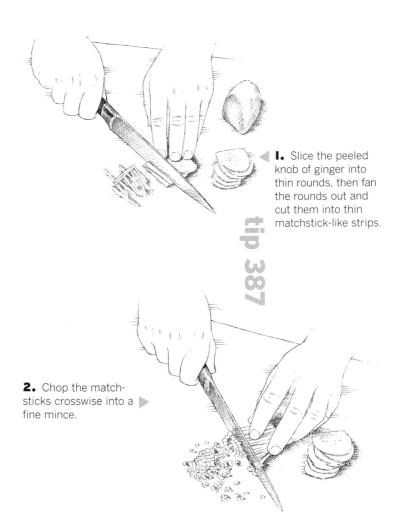

1. Slice the peeled knob of ginger into thin rounds, then fan the rounds out and cut them into thin matchstick-like strips.

tip 387

2. Chop the matchsticks crosswise into a fine mince.

Ginger | GRATING

Most cooks who use fresh ginger have scraped their fingers on the grater when the piece of ginger gets down to a tiny nub. Instead of cutting a small chunk of ginger off a larger piece and then grating it, try this method.

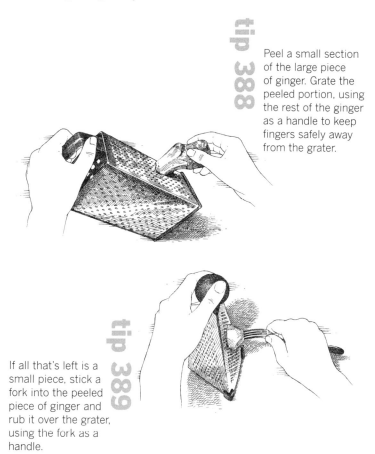

tip 388

Peel a small section of the large piece of ginger. Grate the peeled portion, using the rest of the ginger as a handle to keep fingers safely away from the grater.

tip 389

If all that's left is a small piece, stick a fork into the peeled piece of ginger and rub it over the grater, using the fork as a handle.

Ginger | SMASHING

Smashing ginger is a quick way to release its flavorful oils. This method works equally well with scallions that have been halved lengthwise.

Thinly slice an unpeeled knob and then use the end of a chef's knife to smash each piece.

Gnocchi | MAKING RIDGES

When making gnocchi, it's customary to give each piece distinct ridges using a butter paddle or the tines of a fork. This kitchen utensil works just as well.

Line up the gnocchi pieces on a work surface, then roll a whisk over them to create deep, even ridges.

Goose | RENDERING THE FAT

A goose has a thick layer of fat right under the skin that must be rendered in the oven. If the fat remains, the skin will be flabby and the meat greasy. This technique can be used with duck, too.

1. With a trussing needle or skewer, prick the goose skin all over, especially around the breast and thighs. Hold the needle nearly parallel to the bird to avoid pricking the meat. These holes provide an exit route for rendered fat.

2. Using rubber gloves to protect your hands from possible splashes of boiling water, lower the goose, neck-end down, into a stockpot filled with simmering water, submerging as much of the goose as possible until "goose bumps" appear, about 1 minute. Repeat this process, submerging the goose tail-end down. Dry the goose with paper towels, then set it on a rack in a roasting pan and refrigerate for 1 to 2 days. The boiling and drying process tightens the skin so that during roasting the fat is squeezed out.

tip 392

G

Grater | CLEANING THE CHEESE GRATER

Graters can get coated with the sticky residue from soft cheeses and are a chore to clean.

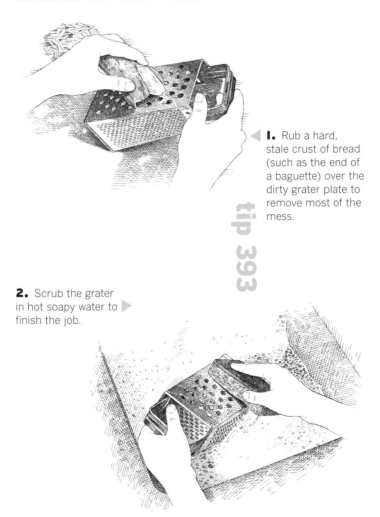

◀ **1.** Rub a hard, stale crust of bread (such as the end of a baguette) over the dirty grater plate to remove most of the mess.

tip 393

2. Scrub the grater in hot soapy water to ▶ finish the job.

Gravy | IMPROVISING A CARAFE

Keeping gravy warm at the table can be a challenge and it can easily spill or drip if placed in a bowl.

Use an insulated coffee carafe. It cuts down on spills and keeps gravy hot throughout the meal.

Greens | PERFECTLY DRY SALAD GREENS

Even a salad spinner may not get salad greens perfectly dry. To make sure that greens are as dry as possible before dressing them, try this trick.

Toss the spun greens in a large bowl with a few sheets of paper towel, each of which has been torn into quarters. The paper towel wicks away the last traces of moisture. Just be sure to pick out all of the towel pieces before dressing the salad.

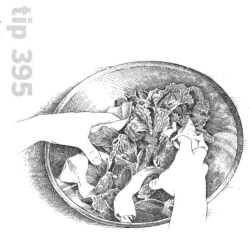

Greens | SEPARATING LEAVES FROM STEMS

Leafy greens such as kale, mustard greens, and collards have thick stems that must be discarded. (Swiss chard stems do become tender when cooked.) Here's a simple way to slice away the leaves from the thick central stalks.

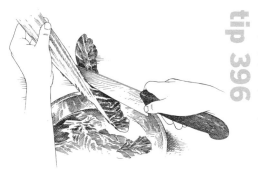

tip 396

Hold each leaf at the base of the stem over a bowl filled with water, and use a sharp knife to slash the leafy portion from either side of the thick stem.

Greens | SPACE SAVER FOR DRAINING

Many recipes for large-leaved greens such as kale and collards recommend adding the greens to the cooking pot with a little water from their washing still clinging to their leaves. Finding a place to temporarily store the bulky, wet leaves without turning your work surface into a watery mess can be a challenge.

As you wash the greens, remove them to the empty dish rack next to the sink.

tip 397

Greens | DRYING BLANCHED GREENS

Many leafy greens, such as broccoli rabe and kale, benefit from quick submerging in boiling water (a process called blanching) before being sautéed with flavorings. After blanching, it's important to squeeze as much water as possible out of the greens before adding them to the pan. Instead of squeezing the greens by hand, try this method.

I. Place the wet greens in the hopper of a potato ricer.

2. Close the handle and squeeze the water from the greens. Don't squeeze harder than is necessary, or you might puree the greens.

tip 398

Grilling | LET THERE BE LIGHT!

Early- or late-season grillers (and diehards who grill through the winter months) often find themselves grilling the evening meal in the dark. In the absence of a well-placed outdoor light, try this technique.

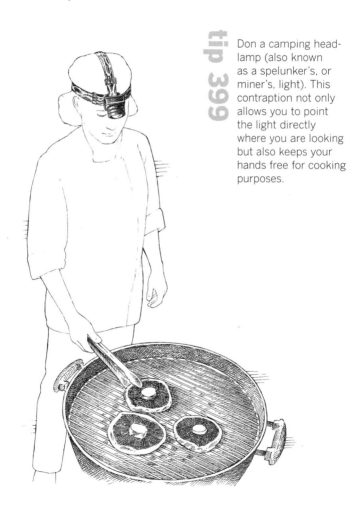

tip 399

Don a camping headlamp (also known as a spelunker's, or miner's, light). This contraption not only allows you to point the light directly where you are looking but also keeps your hands free for cooking purposes.

Grilling | CHECKING THE FUEL LEVEL

There's nothing worse than running out of fuel halfway through grilling. If your grill doesn't have a gas gauge, use this technique to estimate how much gas is left in the tank.

I. Bring a cup or so of water to a boil in a small saucepan or glass measuring cup (if using the microwave). Pour the water over the side of the tank.

tip 400

2. Feel the metal with your hand. Where the water has succeeded in warming the tank, it is empty; where the tank remains cool to the touch, there is still propane inside.

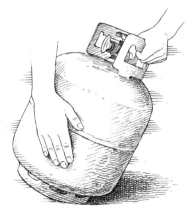

Grilling | LIGHTING THE FIRE

Our favorite tool for lighting a charcoal fire is called a chimney, or flue, starter. A chimney starter is shaped like a can, with both ends open. A wood handle on the side helps you move the can around the grill. Inside, a metal plate divides the lower portion (used to hold crumpled newspaper) from the upper portion (where the charcoal rests).

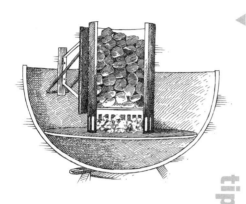

To use a chimney starter, place two or three crumpled sheets of newspaper in the bottom section. Set the starter on the bottom grate in a kettle grill and fill the main compartment with as much charcoal as directed in individual recipes. When you light the newspaper, the flames will shoot up through the charcoal and ignite it. When the coals are covered with light gray ash, they are ready. Simply dump the coals onto the grate and arrange as necessary, using long-handled tongs.

tip 401

Grilling | EASY PREPARATION

Hoisting a huge bag of charcoal to pour some into a chimney starter can be messy and difficult, especially when you are dressed nicely for a summer dinner party. Some advance preparation streamlines the process.

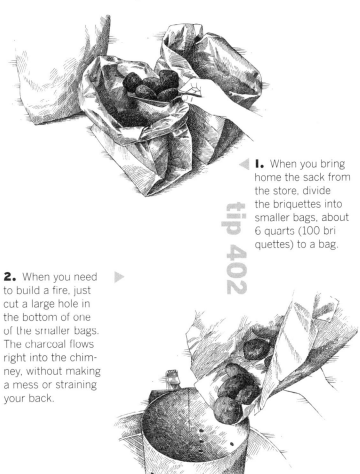

◄ **1.** When you bring home the sack from the store, divide the briquettes into smaller bags, about 6 quarts (100 briquettes) to a bag.

2. When you need to build a fire, just cut a large hole in the bottom of one of the smaller bags. The charcoal flows right into the chimney, without making a mess or straining your back. ▶

tip 402

G

Grilling | MEASURING CHARCOAL

Many recipes call for a particular volume of charcoal, such as 6 quarts. Here's an easy way to measure it out.

Open the top of an empty half-gallon carton of milk or juice and wash the carton thoroughly. Store this carton with the charcoal and use it as a measure. Each full carton equals roughly 2 quarts.

Grilling | FOOLPROOF CHIMNEY LIGHTING

Anyone who enjoys grilling well into autumn knows how frustrating it can be to light a chimney full of charcoal on a blustery fall day. Try these two tricks to help you get the job done.

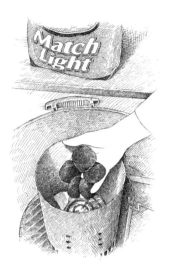

tip 404

Place 4 or 5 briquettes of self-starting charcoal at the bottom of the chimney, then fill the balance with hardwood charcoal. By using just a handful of self-starting briquettes, you're guaranteed both a quick start and food without the acrid taste that comes from using self-starting charcoal exclusively.

G

tip 405

Instead of using a match or lighter, get the fire going with a small butane torch (the kind used for caramelizing crème brûlée).

Grilling | MAKING YOUR OWN CHIMNEY STARTER

Although a chimney starter is relatively inexpensive, you may want to save money and improvise with an empty 39-ounce coffee can that has had both ends removed with a can opener. Note that there are two drawbacks to this method: The improvised starter has no handles so you must maneuver it with long-handled tongs. Also, because of its size, this improvised starter can't light enough charcoal for most grilling jobs; you will need to add unlit coals once the lit coals have been dumped onto the charcoal grate.

I. Using a church-key can opener, punch six holes along the lower circumference of the can.

2. Set the can on the grill's charcoal grate with the triangular holes at the bottom. Load the can about one-half to two-thirds full with crumpled newspaper, then top it off with charcoal.

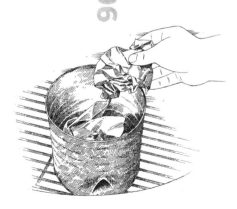

3. Insert a long match through one of the triangular holes at the bottom to set the crumpled paper on fire.

4. When the coals are lit (after about 20 minutes), use tongs to grasp the top of the starter and dump its contents onto the charcoal grate. Place more coals loosely around and on top of the burning coals to build up a cooking fire. ▶

Grilling |
LIGHTING A FIRE WITHOUT A CHIMNEY STARTER

Our preferred method for lighting charcoal calls for a chimney starter. If you don't have a starter, try this.

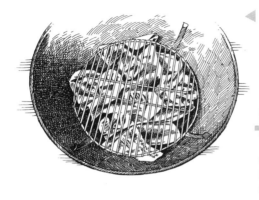

I. Place eight crumpled sheets of newspaper beneath the grate on which the charcoal sits.

tip 407

2. With the bottom air vents open, pile the charcoal on the grate, then light the paper. After about 20 minutes, the coals should be covered with light gray ash and ready for cooking.

Grilling | RESTARTING A FIRE

When your charcoal fire peters out before really getting started, you can douse the coals with lighter fluid, toss in a match, and create a thrilling fireball, or you can try this safer, tamer method.

tip 408

Turn an electric hair dryer to high and aim it toward the base of the pile of coals. The hair dryer acts as a bellows to get the fire going again in just a few minutes.

G

Grilling | BUILDING A TWO-LEVEL FIRE

In many cases, we like to grill over a two-level fire. With this arrangement, one part of the grill is very hot, while the other side is cooler. This setup works well for chops and chicken parts, which can be seared on the hot part of the grill and then cooked through more slowly on the cool part without causing the exterior to char. Having a cool section of the grill also gives the cook a place to drag foods if flames engulf the hot section.

To build a two-level fire, pile the lit charcoal on half of the grill and leave the other half free of coals. Use long-handled tongs to move briquettes into place as necessary.

tip 409

Grilling | MAKING A PACKET FOR WOOD CHIPS

Hickory, mesquite, and other wood chips can be added to a charcoal fire to flavor foods. Here's the best way to keep the chips burning slowly and thus prolong their smoking time.

1. Soak the chips in a bowl of water for at least 1 hour to slow down the rate at which they will burn. Drain the chips and place them in the center of an 18-inch square of aluminum foil. Fold in all four sides of the foil to completely enclose the chips.

2. Turn the foil packet over. Tear about six large holes (each the size of a quarter) through the top of the foil packet with a fork to allow smoke to escape. Place the packet, with the holes facing up, directly on top of a pile of lit charcoal.

tip 410

Grilling | SOAK-AHEAD WOOD CHUNKS

Barbecue aficionados like to smoke ribs over wood chunks, but don't always like having to plan to soak the chunks an hour ahead of time. Here's what to do to make sure soaked wood chunks are always at the ready when starting up the grill.

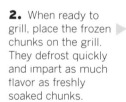

I. Soak as many chunks as you like at the same time. Drain the chunks, seal them in a zipper-lock bag, and store them in the freezer.

G

2. When ready to grill, place the frozen chunks on the grill. They defrost quickly and impart as much flavor as freshly soaked chunks.

Grilling | BRUSHLESS GRATE CLEANING

Food that is being grilled is much less likely to stick to a clean grate. We recommend cleaning the hot grate with a wire brush designed specifically for that purpose, but if you find yourself without a grill brush, try one of these frugal alternatives.

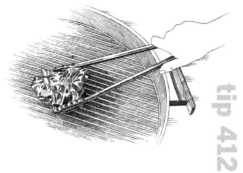

tip 412

A pair of tongs and a crumpled wad of aluminum foil will clean your cooking grate beautifully.

tip 413

A welder's brush, which can be purchased for a mere $2 at a hardware store, has a long wooden handle attached to a wire brush, just like those grill brushes that cost 10 times as much. Its long wires and narrow design allow for deep scrubbing between the bars on the cooking grate.

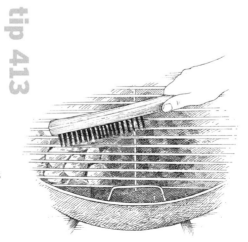

Grilling | OILING THE COOKING GRATE

For foods such as fish, which tend to stick to the grill, take this extra precaution after the hot grate has been cleaned with a grill brush.

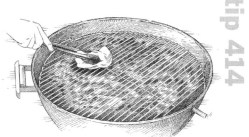

Dip a large wad of paper towels in vegetable oil, grab the wad with tongs, and wipe the grid thoroughly to lubricate it. This extra step also removes any remaining residue on the grate, which might mar the delicate flavor of fish.

Grilling | MEASURING THE HEAT LEVEL

Before grilling, use this technique to determine how hot your fire is. Some foods require a blazing hot fire, while others are best cooked over cooler coals.

Hold your hand 5 inches above the cooking grate. When the fire is hot, you won't be able to leave your hand there for more than 2 seconds; when the fire is medium, 4 or 5 seconds; and when the fire is medium-low, you will be able to leave your hand in place for about 7 seconds.

Grilling | MEASURING THE HEAT IN A CLOSED KETTLE

When grill-roasting a chicken or barbecuing ribs with the lid on, use this method to gauge the grill temperature. For poultry and small roasts, the temperature should be between 300 and 400 degrees. If slow-cooking ribs or thick roasts, keep the temperature between 200 and 300 degrees.

tip 416

Put the food on the grill and set the lid in place. Open the air vents slightly and insert a grill thermometer through the vent.

Grilling | THERMOMETER HOLDER

Avid grillers know that a thermometer is essential to monitor temperature, but it can get quite hot when touching the metal surface of the grill.

An ordinary wooden clothespin makes an ideal holder for the thermometer. It has the benefit of staying cool to the touch while also protecting the head of the thermometer from the hot metal surface of the grill.

tip 417

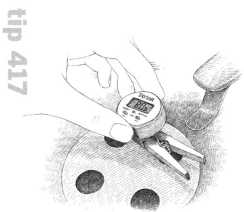

Grilling | DOUSING FLAMES

No one wants an uncontrolled fire that chars food on the grill. Here's an excellent way to prevent a grease fire from ruining your meal.

Keep a squirt bottle or plant mister filled with water near the grill. At the first sign of flames, try to pull foods to a cool part of the grill and douse the flames with water.

Grilling | RIB-RACK STAND-IN

A rib rack is a wonderful piece of equipment to have, as it lets you barbecue twice as many slabs of baby back ribs at once. If you don't have one, you might already own something else you can use.

If placed upside down on the cooking grate, any fixed V-rack used for roasting easily serves as a rib rack, holding up to six slabs of baby back ribs.

Grilling | IMPROVISING A BASTING BRUSH

Not many households stock extra pastry brushes designated for basting, especially for foods on the grill. Here are some good substitutions.

tip 420

Try using a large lettuce leaf as a brush for marinades and sauces.

tip 421

Spear a juiced lemon half onto a fork. The lemon baster works especially well when you're basting with a lemony sauce.

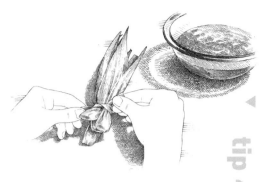

tip 422

1. Gather a fistful of cornhusks and tie them together at one end with an additional husk.

2. To make the brush bristles, fray the loose husks at the opposite end. Tie the middle with another husk to secure.

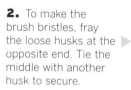

G

3. Dip the cornhusk brush into your sauce and apply to the food; when finished, you can simply toss out the brush.

Grilling | SOAKING BAMBOO SKEWERS

Soaking bamboo skewers before grilling helps keep the wood from burning before the food is cooked. But when the skewers are placed in water, they tend to float to the surface. Here's how to keep them submerged.

tip 423

Fill a rinsed-out 2-liter soda bottle with fresh water. Slip the skewers in the bottle and screw the cap in place. The skewers will remain submerged until you remove the cap.

Grilling | WOODEN SKEWERS AT THE READY

An impromptu dinner from the grill is a great idea during warmer months, but if the menu involves kebabs, waiting for the skewers to soak in water can take too long.

Soak the skewers ahead of time, seal them in a zipper-lock bag, and then store them in the freezer so they won't dry out. They'll be ready to use at a moment's notice.

tip 424

Grilling | GETTING SAUSAGES STRAIGHT

Grilled sausages make a great summer sandwich, but fitting a curved link into a flat bun can be downright frustrating. We're pretty sure curved buns don't exist, but there's still a good solution.

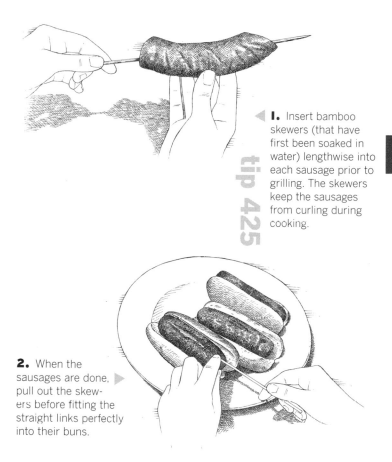

1. Insert bamboo skewers (that have first been soaked in water) lengthwise into each sausage prior to grilling. The skewers keep the sausages from curling during cooking.

tip 425

2. When the sausages are done, pull out the skewers before fitting the straight links perfectly into their buns.

Grilling | HANDLING GRILLED PIZZA EASILY

Once the toppings on a grilled pizza are heated through, it is important to remove the pizza from the grill swiftly to make sure that the crust does not burn. This is sometimes more easily said than done, as the pizza can be difficult to maneuver intact with tongs or a spatula.

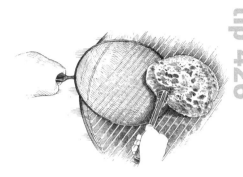

tip 426

Use a splatter screen or rimless baking sheet as a pizza peel: Don an oven mitt on one hand to hold the "peel" and use tongs or a spatula with the other hand to slide the pizza onto the peel.

Grilling | AVOIDING "FISH STICKS" ON THE GRILL

A superclean, superhot, oiled cooking grate should prevent grilled fish steaks, fillets, or kebabs from sticking to the grate, but sometimes you want a little extra insurance.

Place a few thin slices of lemon, lime, or orange (whatever best complements the flavor of the fish) on the cooking grate, and place the fish on the slices. Though you may sacrifice the grill marks on the fish, it will still pick up a great grilled flavor (as well as extra flavor from the citrus), and it will not stick to the grate.

tip 427

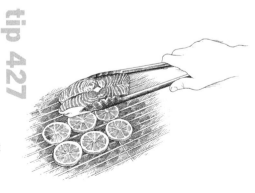

Grilling | MAKESHIFT GRILL BASKET FOR FISH

A grill basket can cut down on the hassles of cooking delicate fish fillets outdoors, but not every griller owns one. Here's how to assemble a basket with equipment most cooks already have.

I. Oil and season the fish and place it on a small oiled wire cooling rack. Place another oiled wire rack on top of the fish and fasten the racks securely together on each side with bendable wire or wire twist ties.

G

2. To flip the basket, use a spatula in one hand to lift the basket and use your other hand (protected with an oven mitt or potholder) to turn it over.

Grilling | ONE PLATTER FOR TWO JOBS

Grilled meat, poultry, and fish should not be returned to the same platter that was used to carry the raw food to the grill. Instead of last-minute fumbling for a new platter, this method uses a single platter for both jobs, which also saves on cleanup time.

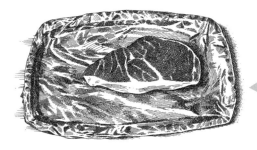

◀ **1.** Cover the platter with foil before placing the raw food on it.

tip 429

2. While the food is ▶ grilling, remove the foil so you can use the same platter when the food comes off the grill.

Grilling | EASY ASH REMOVAL

No matter how you do it, emptying a kettle grill of cool ashes is a messy procedure. A homemade ash scoop can neaten things up.

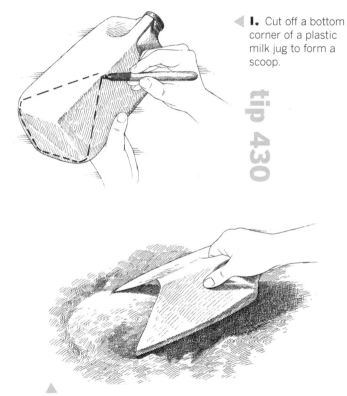

1. Cut off a bottom corner of a plastic milk jug to form a scoop.

2. The plastic conforms to the curve of the grill bottom, which makes it easy to collect ashes with a single sweep.

Grilling | PROTECTING GAS CONTROLS

The ignition and burner control knobs on some gas grills can be persnickety if they get wet or dirty from exposure to the elements, especially if the grill is kept outdoors in the snow during the winter. If your grill has no cover, try this impromptu solution.

Invert a disposable aluminum roasting pan over the control panel and tape it in place on either end with duct or electrical tape.

tip 431

Grocery Shopping |
SHOPPING FOR TOP-RATED PRODUCTS

As you're making your grocery list and shopping, it may be difficult to remember which brands of various products are recommended in taste tests. Here's an easy way to keep track of top-rated ingredients when you are ready to purchase them at the grocery store.

Write notes on index cards that can also double as category dividers in your coupon holder.

tip 432

Grocery Shopping | TRANSPORTING FROZEN FOOD

After a trip to the grocery, it's inevitable that you will think of other errands to be run or that traffic will prevent you from getting home quickly, putting perishable food at risk of getting too warm.

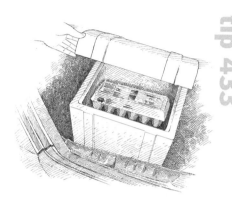

tip 433

Store a Styrofoam cooler in the trunk of your car for holding perishable groceries. The cooler keeps ice cream and other frozen foods from melting and also prevents fragile items like eggs from rolling around and breaking.

G

Guacamole | EASY AVOCADO MASHING

Instead of painstakingly mashing avocados with a fork when whipping up your next batch of guacamole, turn to this other convenient, low-tech kitchen tool.

A pastry blender mashes avocados quickly, and the cleanup is just as quick.

tip 434

Ham | HANDLING A COUNTRY HAM

We love country ham but find its large size makes it unwieldy to cook, especially because the ham should be simmered in a stockpot before being roasted.

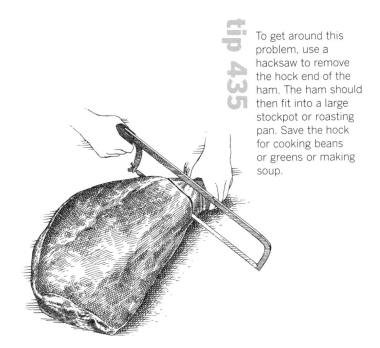

tip 435

To get around this problem, use a hacksaw to remove the hock end of the ham. The ham should then fit into a large stockpot or roasting pan. Save the hock for cooking beans or greens or making soup.

Hamburgers | SHAPING PATTIES

Hamburgers (and crab cakes and other patties) must be uniformly shaped if they are to cook evenly, but gauging their size isn't always a cinch.

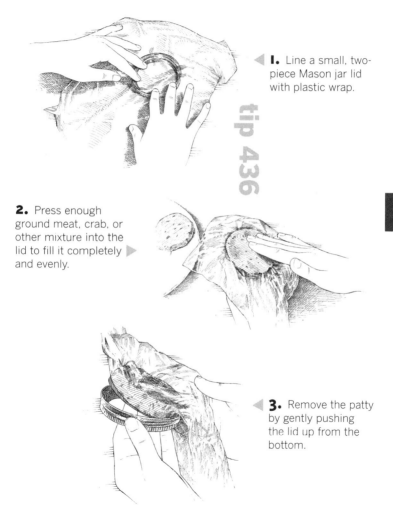

I. Line a small, two-piece Mason jar lid with plastic wrap.

2. Press enough ground meat, crab, or other mixture into the lid to fill it completely and evenly.

3. Remove the patty by gently pushing the lid up from the bottom.

H

Hand Washing | DEODORIZING

After working with pungent ingredients, such as garlic, onions, or fish, lemon juice helps to wash away any lingering odors from hands. When the odor is too strong for citrus, try this method.

tip 437

Wash your hands with a couple of tablespoons of mouthwash. Any inexpensive brand will do the job.

Hash Browns | FLIPPING SAFELY

Hash browns, as well as Chinese noodle cakes and Spanish omelets, must be browned on both sides in a hot skillet. Most recipes suggest inverting the food onto a plate and then sliding it back into the skillet to cook the second side. We find that the removable bottom of a metal tart pan works better than a plate.

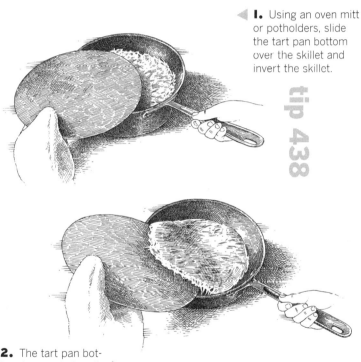

1. Using an oven mitt or potholders, slide the tart pan bottom over the skillet and invert the skillet.

2. The tart pan bottom is easy to handle, lightweight, and has no rim or curvature, so the food slides back into the skillet easily.

tip 438

H

Hazelnuts | TOASTING AND SKINNING

Hazelnuts are covered with a dark brown skin that can be quite bitter. Toasting the nuts in a 350-degree oven until fragrant (about 10 to 15 minutes) improves their flavor and also causes the skins to blister and crack so they can be rubbed off. See tip 440 for an alternative way to rub off the skins.

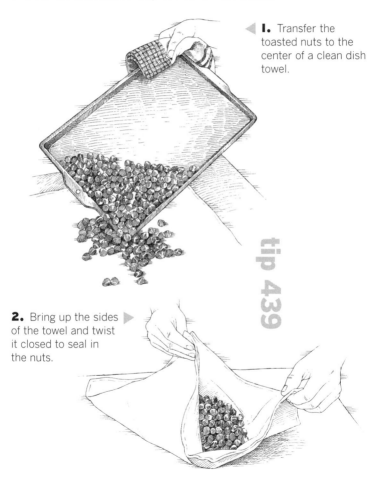

1. Transfer the toasted nuts to the center of a clean dish towel.

2. Bring up the sides of the towel and twist it closed to seal in the nuts.

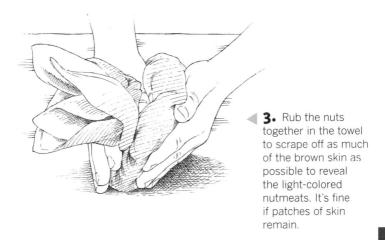

3. Rub the nuts together in the towel to scrape off as much of the brown skin as possible to reveal the light-colored nutmeats. It's fine if patches of skin remain.

4. Carefully open the towel on a flat surface. Gently roll the nuts away from the skins.

Hazelnuts | PEELING

Here's another way to remove the skins from toasted hazelnuts.

After letting the toasted nuts cool slightly, place them in a recycled plastic mesh bag, such as the kind oranges are sold in. With both ends secured, roll the nuts between both hands over a sink or garbage can. The skins are rubbed off and dispensed with in one fell swoop.

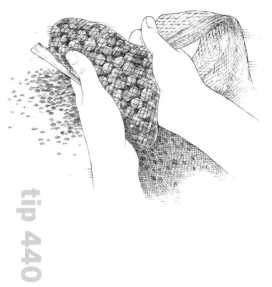

tip 440

Herbs | EASY WASHING

Thoroughly rinsing herbs can be a tedious task. Try this tip to simplify the process.

tip 441

Use a salad spinner to wash herbs. Once the herbs are clean, simply lift the basket with the herbs out of the dirty water, discard the water, fit the basket back into its base, and spin the herbs dry.

Herbs | ADDING FLAVOR

Here's a no-fuss way to add the flavor of hardy herbs to a soup, stew, chowder, or sauce.

H

In recipes that call for thyme or rosemary, there's no need to strip the leaves off the branches and mince them. Simply throw the whole branch into the pan. Remember to remove the spent branch, as you would spent bay leaves, before serving. Rosemary is very strong, so you may want to keep it in the pot for only 15 minutes or so.

tip 442

Herbs | RELEASING FLAVOR FROM DRIED HERBS

Flavorful oils in dried oregano, thyme, and other herbs should be released before the herbs are added to foods. You can crush dried herbs between your fingers or use this method for maximum flavor.

Place the dried herbs in a mesh sieve and push down on them with your fingertips as you shake the sieve back and forth over a bowl.

Herbs | MAKING A BOUQUET GARNI

A bouquet garni is a classic French combination of herbs and spices used to flavor soups, stocks, and stews. Traditional recipes call for wrapping the herbs and spices in cheesecloth for easy removal before serving. A coffee filter, which most modern cooks are more likely to have on hand, can be used in place of the cheesecloth.

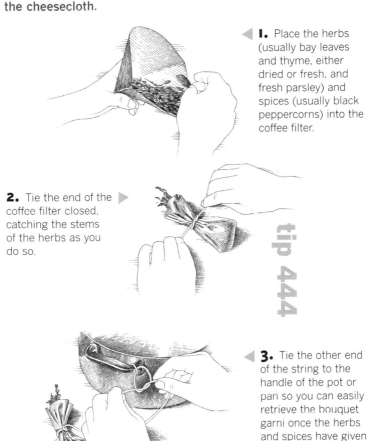

1. Place the herbs (usually bay leaves and thyme, either dried or fresh, and fresh parsley) and spices (usually black peppercorns) into the coffee filter.

2. Tie the end of the coffee filter closed, catching the stems of the herbs as you do so.

3. Tie the other end of the string to the handle of the pot or pan so you can easily retrieve the bouquet garni once the herbs and spices have given up their flavor.

Herbs | HANDY SCISSORS FOR GARDEN CLIPPING

If you're tired of trekking back into the house for the scissors you forgot to bring into the garden, try this handy solution.

Bend a wire coat hanger or heavy floral wire to form a stand with a hooked end. Stick the wire in the soil and hang a small pair of inexpensive scissors on it and they'll be there whenever you are.

Herbs | STORING HARDY HERBS

Perennials such as sage and thyme are hardy enough to tolerate cold outdoor temperatures, and thus can be stored in the refrigerator.

In plastic containers with tight lids, stack the clean, dry herbs in loose layers separated by parchment paper or paper towels to allow for maximum air flow, then seal tightly. Smaller amounts of herbs can be placed in food storage bags.

Herbs | STORING DELICATE HERBS

Delicate leafy herbs like basil, cilantro, mint, and the like should be stored in water in the refrigerator, but not in a drinking glass. This setup will be top-heavy and prone to slips and spills.

For a more stable herb container, cut off the top of a plastic 1-quart or ½-gallon milk or water jug.

Herbs | PRESERVING LEFTOVER HERBS

H

If you find yourself with a plethora of herbs growing in the garden, don't watch them go to seed. Try this quick, easy way to dry and store them.

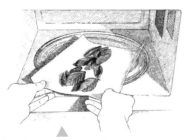

2. Crumble the dried herbs and store in an airtight container (up to 3 months, for best flavor).

I. After washing and drying the herbs, place them on a clean paper towel and microwave on high power for 30 to 40 seconds.

Herbs | FREEZING FRESH HERBS

Recipes usually call for a fairly small amount of parsley, but it's sold only in large bunches. Rather than let the rest of the parsley go bad, try this method to keep it fresh indefinitely (this also works well with sage, rosemary, and thyme).

I. Chop leftover fresh herbs by hand or in the food processor, transfer by the spoonful into ice cube trays, and top with water to cover. For a standard ice cube tray, place 2 tablespoons chopped herbs and approximately 1 tablespoon water in each cube.

2. Once the cubes are frozen, transfer them to a zipper-lock bag and seal. Store until you want to add them to sauces, soups, or stews.

Herbs | ALTERNATE USES FOR FRESH HERBS

Fresh herbs such as parsley or basil are sold in bunches much larger than needed to make just one or two recipes. Cut down on rotting herbs in your refrigerator with this idea.

tip 450

In place of lettuce or other greens, use fresh herbs to give your sandwich an unexpected flavor boost.

Honey | REVIVING CRYSTALLIZED HONEY

All honey hardens and crystallizes over time, but there's no need to toss it. There's an easy way to bring honey back to its translucent, liquid state.

tip 451

Place the opened jar of honey in a saucepan filled with about an inch of water and place over very low heat, stirring the honey often, until the crystals melt. Alternatively, heat the opened jar in the microwave on high power in 10-second increments, stirring intermittently, until it has liquefied. Once cooled, use the honey or screw the lid back on for storage.

Honey | IMPROVISING A DIPPER

Here's what to do if you need to get a small amount of honey out of a jar and don't have a honey dipper.

tip 452

Use a fork, not a spoon. Dip the tines of the fork into the honey pot, spin the fork around, and grab some honey for streaming into a cup of tea or onto buttered toast.

Honey | MEASURING

Sticky ingredients like honey and molasses take their time flowing out of a measuring cup and require a spoon to scrape out the remaining bits. This method makes neat and quick work of the task.

tip 453

Spray the measuring cup with nonstick cooking spray before filling it. When emptied, the liquid will slip right out of the cup.

Ice | EXTRACTING FROM THE TRAY

Trying to coax ice cubes out of their plastic tray can be a no-win proposition. They either stick stubbornly in their slots or tumble out all at once when you want only one or two.

First, twist the tray to loosen the cubes. Then touch the tip of your finger very lightly to the cube you want. Most of the time, your body heat will melt a bit of the ice, which quickly refreezes and sticks your finger to the cube just long enough to pick it up and drop it in a glass. Dampening your fingertip slightly under running water helps the ice stick even more tightly.

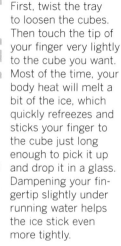

Ice | HOMEMADE ICE PACKS

It can be a tiresome and time-consuming task to fill, empty, and refill ice cube trays when stocking up on ice to chill beverages for a party. Make your own ice packs with zipper-lock bags—it's faster, and they keep drinks cool a lot longer than ice cubes do.

I. Fill quart- or gallon-sized zipper-lock bags to within 2 inches of the top with water (to prevent the bags from bursting when the water expands as it freezes).

tip 455

2. Place the bags in the freezer, letting them lie flat so they can be stacked, thereby making the most economical use of freezer space.

Ice Cream | SLOWER MELTING

Summer heat wreaks speedy havoc on a cool dish of ice cream.

Keep sundae dishes in the freezer until needed. The cool dishes slow the melting of homemade ice cream sundaes (or just plain dishes of ice cream).

Ice Cream | FROSTBITE-FREE SCOOPING

Spring and summer are packed with parties, and whether it's a birthday or a holiday that's being celebrated, ice cream is almost always involved—and frozen fingers inevitably follow from clutching tubs of ice cream while dishing it out. Try this tip to stave off frostbite.

Wrap a kitchen towel around the middle of the ice cream carton and twist the ends together. To scoop, grasp the twisted section of the towel firmly; this will give you a good grip— without the frostbite.

Ice Cream | LEAK-FREE CONES

Anyone who savors ice cream cones slowly knows that the melting ice cream often saturates the tip of the cone, which can result in a messy leak. Here's how to keep the cone from dripping.

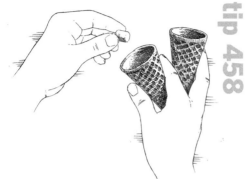

tip 458

Place a mini marshmallow or upside-down Hershey's Kiss in each cone before loading it up with ice cream, creating a barrier between the melting ice cream and the fragile cone tip.

Ice Cream | KEEPING FRESH

If not eaten right away, ice cream can lose its fresh taste and form ice crystals on the surface as it sits in the freezer. An extra layer of insulation prevents this from happening.

tip 459

Before returning the ice cream to the freezer, cover the portion remaining in the carton with heavy-duty plastic wrap, pressing the wrap flush against the surface of the ice cream. Replace the carton cover and return it to the freezer.

Ice Cream | QUICK AND EASY SINGLE SCOOPS

Some home refrigerators freeze ice cream so hard that the ice cream has to sit on the counter to soften before it can be scooped. To avoid the wait, we like this advance preparation method.

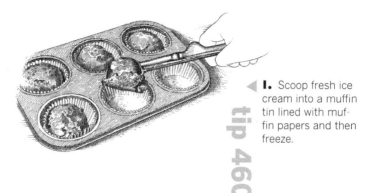

tip 460

I. Scoop fresh ice cream into a muffin tin lined with muffin papers and then freeze.

2. Once frozen, the paper-lined portions can be stored in a plastic bag in the freezer for easy, ready-when-you-are servings. Just peel off the paper and place the ice cream in a bowl. This is also a great method for quickly firming up homemade ice cream, which is notoriously soft when it comes out of the machine.

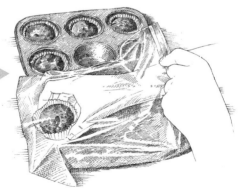

Ice Cream | SERVING SUGGESTION

Taken straight from the freezer, small pint-sized containers of premium ice cream often are frozen too hard to scoop easily. Next time you're faced with this problem, try this creative solution.

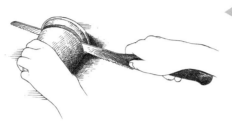

◄ **1.** Place the ice cream container on its side on a cutting board and cut off slices, right through the cardboard, with a serrated or electric knife.

2. Peel the cardboard off the sides of the ice cream disk and serve. The lid will ► sit flush against the ice cream left in the container for easy storage.

tip 461

◄ **3.** The slice-and-serve method also lends itself to artful presentation. Cut the disks into interesting shapes using cookie cutters.

Ice Water | NO-FUSS ICE WATER

Try this easy method for measuring ice water the next time you need it for pie pastry or any recipe requiring ice water.

Put ice cubes and water into a fat separator. You can then measure out the water you need through the spout, leaving the ice behind.

tip 462

Icing | MESS-FREE GLAZING

A simple glaze of milk or lemon juice mixed with powdered sugar adds a flavorful finish to quick breads, muffins, cinnamon buns, and the like, but mixing and applying the glaze can be a messy process. We like this neater method, which also eliminates the need to dirty a bowl and utensil.

tip 463

2. To apply the glaze with precision, just snip off a small corner of the bag and squeeze.

1. Add the powdered sugar and liquid to a zipper-lock sandwich bag, seal it, and knead the ingredients into a soft glaze.

Instant-Read Thermometer | RECALIBRATING

There's no point in using an instant-read thermometer if it's not accurate. To test accuracy, insert the probe into a pan of boiling water. The thermometer should register 212 degrees at sea level. (The boiling point drops about one degree for every 500-foot increase in altitude, so compensate accordingly.) If your dial-face thermometer is inaccurate, it can be adjusted.

Turn over the thermometer and use a pair of pliers to adjust the nut beneath the head. Keep adjusting until the thermometer reads 212 degrees when inserted into boiling water.

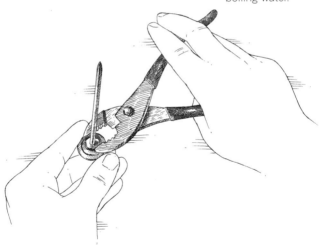

Instant-Read Thermometer |
PROTECTING HANDS FROM POTS

Most instant-read thermometers come in a protective plastic sleeve with a metal clip (for clipping to aprons) that forms a loop at the very top. Use this clip and plastic sleeve to distance your hand from hot pots when taking a temperature.

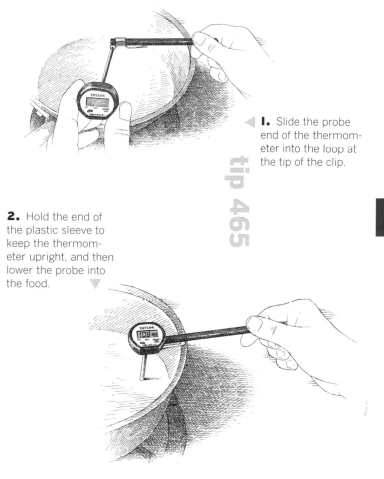

◀ **1.** Slide the probe end of the thermometer into the loop at the tip of the clip.

2. Hold the end of the plastic sleeve to keep the thermometer upright, and then lower the probe into the food. ▼

tip 465

Instant-Read Thermometer |
MEASURING SHALLOW LIQUIDS

Recipes for custards, curds, pastry creams, and other delicate or heat-sensitive mixtures often indicate the temperature at which the mixture should be taken off the heat. If you are cooking a small quantity, use this technique to get an accurate reading with an instant-read thermometer.

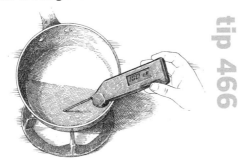

tip 466

Tilt the pan so that the liquid collects on one side, creating enough depth to get an accurate reading.

Jam | JUICING FRUIT

When making jams and jellies from fruits such as grapes, cherries, and plums, it's necessary to juice some of the fruit, but it can be difficult to do without nicking the seeds or pits, which, when cut, release bitter flavors into the fruit. Try this gentler method.

Fit a food processor with the short plastic dough blade. The processor will break down the fruit without nicking the seeds or pits.

tip 467

Jello | UNMOLDING SALADS

Jello salads can be difficult to remove from their molds. Using a mold with a hollow center, such as a Bundt pan, will make things easier, as will following these steps.

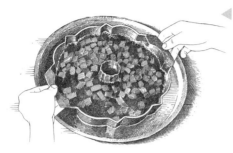

1. Gently lower the bottom of the mold into a bowl filled with hot water and keep it in place for about 5 seconds.

2. With your finger, lightly press the edges of the jello away from the mold to loosen the salad from the pan.

tip 468

J

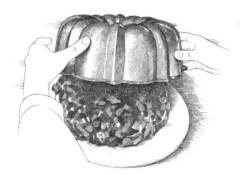

3. Place a large serving plate on top of the mold. Holding the plate securely in place, carefully invert the mold and release the jello salad onto the plate.

Jícama | PREPARING

Jícama, often available in supermarkets, is a sweet, nutty root vegetable common in Mexican and South American cuisines. Jícama can be eaten raw or cooked and should be peeled just before using.

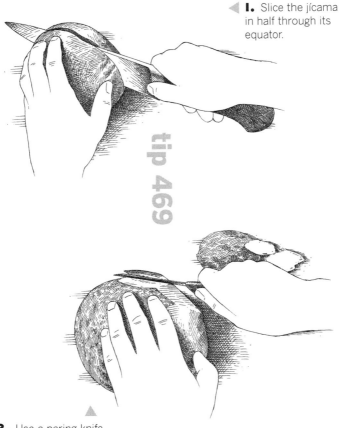

I. Slice the jícama in half through its equator.

2. Use a paring knife to peel the brown outer skin.

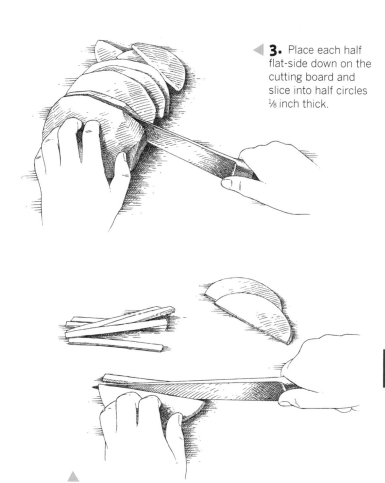

3. Place each half flat-side down on the cutting board and slice into half circles ⅛ inch thick.

4. Stack the half circles and slice lengthwise into thin matchsticks.

J

Kitchen Efficiency | USES FOR A TAMPER

Just because your espresso machine is seldom in use doesn't mean the tamper has to sit idle. It can perform other tasks.

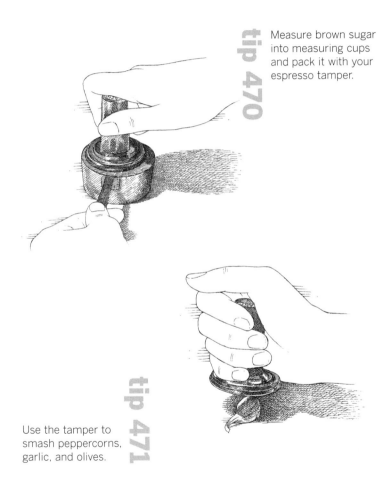

tip 470

Measure brown sugar into measuring cups and pack it with your espresso tamper.

tip 471

Use the tamper to smash peppercorns, garlic, and olives.

Kitchen Efficiency | MAKESHIFT COLANDER

For those times when you don't want to dirty a large colander for a small cleaning job, try this alternative.

I. Place the items to be cleaned in an empty plastic fruit container and rinse, letting the water drain out through the holes.

tip 472

2. Once thoroughly cleaned, transfer the items to paper towels to dry.

K

Kitchen Efficiency | KNIFE SAVERS

Instead of using a knife to break apart chocolate or frozen liquids, try this inexpensive hardware store alternative.

tip 473

Keep a cheap chisel on hand. The chisel's sturdy edge does a better job and keeps your knives' sharp, delicate edges out of harm's way. Place the chisel on chocolate or ice, angled away from you. Using short, quick strokes, chip into pieces of desired size.

Kitchen Efficiency | NONSKID CAKES AND CASSEROLES

Here's a good way to make use of leftover nonskid shelf liner.

tip 474

Use nonskid shelf liner to safely transport cakes, casseroles, and other large serving dishes. Line the bottom of a cake carrier, box, or other container with a small piece to keep the contents from sliding into the walls of the carrier while in transit.

Kitchen Efficiency | PAPER TOWEL SUBSTITUTE

Here's an economical, earth-friendly way to conserve paper towels and recycle newspapers.

tip 475

When you need several layers of paper towels to absorb water or grease, spread out a few layers of newspaper and top them with a single layer of paper towels. The newspapers are wonderfully absorbent and much less expensive than paper towels.

K

Kitchen Efficiency | TWINE REPLACEMENTS

Here's what to do when you need a short length of food-safe string to tie a spice bag or secure a bunch of herbs and don't have any kitchen twine handy.

tip 476

Clip the string off of a tea bag—it is the perfect size for such small tasks. If a longer string is required, two strings can be tied together.

Tie meat, poultry, and bouquets garnis with unflavored, unwaxed dental floss.

tip 477

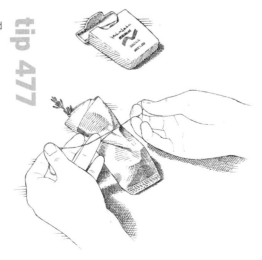

Kitchen Efficiency | EDIBLE SPOON REST

A spoon rest is a nice extra to have in the kitchen, but many cooks don't want to bother with them.

Use a slice of bread instead. The bread catches bits of food and soaks up juices, becoming a savory treat for the family dog (or the cook) in the process.

Kitchen Efficiency | QUICKER SINK CLEANUP

Whether they have built-in disposals or not, many cooks peel and pare fruits and vegetables directly into the sink. Those without disposals are then left with the task of fishing all of the scraps out of the sink and rinsing it out.

2. When you're finished peeling, all you have to do is gather up the paper and its contents and put them in the trash (or the compost heap) in one fell swoop.

K

1. Line the empty sink with newspaper before beginning any prep work.

Kitchen Efficiency |
ALTERNATIVE MISE EN PLACE CUPS

Cooking almost any recipe goes much faster when the ingredients are prepped, measured, and ready. The downside of laying out the ingredients, called mise en place, is that it means washing more dishes—bowls, ramekins, plates, and other containers. Here are some easy substitutes you can use for small quantities of ingredients.

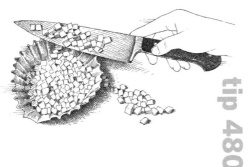

Use flat-bottomed paper coffee filters in place of bowls or ramekins. When you are done, just throw the dirty filters in the trash. Paper cups can serve the same purpose.

tip 480

tip 481

If you are looking for a reusable alternative to ramekins, try clean, dry single-serving yogurt cups.

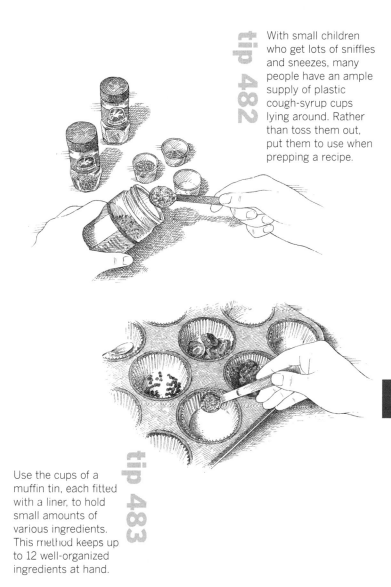

With small children who get lots of sniffles and sneezes, many people have an ample supply of plastic cough-syrup cups lying around. Rather than toss them out, put them to use when prepping a recipe.

K

Use the cups of a muffin tin, each fitted with a liner, to hold small amounts of various ingredients. This method keeps up to 12 well-organized ingredients at hand.

Kitchen Efficiency | SPACE-SAVING VEGETABLE PREP

If your kitchen is tight on counter space, it can be a hassle to
prepare dishes like soups, stews, and stir-fries, all of which
require a number of chopped vegetables and other ingredients.

tip 484

Layer the chopped
ingredients in a bowl
in order of use, sepa-
rating each layer with
a sheet of waxed
paper or plastic wrap.

Kitchen Efficiency | MEASURING WATER ACCURATELY

To get an accurate measurement of water in a liquid measuring cup, you must rest the cup on a flat surface so the water is
level. We found this method to be quick, easy, and convenient.

Set a measuring cup
next to your kitchen
sink and fill it with the
sink sprayer.

tip 485

Kitchen Efficiency |
TESTING THE TEMPERATURE OF LEFTOVERS

Judging the interior temperature of reheated leftovers such as lasagna or a casserole can be difficult. To avoid serving leftovers that are tepid in the center, try this method.

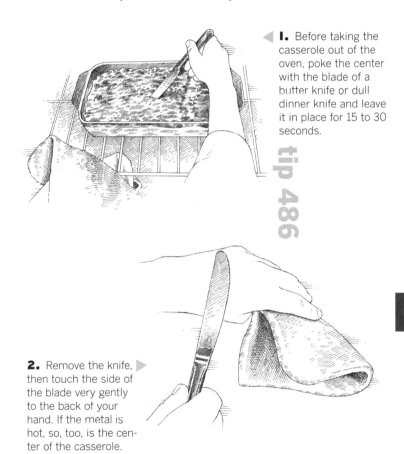

1. Before taking the casserole out of the oven, poke the center with the blade of a butter knife or dull dinner knife and leave it in place for 15 to 30 seconds.

tip 486

2. Remove the knife, then touch the side of the blade very gently to the back of your hand. If the metal is hot, so, too, is the center of the casserole.

K

Kitchen Efficiency | LABELING

Broccoli and some other vegetables come neatly contained in thick rubber bands. Rather than toss them out, recycle the bands for another use.

tip 487

Use them to label items destined for the freezer. Stretch a band around the top and bottom of a container (which also helps keep a loose lid in place) and write the container's contents on the band. You can even flip the band over to get one more use out of it.

Kitchen Efficiency | KEEPING TABS ON LABELS

It's a good idea to label and date containers of leftover food stored in the refrigerator or freezer. Using masking tape is a great way to avoid marking up your Tupperware, but it can be tricky to pry off. This simple trick keeps labels easy to remove.

tip 488

2. Once the leftovers have been used up, just grab the tab and pull; the tape comes right off.

1. Fold over a small section at the end of the roll of masking tape to create a tab; then tear off a piece of tape and label the container.

Kitchen Efficiency |
PROTECTING RECIPE INGREDIENTS

It can be frustrating to purchase ingredients for a recipe, only to find that hungry family members have raided the pantry. Rather than make repeated trips to the grocery store, try this straightforward tip.

Place brightly colored stickers on any items reserved for use in a recipe as soon as you unpack the groceries. Anything without a sticker is fair game.

Kitchen Efficiency | CHOPSTICKS TO THE RESCUE

Most cooks like to keep a pump soap dispenser near the kitchen sink for hand washing. But it's wasteful to discard the last drops of soap that always collect in the bottom of the bottle. Here's a fast, neat way to get the soap from one bottle to another.

Insert a long chopstick into the neck of the newer bottle and invert the older bottle on top. The soap will cling to the chopstick and trickle down more readily.

K

Kitchen Efficiency | MAXIMIZING OVEN SPACE

A large Dutch oven often leaves little room in the oven for anything else, but there's an easy way to maximize the space.

Invert the lid, cover it with foil, and roast a side dish of potatoes or vegetables right on top.

tip 491

Kitchen Efficiency | REACHING BEYOND YOUR GRASP

The next time you need to access a lightweight kitchen item that is just out of reach, try this easy alternative to pulling out the step stool.

Use a pair of tongs to grab things like bags of pasta, cereal boxes, or spices from the top shelves of the cupboard or pantry.

tip 492

Kitchen Efficiency | MAGAZINE RECIPE STAND

Here's a clever way to keep magazine recipes in plain view (and out of harm's way) when cooking.

tip 493

Place the open magazine in an empty napkin holder.

K

Kitchen Efficiency | ORGANIZING YOUR SPACE

Here are a few tips to make it easier to locate frequently used items in your kitchen.

Utilize deep kitchen drawers by stacking cutlery trays on top of each other. For easy access, use the top tray for the most frequently used items (everyday utensils, such as can openers, spatulas, and large spoons) and the bottom tray for less frequently needed items (such as spreaders, skewers, straws, and chopsticks). It's a simple matter to grasp the top tray and lift it aside when access to the bottom layer is desired.

Playing hide-and-seek with spices stored in the kitchen cabinet gets old fast. Here's a simple way to keep them organized.

Arrange the spices in labeled rectangular baskets alphabetically or according to type; you can quickly identify their location and retrieve whatever is needed by pulling down the appropriate basket.

A permanent marker and masking tape are all that's needed to keep a refrigerator neat and organized.

Every time a new bottle or jar is opened or leftovers are packaged up, write the date on a piece of tape and stick it to the side of the container in a highly visible spot.

K

Kitchen Efficiency | ORGANIZING YOUR FRIDGE

Many refrigerators are jam-packed with jars and bottles of every type of sauce and condiment imaginable. And the hunt for any one of them—say, raspberry jam—occasions an often frustrating search through every last bottle. Here's how to avoid wasting any more time in front of an open refrigerator door.

tip 497

Group similar products in their own labeled food storage bin. Wide, shallow shapes work well. For instance, all the jams and jellies go into one container, all the Asian sauces and condiments in another, and all mustards, ketchups, and relishes in another. This is especially convenient if you are preparing, say, a stir-fry sauce that calls for several items likely to be kept in the same container. This system also limits messes on refrigerator shelves from sticky jars.

Kitchen Efficiency |
HERB, SPICE, AND CONDIMENT INVENTORY LIST

It's easy to lose track of the contents of an overstuffed spice or condiment cabinet. Inevitably, some jars and bottles will work their way to the back of the cabinet never to be seen again—or at least not until spring cleaning.

tip 498

Keep a typed list of the cabinet contents taped to the inside of the door. Your computer makes it easy to alphabetize and update the list, and the list enables you to keep track of unique items and to use them more often. The list also makes it easy to compile shopping lists for new recipes and can save you from buying items you already have on hand.

K

Kitchen Efficiency | HOMEMADE TIERED SHELF

Small items, such as spice jars or extract bottles, can get lost in a well-stocked cabinet. Here's how to keep all items, even those at the back, visible at a glance.

tip 499

Stack 2-by-4 pieces of lumber, cut to the right length, to create different height levels within the cabinet. Stack more wood in the back of the cabinet so that items in the rear will be visible above those placed in the front.

Kitchen Efficiency |
PROTECTING SINKS FROM CRACKS AND CHIPS

With soapy, slippery hands, it's easy to drop a heavy pot or pan into the sink while you're washing it. If you have a porcelain or enameled sink, this can result in an ugly chip or crack.

To protect your sink, lay several wooden spoons in it to cushion the blow in case you drop a heavy pot or pan.

tip 500

Kitchen Efficiency |
SECURING THE SILVERWARE TRAY

Most silverware organizers are shorter than the drawers they're meant to organize. The result is that the organizer and its contents slide to the back of the drawer every time you open it. If you are tired of pulling the organizer forward all the time, here's how to anchor it to the drawer.

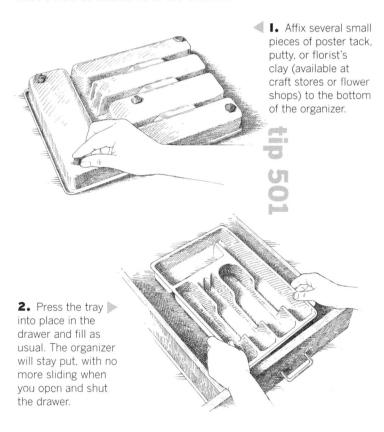

1. Affix several small pieces of poster tack, putty, or florist's clay (available at craft stores or flower shops) to the bottom of the organizer.

2. Press the tray into place in the drawer and fill as usual. The organizer will stay put, with no more sliding when you open and shut the drawer.

K

Kitchen Efficiency | EXTENDING COUNTER SPACE

Not everyone has the luxury of ample counter space, and finding room for multiple wire racks when baking cookies can be a challenge.

tip 502

To extend counter space, set the rack directly over the sink, which has the added benefit of making it easy to clean up the crumbs that fall through the rack.

Kitchen Efficiency | INSTANT COUNTER SPACE

No matter the size of the kitchen, a little extra counter space for resting bowls, platters, or cooling racks is always welcome.

Create extra counter space by opening a drawer and resting a cutting board across the top.

tip 503

Kitchen Efficiency |
EASY-TO-REACH KITCHEN TOOLS

Many cooks keep measuring cups and spoons in a drawer, where they can get buried deep among other utensils. Here's a way to keep these items within easy reach.

tip 504

Mount a simple hardware-store key holder near your workspace, and instead of using it to safeguard keys, hang your measuring cups and spoons from it.

Kitchen Efficiency |
KEEPING THE REMOTE CONTROL CLEAN

Many cooks enjoy listening to music or watching TV as they cook. But sticky hands can make a real mess of the remote control.

tip 505

Before cooking, wrap the remote control unit in a layer of clear plastic wrap. The buttons will remain visible and operable but won't get smeared by sticky hands.

K

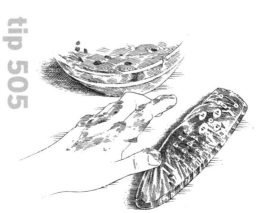

Kitchen Efficiency |
KEEPING DISHES SPOTLESS BETWEEN USES

Many home kitchen pantries, especially the oversized butler's pantries in older houses, feature open storage for platters and serving dishes. The downside of this system is that the open shelves allow the dishes to get dusty between uses. That won't be a problem if you take this precaution.

tip 506

Wrap your dishes tightly with plastic wrap before storing them.

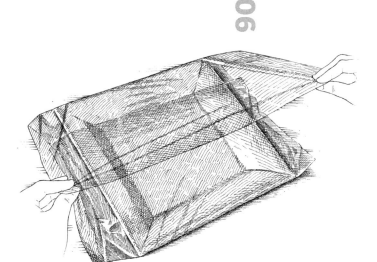

Kitchen Efficiency |
MAKESHIFT DISH-DRYING RACKS

Everyone dreads the huge pile of dishes that builds up after a dinner party or holiday gathering. In these situations, when the dishwasher and dish rack are full, drying space can be hard to come by. Try these two methods to create extra space.

tip 507

Cooling racks used for baking are an ideal source of drying space, especially for delicate wine glasses. Place a towel underneath the rack to absorb the water that drips off the glasses.

Alternatively, set an oven rack over the sink. The air circulating on all sides of the rack will help dry dishes, glasses, and other items.

tip 508

K

Kitchen Efficiency | WARMING DINNER PLATES

Warm dinner plates make any meal special and are especially welcome in cold winter months. Try this trick for getting all the plates and any serving bowls you need warmed at once.

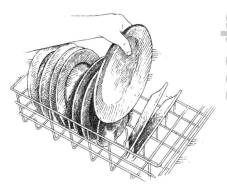

tip 509

Run all the plates, platters, and bowls you want to warm through the dish-washer on the dry cycle.

Kitchen Efficiency | MINIMIZE SAUTÉ SPLATTER

When you are browning meat for a soup or stew, grease splatters on the stovetop and burners, resulting in an unpleasant cleanup job. The stovetop is easy to wipe off, but not the burners and burner plates. Here's a way around this chore.

Position inverted disposable aluminum pie plates over the unused burners. The pie plates can be wiped clean and used again.

tip 510

Kitchen Efficiency | DOUBLE DUTY FOR POT LIDS

Most stews start with browning the meat, which must then be removed from the pan so the other ingredients can be browned, occasioning a dirty dish.

tip 511

Instead of using a clean dish, invert the lid of the pan in which you're cooking over another bowl or pot (so that it won't tip). The lid, which you need to wash any-way, now serves as a spoon rest and receptacle for the sautéed food.

K

Kitchen Efficiency | AN EXTRA-LARGE TRIVET

Many cooks, especially those whose kitchen countertops cannot accommodate hot pots and pans, often have problems finding a spot to put down a hot roasting pan right out of the oven.

To solve this problem, we place an overturned baking sheet on the counter and use it as a trivet on which to rest a hot roasting pan or Dutch oven.

tip 512

Kitchen Efficiency | PAN FLIP THAT STOPS DRIPS

Pouring melted butter, warm oil, sauce, or almost any liquid from a pan often creates a drip down the outside of the pan. This not only makes a mess on the pan's exterior but can burn onto the pan bottom if you place the pan back on a hot burner. Try this the next time the occasion arises.

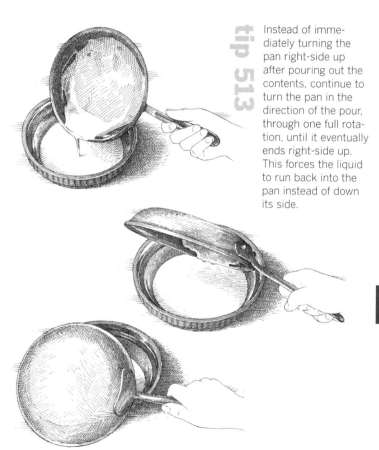

tip 513

Instead of immediately turning the pan right-side up after pouring out the contents, continue to turn the pan in the direction of the pour, through one full rotation, until it eventually ends right-side up. This forces the liquid to run back into the pan instead of down its side.

K

Opening a stubborn jar lid sometimes takes a little more than muscle. Here are four tricks we like.

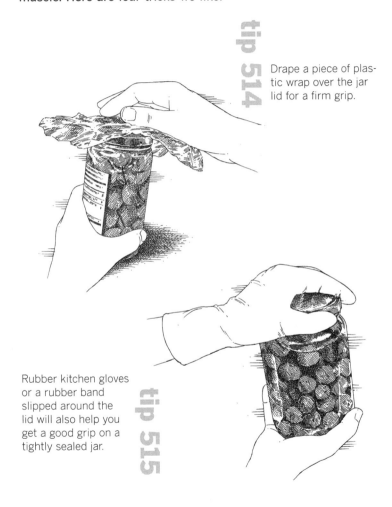

tip 514

Drape a piece of plastic wrap over the jar lid for a firm grip.

Rubber kitchen gloves or a rubber band slipped around the lid will also help you get a good grip on a tightly sealed jar.

tip 515

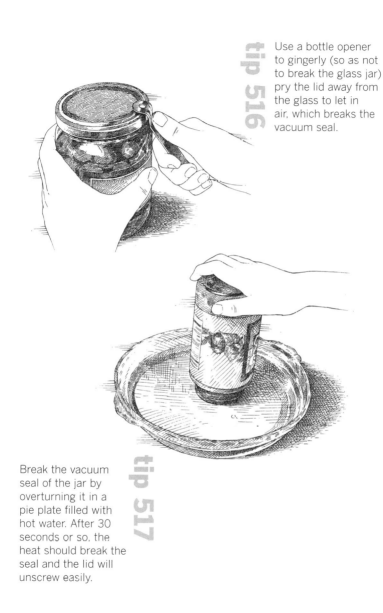

tip 516

Use a bottle opener to gingerly (so as not to break the glass jar) pry the lid away from the glass to let in air, which breaks the vacuum seal.

K

tip 517

Break the vacuum seal of the jar by overturning it in a pie plate filled with hot water. After 30 seconds or so, the heat should break the seal and the lid will unscrew easily.

349

Kitchen Efficiency | PREVENTING STICKY LIDS

The lids of jars with gooey contents such as jelly or molasses often stick as if cemented in place. Instead of struggling with sticky lids, try one of these tips.

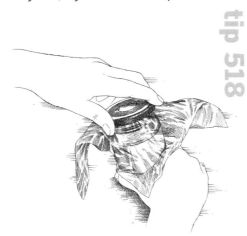

tip 518

Cover the top of the jar with plastic wrap before screwing on the lid. The plastic prevents any serious sticking, so the lid always unscrews.

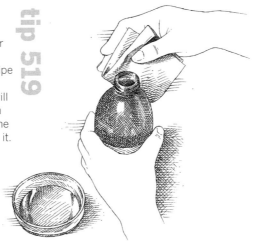

tip 519

Alternatively, dip a small piece of paper towel into a bit of vegetable oil and wipe the threads of the jar. The film of oil will prevent the lid from sticking to the jar the next time you open it.

Kitchen Efficiency | BOTTLE OPENER AIDE

When the small cap to a bottle of ketchup, Worcestershire or soy sauce, vinegar, or the like sticks and won't unscrew easily, try this method.

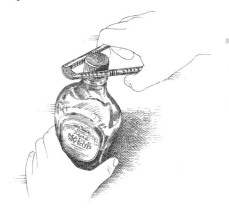

tip 520

Use a nutcracker, which should grip and twist off the cap easily.

Kitchen Storage | REUSING CRATES

Instead of discarding empty clementine orange containers, put them to good use.

tip 521

Keep the stackable crates in your pantry for storing onions, potatoes, and other items that benefit from exposure to air.

K

Kitchen Storage | PASTRY TOOLBOX

Baking buffs know how quickly all the necessary tools of the trade can overtake the limited space in their kitchen drawers, but there's an easy way to avoid this problem.

Store baking gadgets (cookie cutters, icing spatulas, measuring cups, and the like) in an inexpensive plastic toolbox, purchased from a hardware store.

Kitchen Storage | EXTENDED PANTRY SPACE

When faced with less-than-ample pantry space in your kitchen, try this creative solution.

Extend storage space by hanging an inexpensive plastic shoe rack over the inside of the pantry door. Racks with clear plastic pockets work best, providing quick visual access to all of the small items that might normally take up room on a shelf.

Kitchen Storage | DUST BUSTERS

It makes sense to store the attachments for an electric mixer inside the bowl, but doing so can also expose them to dust.

Use a clean shower cap as a portable cover for the bowl and the attachments stored inside. This trick also keeps dust from collecting on utensils stored upright in a crock. When you're cooking or have company, simply slip off the cap and stick it in a kitchen drawer.

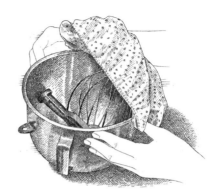

tip 524

Kitchen Storage | ROLLING PIN

Storing large, awkward rolling pins with handles and ball bearings is often difficult, especially with limited drawer and cupboard space.

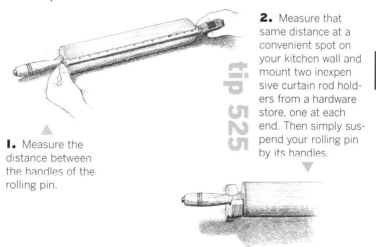

tip 525

2. Measure that same distance at a convenient spot on your kitchen wall and mount two inexpensive curtain rod holders from a hardware store, one at each end. Then simply suspend your rolling pin by its handles.

I. Measure the distance between the handles of the rolling pin.

K

Kitchen Storage | SHARP UTENSILS

Fondue forks, paring knives, skewers, and all manner of small, sharp objects can present a danger when tossed haphazardly into a kitchen drawer. The next time you reach into the drawer, you could let yourself get poked, or you can try this tip instead.

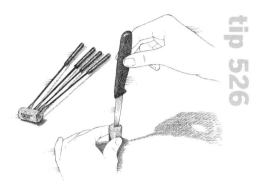

tip 526

Secure those pointy tips in leftover wine corks, which not only protect hands but also keep sharp edges from getting dull.

Kitchen Storage | IMPROMPTU BOWL COVER

When there's no plastic wrap around to cover leftovers for storage, try this alternative.

tip 527

A clean, unused shower cap (often found in complimentary toiletry packs in hotel rooms) makes a perfect bowl cover. It is big enough to fit most large mixing bowls and creates a more reliable seal than most plastic wraps.

Kitchen Storage | NO-FUSS WRAPPER STORAGE

Opened boxes of aluminum foil and plastic wrap often catch on the kitchen drawer frame, causing it to jam.

tip 528

When you return a box of foil or plastic wrap to its storage drawer, turn the box lid-side down. The next time you open the drawer, the lids won't stick up and catch to prevent the drawer from opening.

Kitchen Storage | BOXES OF FOIL AND WRAP

The boxes containing plastic sandwich bags, rolls of aluminum foil, plastic wrap, and the like can use up a lot of valuable drawer space. Here's an efficient way to store these boxes in a cabinet under the counter.

Store the boxes upright in the slots of a cardboard six-pack container that once held beer or soda bottles.

tip 529

K

Kitchen Storage | SPACE SAVING

Cooks with limited storage space will appreciate this method of storing baking sheets upright.

A metal vertical file holder is ideal for storing cutting boards and baking sheets. They not only take up less space this way but also are easy to grab when you need one.

Kitchen Storage | PLASTIC PRODUCE BAGS

Many home kitchens sport a drawer filled to the gills with crumpled plastic produce bags. Reclaim your drawer with this space-saving solution.

Stuff the plastic bags into empty tissue boxes. A box will accommodate many, many bags, which are then easy to remove one at a time when the need arises.

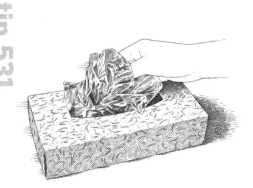

Kitchen Torch | ALTERNATE USES

Crème brûlée aficionados use their kitchen torch to caramelize the sugar layer on their favorite dessert, but not for much else.

tip 532

Get more from your kitchen torch by using it to brown already-baked meringue-topped pies, tartlets, and cakes.

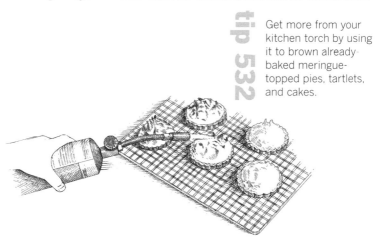

Kitchen Towel | USING THAT LOOPHOLE

Many kitchen towels come with a loop sewn into the hem. Here's a way to put it to good use, so your towel is always at the ready.

tip 533

Sew a button into the waist of an apron, so you can hang the towel from it for easy access.

K

Kiwi | PEELING

A vegetable peeler or knife can be ineffective for removing the hairy skin from a kiwi, tending to crush the soft flesh. We like the following method.

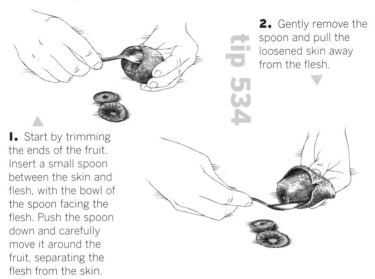

2. Gently remove the spoon and pull the loosened skin away from the flesh.

I. Start by trimming the ends of the fruit. Insert a small spoon between the skin and flesh, with the bowl of the spoon facing the flesh. Push the spoon down and carefully move it around the fruit, separating the flesh from the skin.

Knives | DETERMINING SHARPNESS

Don't wait until an accident occurs to find out if your knife blade is dull.

Put your knife to the paper test. Hold a sheet of paper by one end and try slicing clean ribbons from it. If the knife snags or fails to cut the paper, it needs to be steeled or sharpened.

Knives | DETERMINING HONING ANGLE

When honing a knife on a steel or a stone, it's best to hold the blade at a 20-degree angle. But what is a 20-degree angle? Here's an easy way to approximate the angle.

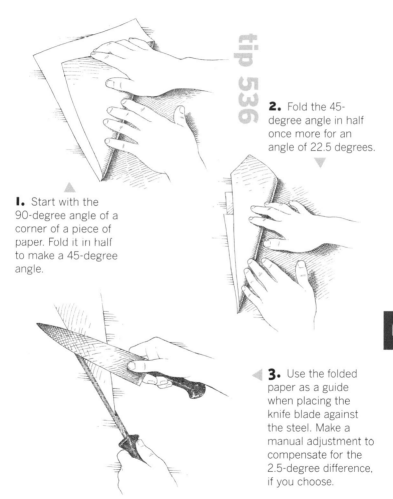

2. Fold the 45-degree angle in half once more for an angle of 22.5 degrees.

I. Start with the 90-degree angle of a corner of a piece of paper. Fold it in half to make a 45-degree angle.

3. Use the folded paper as a guide when placing the knife blade against the steel. Make a manual adjustment to compensate for the 2.5-degree difference, if you choose.

Most home cooks do not have a sheath in which to carry a knife when traveling. Here are two homemade carriers that work well.

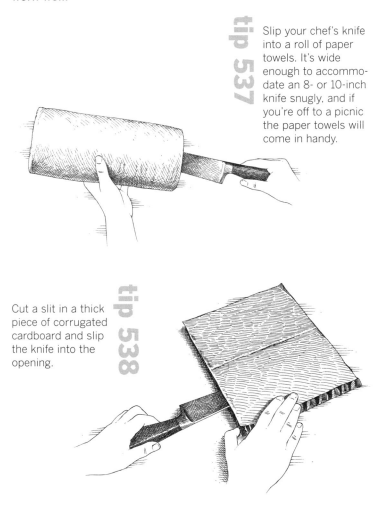

tip 537

Slip your chef's knife into a roll of paper towels. It's wide enough to accommodate an 8- or 10-inch knife snugly, and if you're off to a picnic the paper towels will come in handy.

tip 538

Cut a slit in a thick piece of corrugated cardboard and slip the knife into the opening.

Lasagna | MAKING SMALLER BATCHES

Most lasagna recipes produce enough to feed a big crowd, but cooks who are feeding fewer people may not want to make that much.

tip 539

For single-serve portions, make lasagna in mini-loaf pans. Pans that measure 5¾ by 3 inches are the perfect size for most standard lasagna noodles, which will fit perfectly if cut in half after cooking. The individual loaf pans can be wrapped, frozen, and baked one at a time as needed.

L

Leeks | CLEANING

Leeks are often quite dirty and gritty, so they require thorough cleaning. Both of the following methods require that you first cut the dark green portion into quarters lengthwise, leaving the root end intact.

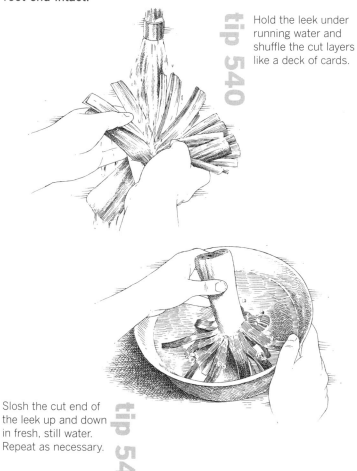

Hold the leek under running water and shuffle the cut layers like a deck of cards.

tip 540

Slosh the cut end of the leek up and down in fresh, still water. Repeat as necessary.

tip 541

Lemon Slices | FREEZING FOR BEVERAGES

Lemon slices are a refreshing addition to a glass of water and many other beverages, but if you need just a slice at a time, it can seem a bother. This method makes adding lemon slices to your drink as convenient as adding an ice cube.

tip 542

Slice a few lemons and lay the slices flat on a parchment paper–covered baking sheet and freeze, then store frozen in a zipper-lock bag.

L

Lemons and Limes |
SHORTCUT FOR SQUEEZING JUICE

If you need to squeeze a large amount of citrus juice, as when making lemonade or a Key lime pie, try this method.

tip 543

Place two or three quartered limes or lemons in the hopper of a potato ricer and squeeze the handles together.

Lemon Reamer | IMPROVISING

If you find yourself in a kitchen without a citrus reamer, don't despair. This common kitchen tool makes a fine substitute.

tip 544

A beater from a handheld mixer can be used to ream lemons beautifully.

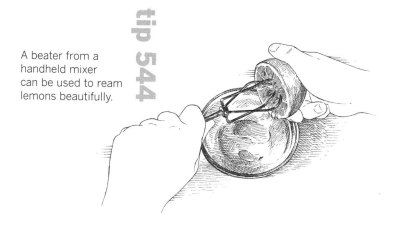

Lemonade | TWO WAYS TO MASH SLICED LEMONS

We find that sugaring sliced lemons and then mashing them to release their flavorful oils creates the best lemonade ever. Although you can mash the sugared lemons with a potato masher or wooden spoon, here are two ways to work more quickly.

tip 545

Place the sliced lemons and sugar in the bowl of a standing mixer fitted with the paddle attachment. Turn the mixer to low and mix for about 45 seconds. (Longer mixing can mash the lemons too much and make the lemonade bitter.) To prevent splatters, drape a kitchen towel over the mixer.

tip 546

An alternative method is to let sugared lemon slices macerate for about 15 minutes, or until softened, and then mash them in batches with a potato ricer. Set the ricer right over the lemonade pitcher.

L

Lemons | REMOVING PEEL FROM A GRATER

Lemon zest often becomes trapped in the teeth of a box grater and ends up being wasted. Here are two ways to get around this problem.

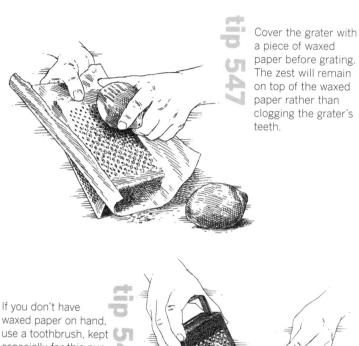

tip 547

Cover the grater with a piece of waxed paper before grating. The zest will remain on top of the waxed paper rather than clogging the grater's teeth.

tip 548

If you don't have waxed paper on hand, use a toothbrush, kept especially for this purpose in the kitchen, to scrape the trapped zest off the grater.

Lemons | JUICING

Everyone has a trick for juicing lemons. We find that this one extracts the most juice possible from lemons as well as limes.

1. Start by rolling the lemon on a hard surface, pressing down firmly with the palm of your hand to break the membranes inside the fruit.

2. Cut the lemon in half. Use a wooden reamer to extract the juice into a bowl. To catch the seeds, place a mesh strainer over the bowl.

L

Lemons | FREEZING SPENT SHELLS

Here's a nifty use for the spent shells from juiced lemons and limes.

tip 550

Place spent shells in a zipper-lock bag in the freezer. When you need acidulated water to hold peeled apples, potatoes, or artichokes, don't waste a fresh lemon—just take a spent shell from the freezer. It has enough juice and acidity to keep these foods from turning brown.

Lemon Grass | BRUISING

Bruising a whole stalk of lemon grass is the best way to release its flavorful juices when infusing a liquid like stock.

Smack the stalk with the back of a large chef's knife and use immediately.

tip 551

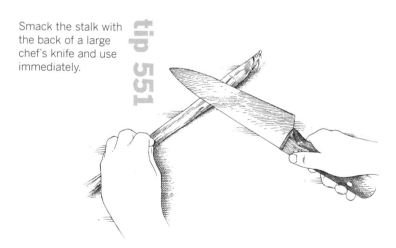

Lemon Grass | MINCING

Because of its tough outer leaves, lemon grass can be difficult to mince. We like this method, which relies on a sharp knife.

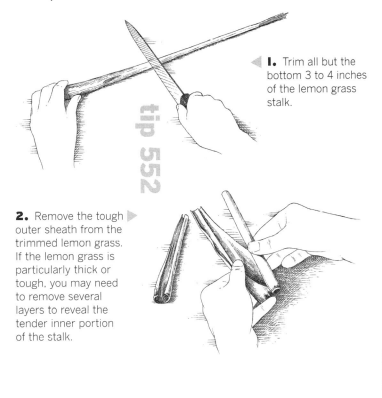

I. Trim all but the bottom 3 to 4 inches of the lemon grass stalk.

2. Remove the tough outer sheath from the trimmed lemon grass. If the lemon grass is particularly thick or tough, you may need to remove several layers to reveal the tender inner portion of the stalk.

3. Cut the trimmed and peeled lemon grass in half length-wise, then mince fine.

L

Lettuce | CORING AND WASHING

Here's a simple way to core and wash a head of iceberg lettuce with just one motion.

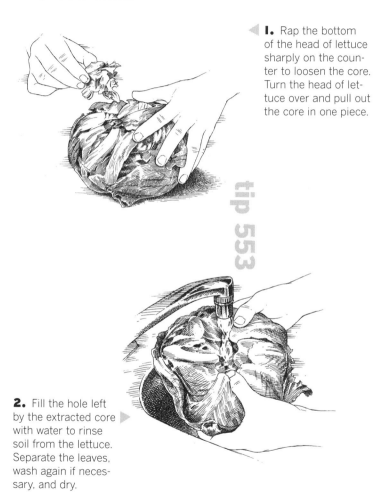

I. Rap the bottom of the head of lettuce sharply on the counter to loosen the core. Turn the head of lettuce over and pull out the core in one piece.

tip 553

2. Fill the hole left by the extracted core with water to rinse soil from the lettuce. Separate the leaves, wash again if necessary, and dry.

Lobster | DISTINGUISHING HARD-SHELLS FROM SOFT

Right after molting, a lobster has a soft shell that is easy to crack. However, hard-shelled lobsters are much meatier. Here's how to tell the difference between the two stages in the lobster's life cycle.

Squeeze the sides of the lobster's body, just in front of the tail. A soft-shell lobster will yield to pressure, while a hard-shell lobster will feel hard and tightly packed with meat.

Lobster | CONTROLLING MESS

Whether eaten at home or in a restaurant, lobster dinners inevitably make a sticky mess when fluid escapes in gushes and geysers from the shells as you crack them to get to the meat. Here's an easy way to stem the tide.

Using tongs, hold the cooked lobster by the tail above the cooking pot, so the claws are pointing down into the pot. Then use kitchen shears to cut about ¼ inch off the tip of each claw and continue holding the lobster as the water in its shell drains back into the pot through the holes in the claws.

L

Mangoes | PEELING

Mangoes are notoriously hard to peel, owing to their odd shape and slippery texture. Here's how we handle this tough kitchen task. This method ensures long, attractive strips of fruit.

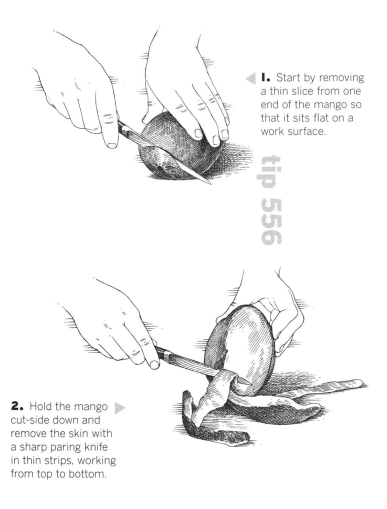

1. Start by removing a thin slice from one end of the mango so that it sits flat on a work surface.

tip 556

2. Hold the mango cut-side down and remove the skin with a sharp paring knife in thin strips, working from top to bottom.

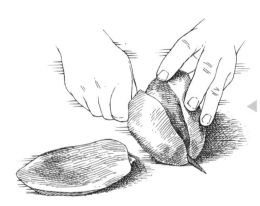

3. Cut down along the side of the flat pit to remove the flesh from one side of the mango. Do the same on the other side of the pit.

4. Trim around the pit to remove any remaining flesh. The mango flesh can now be chopped or sliced as desired.

Mayonnaise | DRIZZLING IN THE OIL

Homemade mayonnaise is made by slowly whisking oil into beaten egg yolk and lemon juice. It can be difficult to whisk with one hand and pour evenly from a heavy measuring cup with the other hand.

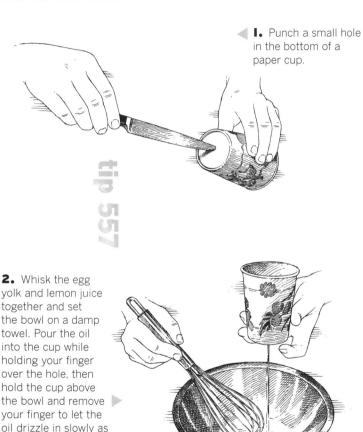

I. Punch a small hole in the bottom of a paper cup.

2. Whisk the egg yolk and lemon juice together and set the bowl on a damp towel. Pour the oil into the cup while holding your finger over the hole, then hold the cup above the bowl and remove your finger to let the oil drizzle in slowly as you whisk.

Measuring Cups | IMPROVISING

If you are cooking in a kitchen without a set of measuring cups, turn to this clever substitution.

tip 558

Cleaned-out yogurt cups make great homemade measuring cups. Use the 4-ounce size for a ½-cup measure, the 6-ounce size for a ¾-cup measure, and the 8-ounce size for a 1 cup measure.

Measuring Spoons | KEEPING TOGETHER

Measuring spoons often come with flimsy rings that end up breaking. Here's a way to make sure they all stay together.

tip 559

Attach the spoons to a simple "split" key ring to keep them all together and in one place no matter how many times they go through the dishwasher.

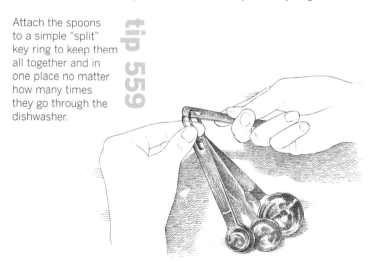

Meat | SPACING TIES ON A ROAST

Roasts cook more evenly when tied at even intervals. Tying also makes the roast more attractive. Here's an easy way to make sure that you space the pieces of kitchen twine evenly.

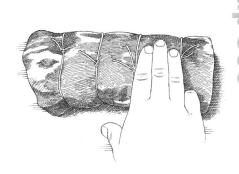

tip 560

Space the ties about three fingers apart down the entire length of the roast.

Meat | FREEZING FOR EASY SLICING

Many recipes, including stir-fries, soups, and pasta sauces, call for thinly sliced pieces of flank steak, pork tenderloin, or other meats. Here's how to make the slices as thin as possible.

tip 561

Place the meat in the freezer until partially frozen, 1 to 2 hours, depending on the thickness of the meat. It's much easier to slice through partially frozen meat and turn out thin, even slices.

Roasts and other meats need to rest for several minutes before being carved to give the juices a chance to redistribute throughout the meat, but tenting a roast takes a lot of aluminum foil, which you might not want to spare for this use. Try one of these alternatives instead.

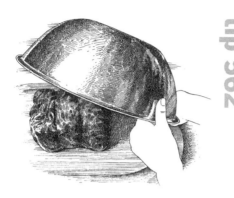

tip 562

Cover the roast with a large overturned metal bowl.

tip 563

Place the roast in a large, covered Dutch oven or stockpot. The roast stays warm, and any juices given off by the roast are contained and can be added easily to a *jus* or pan sauce. (This method is better suited to beef, pork, lamb, or veal roasts than to poultry because crisp skin will soften.)

Meat | PROTECTING ROAST CRUST

As your roast rests before carving, don't let the accumulated juices soggy its crusty bottom.

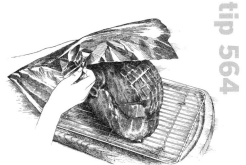

Place the roast on a rack set over a rimmed baking sheet or a roasting pan, which will keep the roast and its crisp exterior above and away from the dampening juices.

Meat | STEADYING A ROAST FOR CARVING

When carving a roast, it's necessary to steady it, usually with a large fork, but we don't like how the fork punctures the meat and causes juices to leak. This method keeps the juices inside the meat.

A pair of kitchen tongs grasps a roast or large bird without puncturing the meat.

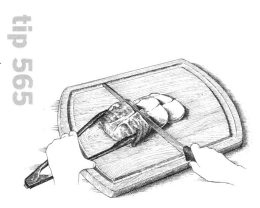

Meat | FREEZING

If you'd like the convenience of pulling out frozen chops, burgers, or steaks as you need them, follow this easy method.

Separate chops, steaks, and burgers with sheets of parchment paper, place the meat in freezer bags, and freeze. The paper makes it much easier to pull individual pieces from the frozen package.

tip 566

Meatballs | EMERGENCY MEATBALLS

Throwing together an impromptu spaghetti dinner is always fun, but meatballs aren't usually a quick project. Here's a way to shortcut the process.

tip 567

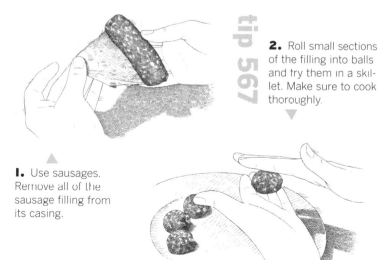

2. Roll small sections of the filling into balls and fry them in a skillet. Make sure to cook thoroughly.

I. Use sausages. Remove all of the sausage filling from its casing.

Meatballs | ENSURING EVEN BROWNING

Meatballs must be cooked through and taste best when browned evenly on all sides. Their round shape can make this a challenge.

tip 568

Once the meatballs have been browned on their two broader sides, use tongs to stand them on the remaining sides to finish cooking. If necessary, lean the meatballs up against one another to get the final sides browned.

Melon | NOVEL WAY TO SERVE

Instead of serving plain wedges of cantaloupe or other melon, try adding a handy touch that also facilitates eating.

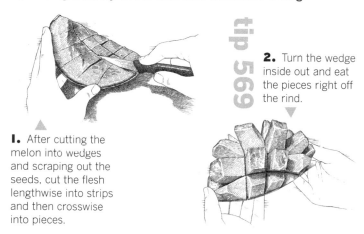

tip 569

2. Turn the wedge inside out and eat the pieces right off the rind.

I. After cutting the melon into wedges and scraping out the seeds, cut the flesh lengthwise into strips and then crosswise into pieces.

Meringue | MAKING ITALIAN MERINGUE

Italian meringue is made with hot sugar syrup, which cooks the egg whites and ensures a stable meringue. If the syrup is allowed to make contact with the metal beater or bowl, it can solidify into small, hard pieces that won't mix with the whites. Here's how to avoid the problem.

Carefully pour the hot sugar syrup into the egg whites, making sure the syrup doesn't touch the metal beater or the sides of the bowl.

tip 570

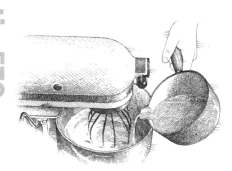

Microwave Oven | CLEANING

Cleaning dried-on spills and splatters in your microwave oven needn't be a time-consuming chore.

1. Place a microwave-safe bowl full of water in the oven and heat it on high for 10 minutes. The steam loosens any dried food particles, which can then be wiped off with ease.

tip 571

2. For hard-to-reach corners, a small disposable foam paintbrush is just the right size to brush away any crumbs or other residue.

Mixer | KEEPING BOWLS IN PLACE

Here's how to secure a mixing bowl so that you can hold a mixer in one hand and add ingredients with the other.

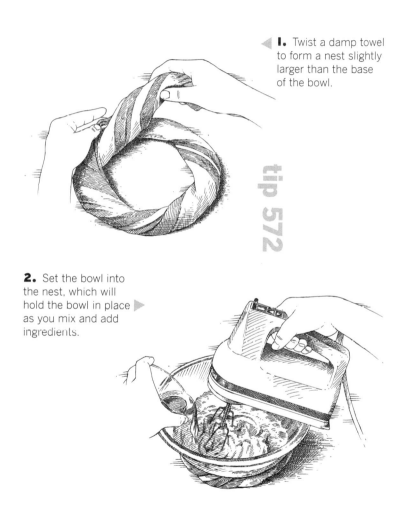

1. Twist a damp towel to form a nest slightly larger than the base of the bowl.

tip 572

2. Set the bowl into the nest, which will hold the bowl in place as you mix and add ingredients.

Mixer | SPLATTER-FREE MIXING

Handheld mixers often cause an excessive amount of splashing, especially when you are beating a thin, liquid batter or whipping cream. Here's how to keep the mess under control.

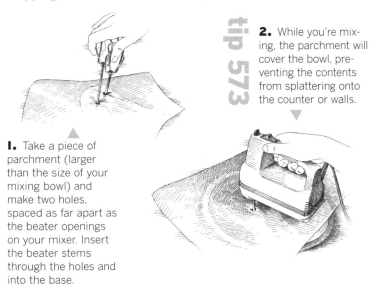

tip 573

2. While you're mixing, the parchment will cover the bowl, preventing the contents from splattering onto the counter or walls.

1. Take a piece of parchment (larger than the size of your mixing bowl) and make two holes, spaced as far apart as the beater openings on your mixer. Insert the beater stems through the holes and into the base.

Mixer | EASY CLEANUP

Avoid a messy cleanup when using a standing mixer with this tip.

tip 574

Put a plastic serving tray (like the kind found in cafeterias) under the mixer. Not only is it easier to slide the mixer on the countertop, but any mess can be easily cleaned up with a quick rinse of the tray.

Mixer | MOVING HEAVY MIXERS

Many standing mixers, as well as food processors, are heavy and don't slide easily. They can be difficult for many people to lift. Here are two good ways to move them around the counter with ease.

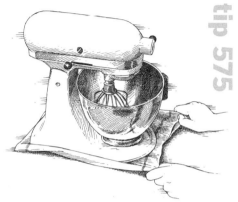

tip 575

Place your mixer on a towel or cloth place mat, which then can be pulled anywhere on the counter with little effort.

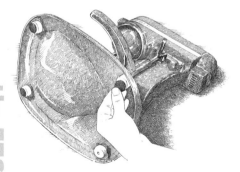

Stick self-adhesive floor-protector pads made of felt (normally used on furniture) to the bottom of food processors, blenders, and standing mix-ers. The pads allow the heavy appliances to glide across the counter.

tip 576

Mixer | KEEPING THE MESS UNDER CONTROL

Dry ingredients can puff out in a cloud of fine particles when mixed, while wet ingredients, such as cream or liquid batters, can splatter. Here's a good way to keep your counter clean when using a standing mixer.

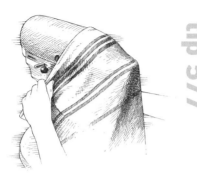

tip 577

Once the ingredients are in the bowl, drape a clean, very damp dish towel over the front of the mixer and bowl. Draw the towel snug with one hand and then turn on the mixer. When done, simply wash the towel.

Mortar and Pestle | IMPROVISING

Mortars and pestles are great for grinding chiles, spices, nuts, or even herbs. Many modern kitchens are not equipped with this tool, however. Here's how to make a mortar and pestle with objects likely to be found in any kitchen.

Place the ingredients to be ground in a shallow, diner-style stoneware coffee cup (which will be the mortar), and use a heavy glass spice bottle as the pestle.

tip 578

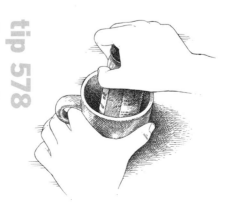

Muffin Tin | MUFFIN-TIN SHIELDS

Tired of scrubbing off the burnt batter from muffin tins?
Opt for an ounce of prevention with this technique.

1. Cover the muffin tin tightly with aluminum foil. Cut slits in each hole and press the foil into each indentation.

tip 579

2. Drop paper or foil liners into each hole and fill with your favorite muffin batter.

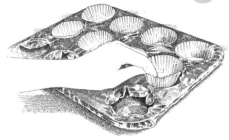

3. After removing the muffins, simply peel off the dirty foil.

Muffin Tin | LIBERATING TRAPPED MUFFINS

Sometimes muffins will stubbornly stick in the pan. Here's a way to pry them out with little likelihood of tearing the muffin apart.

tip 580

The thin, slightly curved blade of a grapefruit knife is particularly suited to getting under a stubborn muffin with little chance of damage.

Mushrooms | STUFFED MUSHROOM CUPS

Here's an easy way to ensure that stuffed mushrooms remain upright when transporting them to a party.

Use mini-muffin tins. Each mushroom perches neatly in a muffin cup, and not a single bread crumb is lost on the way to the party.

tip 581

Mushrooms | CLEANING

Mushrooms—with all of their hard-to-reach spots—can be difficult to clean. Here's an inexpensive way to get the job done.

tip 582

Use a clean, soft-bristled toothbrush. It provides a comfortable handle, and the small head slips easily under the gills to capture every stray bit of dirt. A run through the dishwasher cleans the soiled brush.

Mushrooms | FLAVORING PORTOBELLOS

Big, meaty portobello caps can be studded with garlic and herbs, just like a piece of meat.

tip 583

2. Insert a sliver of garlic into each slit along with a sage leaf, some fresh rosemary, or maybe a tiny sprig of thyme. The garlic and herbs will remain inside the portobello as it cooks.

1. Use the tip of a paring knife to make 10 or 12 narrow slits in the top of each portobello cap.

Mushrooms | SLICING WHITE MUSHROOMS QUICKLY

Slicing white mushrooms thin takes some patience. Here's a novel way to speed up the process.

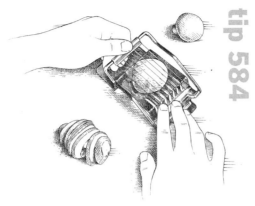

tip 584

Trim a thin piece from the stem end of each mushroom, then cut the trimmed mushrooms, one at a time, in an egg slicer. The pieces will be even and thin.

Mushrooms | GRILLING WHITE MUSHROOMS

Grilling gives white mushrooms a rich brown crust and meaty flavor. Proper skewering keeps them from falling through the grill grate and allows for even grilling.

Once the mushrooms have been cleaned and any dry ends trimmed from the stems, slide each one onto a skewer through the stem up through the cap. This method keeps the mushrooms from rotating on the grill, so they can be turned easily for even cooking.

tip 585

Mushrooms | SOAKING DRIED MUSHROOMS

Dried porcinis, as well as shiitakes, oysters, and other dried mushrooms, must be reconstituted before being added to recipes. Soak the mushrooms in hot tap water (about 1 cup per ounce of dried mushrooms) in a small bowl until softened, about 20 minutes. Here's how to make sure any sand or dirt released by the mushrooms doesn't end up in your food.

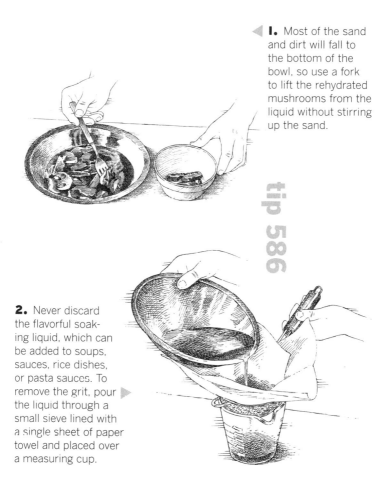

1. Most of the sand and dirt will fall to the bottom of the bowl, so use a fork to lift the rehydrated mushrooms from the liquid without stirring up the sand.

tip 586

2. Never discard the flavorful soaking liquid, which can be added to soups, sauces, rice dishes, or pasta sauces. To remove the grit, pour the liquid through a small sieve lined with a single sheet of paper towel and placed over a measuring cup.

Mushrooms |
KEEPING DRIED MUSHROOMS SUBMERGED IN LIQUID

To keep dried mushrooms (or tomatoes or chiles) submerged in water as they hydrate, try one of these tips.

tip 587

Place the food in the carafe of a French press coffee maker (also called a plunger pot), fill the carafe partway with water, and depress the plunger a bit to keep the food submerged. Just make sure to choose a model with a glass carafe that will not retain flavors and ruin subsequent pots of coffee.

tip 588

Alternatively, place the items to be hydrated in a zipper-lock bag, fill the bag with enough water to submerge the food, and zip it shut, squeezing out as much air as possible as you go.

Mussels | DEBEARDING

Mussels often contain a weedy beard protruding from the crack between the two shells. It's fairly small and can be difficult to tug out of place. Here's how we handle this task.

tip 589

Trap the beard between the side of a small knife and your thumb and pull to remove it. The flat surface of the paring knife gives you some leverage to extract the pesky beard.

Nutmeg | MAKING THE MOST OF WHOLE NUTMEG

When you have grated a whole nutmeg seed to the point at which you are risking your fingertips, don't throw the little nub away. There's an easy way to eliminate waste.

Grind the leftover nutmeg with a mortar and pestle. It is actually fairly soft and pulverizes quite easily.

tip 590

Nuts | TOASTING

Here's a good reason to dust off that old hot-air popcorn popper that hasn't been used in years.

Toast nuts in it. Place ¼ cup nuts in the popper and turn on the contraption for about 1 minute, until the nuts turn golden brown.

tip 591

Nuts | KEEPING IN PLACE

Chopping nuts on a cutting board can send projectiles flying across the kitchen. A tool found in most kitchens can help keep them in check.

tip 592

Use a sharp-edged pastry blender to chop soft nuts like walnuts and pecans in a mixing bowl.

Nuts | CRACKING TOUGH NUTS

Few nutcrackers are strong enough to crack the hard shells of many nuts, especially walnuts. You can find a better alternative at the hardware store. A vise-grip, also known as curved-jaw locking pliers, is perfect for the job.

1. The adjustable rounded jaws can accommodate nuts of almost any shape or size.

tip 593

2. The grip is strong enough to break through the hardest shell, leaving the tender flesh intact.

Nuts |

MICROWAVE-TOASTED NUTS AND SESAME SEEDS

If you are cooking multiple dishes at once, it can be difficult to find available stovetop or oven space when you need to toast nuts or sesame seeds. Use the microwave for this task.

tip 594

1. For fragrant, browned results, place ½ cup of sesame seeds or nuts in a microwave-safe bowl and microwave at full power for about 2 minutes, checking and stirring every 30 seconds, until the seeds or nuts are golden brown.

2. Spread the seeds or nuts on paper towels to cool and absorb oils. This technique works best for cashews, almonds, pine nuts, hazelnuts, and sesame seeds.

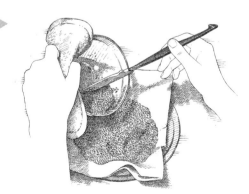

Nuts | DE-SALTING

Here's a quick and easy way to make salted nuts usable in recipes that call for the unsalted variety.

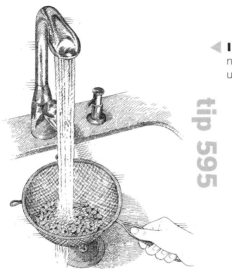

1. Rinse the shelled nuts in a strainer under cool water.

tip 595

2. Spread the nuts evenly on a toaster oven tray and cook at 350 degrees for about 6 minutes, or until the nuts are dry and slightly toasted. (A regular oven works just as well.)

Nuts | CHOPPING QUICKLY

Chopping a large batch of nuts can be a tedious task. Here's how to speed up the process.

Place the nuts on a cutting board and hold two chef's knives parallel to each other in one hand and chop. Use the other hand to guide the knives through the nuts.

Nuts | CHOPPING NEATLY

Chopping hazelnuts or peanuts can sometimes mean a wild chase around the cutting board as the nuts roll every which way. Here is an easy way to contain the nuts.

2. Lay the rope on the board in a ring around the nuts. Leave enough room in the center of the ring to fit the knife, and chop away.

1. Wet a kitchen towel (or two, depending on how many nuts you have to chop), grasp both ends, and twist them in opposite directions to form a tight rope.

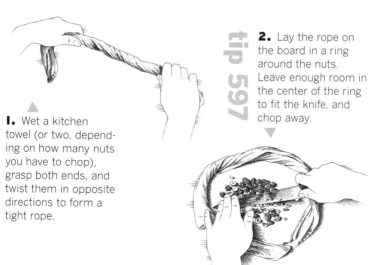

Oil | DISPENSING CONVENIENTLY

Pour spouts are a great way to mete out just the right amount of cooking oil for a sauté or a salad. But if you don't have cupboards tall enough to fit both the bottle and the spout, here's an easy way to get just a splash of oil from the bottle without using a spout.

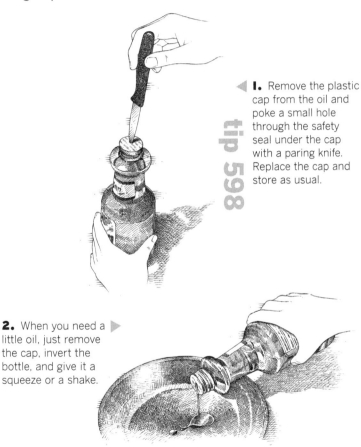

tip 598

I. Remove the plastic cap from the oil and poke a small hole through the safety seal under the cap with a paring knife. Replace the cap and store as usual.

2. When you need a little oil, just remove the cap, invert the bottle, and give it a squeeze or a shake.

Oil | CATCHING DRIPS

Oil that has run down the side of a bottle can create unsightly oil stains on pantry shelves. Here are a couple of ways to prevent this problem.

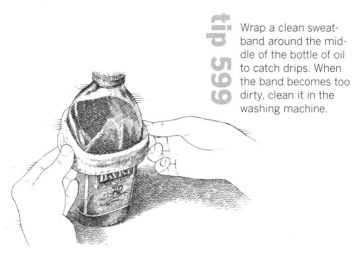

tip 599

Wrap a clean sweatband around the middle of the bottle of oil to catch drips. When the band becomes too dirty, clean it in the washing machine.

tip 600

Alternatively, a band of folded paper towels can be fastened around the bottle with a rubber band and simply thrown away when dirty.

Oil | BETTER CONTAINERS

Frugal shoppers often buy cooking oil in 1-gallon cans, which are bulky to store in the cupboard and are especially difficult to pour.

 tip 601

Transfer the oil to a more manageable receptacle, such as a clean plastic syrup container with a flip top. Now if you need only a tablespoon or two, you can squirt it out in a neat stream. A sports water bottle with a pop-up spout can be used for the same purpose.

O

Oil | POURING SMOOTHLY

Many households buy olive oil in gallon containers, pouring some into a smaller can or bottle for daily use. But pouring from such a huge container can be a problem, especially when the oil glugs and sloshes out.

1. To even out the flow while pouring, use a can opener to punch a hole in the top of the container opposite the pouring spout.

2. Having thus evened out the pressure in the container, you can pour the oil in a smooth, continuous flow.

tip 602

Olives | SMARTER RETRIEVAL

Try this easy method to extract capers and olives from their
narrow jars.

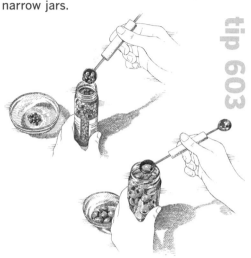

Use the small scoop
of a melon baller to
retrieve capers and
the larger scoop for
olives. As a bonus, the
excess brine drains
through the scoops'
perforations.

Olives | INSTANT PASTE

Finely mincing olives, capers, or sun-dried tomatoes can be a
tedious task.

Use a garlic press.
Place two or three
pitted olives, a tea-
spoonful of capers,
or two oil-packed
sun-dried tomatoes
in the hopper of
a garlic press and
squeeze. The pastes
can be used to flavor
salad dressings, dips,
and sauces or as
a pasta topping or
sandwich spread.

Onions | STORING VIDALIAS

The sugar content of Vidalia, Walla Walla, and Maui onions, which is what endears them to many cooks, also makes them spoil more quickly if they are stored touching one another. Here's how to prolong their freshness.

tip 605

Place one onion in the leg of an old but clean pair of pantyhose. Tie a knot in the hose, just above the onion. Repeat this process up the entire leg of the pantyhose.

Onions | KEEPING ORGANIZED

It's always best to use up onions that have been sitting in the pantry before breaking into a fresh supply. But it's difficult to keep track of the older versus the younger onions.

Using a permanent marker, lightly mark a small X on the skin of each onion now in your storage bin. Leave any new onions you add to the bin unmarked, so that you'll know to reach for the marked onions first. When all of the marked onions have been used, mark the remaining ones.

tip 606

Onions | GETTING A GRIP WHILE SLICING

Here's a tip to make dicing or slicing onions even easier. After trimming the top of the onion and halving it pole to pole, follow the steps below.

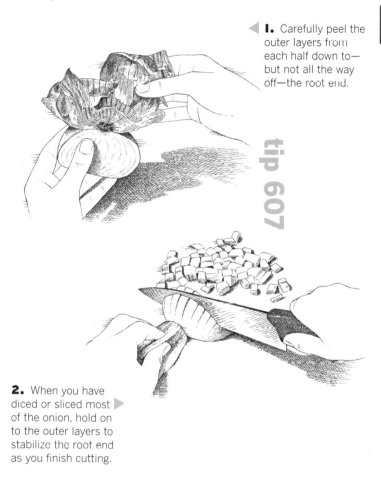

1. Carefully peel the outer layers from each half down to—but not all the way off—the root end.

2. When you have diced or sliced most of the onion, hold on to the outer layers to stabilize the root end as you finish cutting.

Onions | MINCING WITH EASE

Mincing onions can be tedious work, but take heart—there are shortcuts. This one is the easiest we've come across.

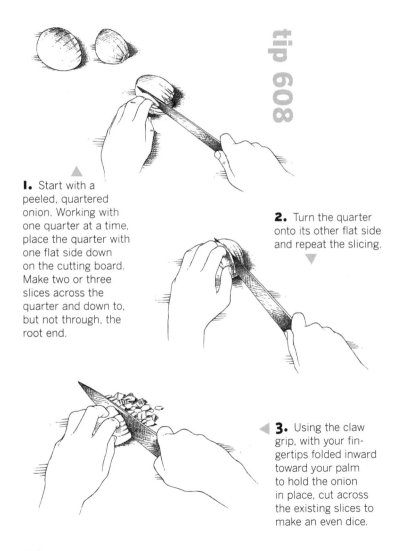

1. Start with a peeled, quartered onion. Working with one quarter at a time, place the quarter with one flat side down on the cutting board. Make two or three slices across the quarter and down to, but not through, the root end.

2. Turn the quarter onto its other flat side and repeat the slicing.

3. Using the claw grip, with your fingertips folded inward toward your palm to hold the onion in place, cut across the existing slices to make an even dice.

Onions | KEEPING MOIST

When browning small amounts of onion, there's a tendency for drying and scorching, even when using a high-quality pan. Here's a way to prevent them from drying out.

Keep small batches of onions moist with a plant mister, spritzing them lightly if they start to look dry. The water not only helps them caramelize evenly but also deglazes any flavorful brown bits (fond) stuck to the bottom of the pan.

tip 609

Onions | GRILLING RINGS

Onion slices can be difficult to handle on the grill, with rings often slipping through the grate and onto the coals. Here's how to grill onions safely and easily.

tip 610

2. The skewered onion slices remain intact as they grill so no rings can fall onto the coals. Best of all, the onions are easily flipped with tongs.

I. Cut thick slices (at least ½ inch) from large onions and impale them with a slender bamboo skewer (it should be about the thickness of a toothpick) or a thin metal skewer. If using long skewers, thread two slices on each skewer.

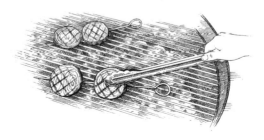

Orange Juice |
SHORTCUTTING FROZEN JUICE PREPARATION

When the craving for orange juice hits, waiting for a can of frozen concentrate to thaw before mixing it with water can be frustrating. Here's a way to avoid the wait.

1. Run the can of frozen concentrate under hot water so it will melt just enough to release from the can.

tip 611

2. Use an immersion blender to mix the still-frozen block of concentrate with water. The action of the blender produces a smooth, lump-free juice—with no waiting.

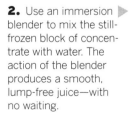

Oranges | ORANGE BOWLS FOR SHERBET

Don't toss out all of the spent orange halves left over after making fresh orange sherbet. Put them to good use with this tip.

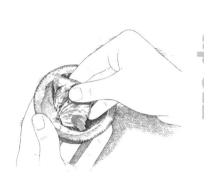

1. After juicing the oranges, carefully peel out the remaining flesh by hand. If necessary, slice a thin section off the bottom of each half to keep the oranges upright.

tip 612

2. After the sherbet has firmed up in the freezer, scoop it neatly into each orange half. Return to the freezer to store until ready to serve.

Oranges | REMOVING SEGMENTS

When presentation matters, you will want to remove segments from an orange without any white pith or membranes. Use the same technique with grapefruit.

I. Start by slicing a small section, about ½ inch thick, off the top and bottom ends.

tip 613

2. With the fruit resting flat, use a sharp paring knife to slice off the rind and the bitter white pith. Slide the knife edge from top to bottom, closely following the outline of the fruit to minimize waste.

3. Working over a bowl to catch the juice, slip the blade between a membrane and a section and slice to the center, separating one side of the section.

O

4. Turn the blade so that it is facing out and is lined up along the membrane on the opposite side of the section. Slide the blade from the center out along the membrane to free the section. Continue until all the sections are removed.

Oven Thermometer | RETRIEVING

Oven thermometers are apt to fall off the rack and onto the oven floor. Retrieval can be a difficult proposition, especially with a hand protected by a bulky oven mitt.

tip 614

Use a pair of tongs to retrieve or reposition the thermometer. Tongs keep your hands a safe distance away from the hot rack while enabling dexterity that's not possible with your hand clad in an oven mitt.

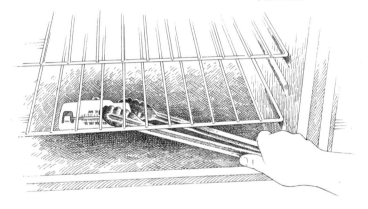

Oysters | SHUCKING

An oyster knife with a slightly angled, pointed tip is the best tool for opening oysters. The long blade can also be used to detach the oyster meat from the shell.

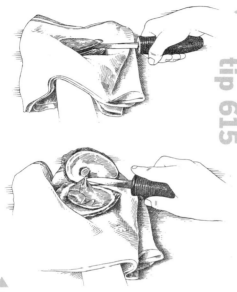

1. Start by holding the oyster cupped-side down in a kitchen towel. (The towel is essential because it will protect your hand in case the knife slips.) Make sure to keep the oyster flat as you work, to keep the flavorful juices from spilling out of the shell. With the tip of the knife, locate the hinge that connects the top and bottom shells. Push between the edges of the shells, wiggling the knife back and forth to pry them open.

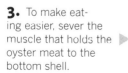

2. Detach the meat from the top shell and discard the shell.

3. To make eating easier, sever the muscle that holds the oyster meat to the bottom shell.

Packing | ORGANIZING ROAD TRIPS

A well-packed car usually means restricted access to snacks. Try this tip to get to the food more easily without forfeiting organization.

tip 616

Recycle the empty box from a case of wine. The cardboard insert (used to separate the bottles) creates compartments for holding soda cans, napkins, utensils, fruit, and the like. It's so easy to find the food that the kids can help themselves.

Packing | DISHES

It's a good idea to protect dishes before boxing them for moving, but newspaper can stain.

tip 617

Use plastic wrap to keep the dishes clean. Crumpled newspaper or bubble wrap can be used to pad the box and keep plastic-wrapped dishes and glassware safe.

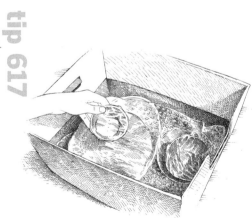

Pancakes | KEEPING WARM

Pancakes are best eaten as soon as they come off the griddle. Of course, this isn't always possible. Here's how to keep them warm for a few minutes while you round up the troops.

tip 618

Place the pancakes on a platter lined with a clean cloth napkin or dish towel. Pull the towel over the pancakes and then cover with an inverted colander to keep them warm.

P

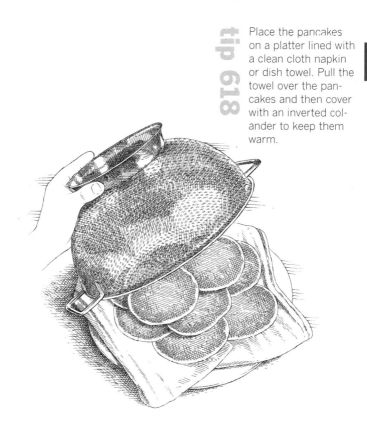

Pan Drippings | EASY DEFATTING

No one looks forward to spooning that thin layer of liquid fat off the drippings from a roast before making a pan sauce or gravy. Yet if the fat remains, the sauce will be greasy. Here's a method that makes the process faster and easier.

1. Deglaze the roasting pan, fat and all, and scrape up and dissolve the brown bits from the bottom of the pan, but stop short of reducing the liquid. Pour the brown, fatty liquid into a small mixing bowl (metal works best because it reacts quickly to changes in temperature), and set the bowl in an ice water bath.

tip 619

2. After a few minutes, as the liquid cools, small bits of fat will solidify and rise to the surface. If you rock the inner bowl very gently to create a small wave of liquid moving around its perimeter, the fat will collect around the upper inside edge of the bowl, where it will be easy to remove.

Parchment Paper | STORING IN BULK

Parchment paper is a must for many baking projects. To save money, we like to buy it in bulk in sheets (rather than in rolls), but storing a large quantity can be a challenge. Here's how to keep parchment safe and out of the way.

Roll a quantity of parchment paper sheets into a tight roll and slide it inside an empty gift-wrap tube, which can be stored in the pantry or kitchen. The sheets can be pulled out easily, one at a time.

tip 620

P

Parsley | STORING

Chopped parsley is an easy, attractive garnish for many dishes, but it's a nuisance to chop at the very last minute, when you've got steaming-hot plates of food to serve to hungry guests waiting at the table.

tip 621

2. Wrap the towel around the parsley, and then twist both ends very, very tight, until you see green parsley juice bleeding through the cloth. Twist as tight as you can to extract as much juice as possible. The dried parsley will stay looking fresh for hours.

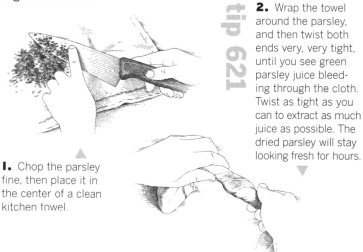

I. Chop the parsley fine, then place it in the center of a clean kitchen towel.

Pasta | IMPROMPTU COLANDER

Rather than dirty an extra piece of equipment to drain pasta, put your salad spinner on double duty.

Use a salad spinner to drain pasta rather than digging out the colander too. After cooking the pasta, simply pour it into the salad spinner insert and drain.

Pasta | MAKING SURE TO SEASON PASTA

Some cooks don't like to add salt to pasta water before it comes to a boil for fear of pitting the pot. But by the time it does come to a boil, you could easily be preoccupied with the rest of the meal and forget to add the salt. To avoid unseasoned pasta, try this clever solution.

Add the salt to the opened box of pasta (we recommend 1 tablespoon of table salt per pound of pasta), then simply dump the contents into the boiling water.

Pasta | RESERVING PASTA WATER

In that last flurry of activity before saucing pasta and getting dinner on the table, it's easy to overlook small details—such as saving a bit of pasta cooking water to add to the sauce when the recipe recommends it. Try this foolproof reminder.

Before cooking the pasta, set up the colander for draining it in the sink, then place a measuring cup inside the colander. It's sure to nudge your memory at the appropriate moment.

tip 624

P

Pasta | DRAINING FOR SALAD

Even when drained well, the curved shape of macaroni and other similar-shaped pasta tends to hold in some cooking water. To thoroughly dry cooked macaroni and prevent the excess water from diluting your pasta salad dressing, try this method.

tip 625

2. Roll the macaroni in the paper towels to blot any remaining moisture, then transfer the macaroni to a bowl.

▼

I. After shaking the macaroni dry in a colander, spread it in an even layer on a rimmed baking sheet lined with paper towels. Let the macaroni dry for 3 minutes.

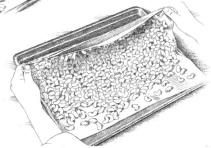

Pasta | DRYING FRESH PASTA

You don't need a fancy pasta rack to dry pasta.

Hang the pasta over the bars of a wooden indoor adjustable clothes rack.

Pastry Bag | FILLING THE BAG

It's always easier to fill a pastry bag when it is propped up and open.

Roll down the top of the pastry bag and, depending on the size of the bag, fit it into a pilsner beer glass, blender jar, or Pringles potato chip can. Fold the cuff at the top of the bag over the top edge, and spoon the frosting down into the bottom of the bag, which is held snugly in place.

Pastry Cream | QUICK COOLING

Pastry cream and puddings come off the stove hot but must be cooled to room temperature, or even chilled, before they can be used. By maximizing the surface area from which steam can escape, you will speed up the process.

1. Spread the pastry cream or pudding across a rimmed baking sheet that has been covered with plastic wrap.

tip 628

2. Once the pastry cream or pudding has been spread to the edges of the pan, cover it with another piece of wrap to keep a skin from forming. Snip a number of holes in the plastic wrap to allow steam to escape.

Peaches | REMOVING THE PIT

If you're tired of wrestling with peaches and nectarines to remove the pit, try this method, in which the peach splits neatly so the pit can be removed.

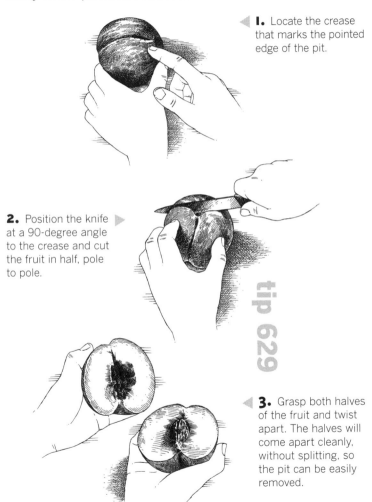

I. Locate the crease that marks the pointed edge of the pit.

2. Position the knife at a 90-degree angle to the crease and cut the fruit in half, pole to pole.

3. Grasp both halves of the fruit and twist apart. The halves will come apart cleanly, without splitting, so the pit can be easily removed.

tip 629

Peaches | PEELING

Some recipes, especially for pies, call for peeled peaches. A vegetable peeler often mashes the fruit, while a knife trims a lot of edible flesh with the skin. Use this method instead, which also works with nectarines.

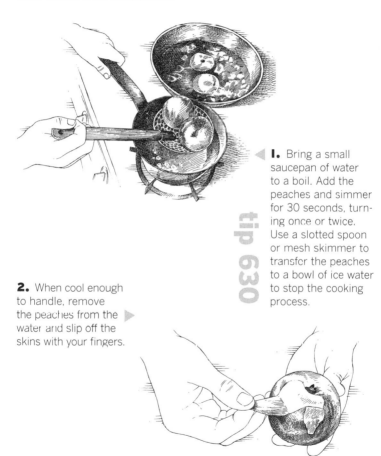

1. Bring a small saucepan of water to a boil. Add the peaches and simmer for 30 seconds, turning once or twice. Use a slotted spoon or mesh skimmer to transfer the peaches to a bowl of ice water to stop the cooking process.

tip 630

2. When cool enough to handle, remove the peaches from the water and slip off the skins with your fingers.

Peanut Butter | MIXING NATURAL PEANUT BUTTER

The layer of oil that separates from natural peanut butter is not always so easy to reincorporate.

Use only one wire beater attachment on your handheld mixer; carefully mix on low until the peanut butter is homogenous.

tip 631

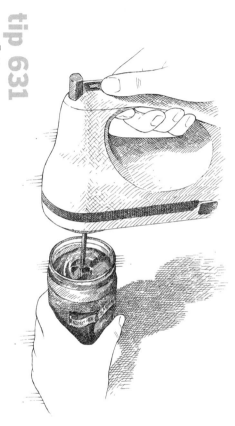

Peanut Butter | HOMEMADE PEANUT BUTTER

Many cooks buy natural peanut butter, preferring it to brands made with added sugar, hydrogenated oil, and salt. Here's an easy way to make pure peanut butter at home.

1. Process salted or unsalted cocktail peanuts with a teaspoon or two of oil (to facilitate processing) until smooth in the workbowl of a food processor or in a blender. Of course, if you like chunky peanut butter, leave the mixture slightly coarse.

2. Another benefit of making peanut butter this way is that it does not readily separate, especially when stored in the refrigerator.

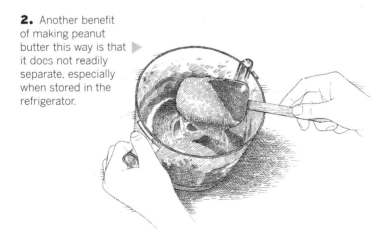

Peanut Butter | BLENDING NATURAL BUTTERS

Fans of natural peanut butter (without sugar or other stabilizers), other nut butters, and tahini, know that the butter often separates into a dense, solid mass beneath a layer of oil that has risen to the surface. Before spreading, the oil and solids have to be reblended. A spoon makes a mess of everything. Try one of these tricks instead.

tip 633

Turn the sealed jar upside down and allow the oil to rise again to the top. As the oil passes through the nut butter, the solids will absorb some oil and become soft enough to spread. Flip the jar right-side up, and the nut butter is ready to use.

Scrape the contents of the jar into a wide food storage container (such as Tupperware) and then mix very well. The extra space allows for mixing without splashing oil, and mixing vigorously and completely keep the oil and butter blended. It also allows you to easily mix in a sweetener, such as honey, if you desire.

tip 634

Pears | PREPARING FOR POACHING

We've found this to be the easiest and best way to prepare pears for poaching.

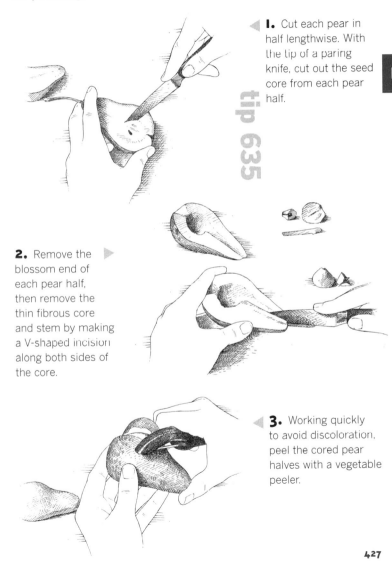

1. Cut each pear in half lengthwise. With the tip of a paring knife, cut out the seed core from each pear half.

tip 635

2. Remove the blossom end of each pear half, then remove the thin fibrous core and stem by making a V-shaped incision along both sides of the core.

3. Working quickly to avoid discoloration, peel the cored pear halves with a vegetable peeler.

Pepper | THE PERFECT GRIND

Measuring fresh-ground pepper for a recipe can be tricky. A coffee grinder works, but if you're like us, you end up grinding much more than you need. This method is a great alternative.

Count the number of grinds a pepper mill requires to produce ¼ teaspoon of pepper and then mark the number on a piece of tape affixed to the mill.

tip 636

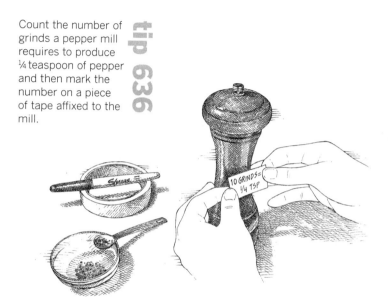

10 GRINDS = ¼ TSP

Peppercorns | THREE WAYS TO CRUSH

For recipes requiring crushed peppercorns, such as steak au poivre, where the pepper forms a crust, it's important that the peppercorns be coarsely crushed. Some households might not have an adjustable pepper grinder with a coarse setting. In that case, try one of these methods, often used by restaurant chefs.

P

tip 637

Spread the peppercorns in an even layer in a zipper-lock bag and whack them with a rolling pin or meat pounder.

tip 638

Use the back of a heavy pan and a rocking motion to grind the peppercorns.

tip 639

Use a Pyrex measuring cup. The cup is heavy enough to crush the peppercorns, and its clear glass bottom allows you to gauge your progress as you work.

Peppercorns | GRINDING LARGE AMOUNTS

At one time or another, many cooks face the task of seasoning a huge quantity of meat with salt and ground black pepper
while preparing for a large dinner party or big outdoor barbecue. Before you break a sweat, try this powerful alternative.

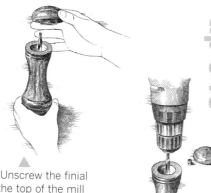

2. Insert the shaft
into the chuck of
a power driver/
drill—and off you go.
Changing the tension
in the connection
between shaft and
driver/drill controls
the grind size, from
fine to coarse.

tip 640

1. Unscrew the finial
at the top of the mill
to reveal the tip of the
square shaft that runs
down the center.

Pepper Mill | JAM-FREE LOADING

Anyone who has filled a pepper mill using a funnel knows how
frustrating it is when the peppercorns jam in the neck.

Cut off the bottom of
a small plastic soda
or water bottle whose
neck is small enough
to fit easily into the
mouth of a pepper
mill but is wider than
a funnel neck, so no
jamming will occur.

tip 641

Pepper Mill | KEEPING THE GRINDER CLEAN

Preparing raw cutlets, ground meat, or poultry for cooking can leave the cook's hands greasy and slippery when it is time to season the meat. Here's how to grind fresh pepper over meats, even when your hands are dirty.

tip 642

Before you handle the meat, drape a small piece of plastic wrap over the pepper mill. Your hand touches only the plastic, which can be removed and discarded once the meat has been seasoned.

Pepper Mill | PREVENTING A MESS

Cooks who use a mill to grind their own pepper know that even the best mill invariably leaves a mess of ground pepper on the surface where it is set down. Here's how to avoid this nuisance and capture every last bit of pepper from your grinder.

When you're done using the mill, set it in a small ceramic dish, such as a ramekin or Japanese soy sauce dish. Excess pepper ends up in the dish, not on the counter, and can even be collected, measured, and used for cooking.

tip 643

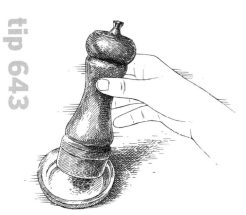

Peppers | ROASTING

Most recipes instruct the cook to roast whole peppers under the broiler until blackened. The uneven shape of a bell pepper means that one part always burns while another remains undercooked. We prefer to flatten the peppers before roasting, which lets them cook evenly and makes them much easier to peel. As an added bonus, the seeds can be removed before roasting, not after, when your hands are slippery and the seeds stick to everything.

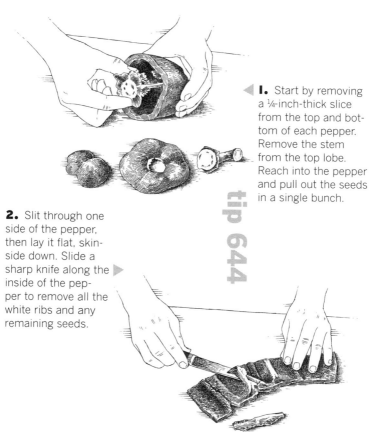

I. Start by removing a ¼-inch-thick slice from the top and bottom of each pepper. Remove the stem from the top lobe. Reach into the pepper and pull out the seeds in a single bunch.

2. Slit through one side of the pepper, then lay it flat, skin-side down. Slide a sharp knife along the inside of the pepper to remove all the white ribs and any remaining seeds.

tip 644

3. Arrange the flattened peppers and the top and bottom pieces, all skin-side up, on a baking sheet lined with foil. Flatten the strips with the palm of your hand.

4. Roast the peppers under the broiler until the skins are charred but the flesh is still firm. Wrap the pan tightly with foil and steam the peppers to help loosen the skins. When the peppers are cool enough to handle, peel off the skin in large strips.

Peppers | KEEPING STUFFED PEPPERS UPRIGHT

Cooks who've made stuffed bell peppers know they have an annoying tendency to topple toward disaster in the roasting pan. Here are a few solutions.

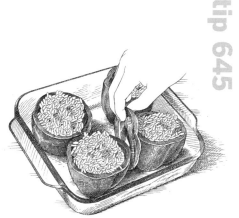

tip 645

Reserve the tops of the peppers—which you have cut off to open the peppers for stuffing—and insert them between the stuffed peppers for added stability.

tip 646

Instead of cooking the peppers in a baking dish or roasting pan, as specified in most recipes, place them in a tube pan. The snug fit makes the peppers sit upright.

Place the peppers in
the cups of a muffin
tin, which will hold
the peppers firmly
in place.

P

Place each pepper
in an individual oven-
proof ramekin or
custard cup. This is
also a great system
when you want to
cook only a couple
of peppers, instead
of a whole batch.

Pepperoni | DEGREASING

Straight from the package, pepperoni slices often leave unsightly puddles of grease when baked atop a pizza. You can prevent this problem with these easy steps.

I. Line a microwave-safe plate with a double layer of paper towels, place the pepperoni on top, then cover with two more paper towels and another plate to keep the meaty disks flat.

tip 649

2. Cook for 30 seconds in a microwave on high, carefully remove the hot plate from the microwave, and uncover.

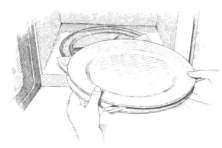

3. Place the degreased pepperoni on the pizza and bake according to the recipe.

Picnics | SANDWICHES FOR PICNICS

Instead of wrapping sandwiches individually when heading off to the beach or park for a picnic, try this easy (and less wasteful) method of packing them for transport.

Stack prepared, unwrapped sandwiches in the bread bag that was emptied to make the sandwiches. You can even recycle the original tab to seal the bag shut.

tip 650

P

Pies | EASY, EVEN LATTICE

A lattice top crust on pie makes an attractive presentation, but achieving strips of dough of even lengths and widths can pose a problem.

Use a thin, inch-wide metal ruler to line up both the length and width of the lattice.

tip 651

Pies | PACKAGING FOR TRANSPORT

Transporting freshly baked pies from home to a holiday party can be hazardous, as the pies slide every which way in the car. Solve the problem with this tip.

tip 652

Get a clean box from the local pizzeria and use it to hold the pie. A small 10-inch-square pizza box is just the right size for keeping flat-topped pies, such as pecan and pumpkin, safe. (This tip won't work with domed pies, like lemon meringue.)

Pies | SPRITZING DOUGH

Anyone who makes pie dough has faced the problem of dough that is too dry and crumbly when it's time to roll it out, but mixing in more water with a spoon or spatula can overwork the dough and make the crust tough.

tip 653

A spray bottle full of ice water helps control the flow and distributes just the right amount of water.

Pies | A NEATER FIRST SLICE

Extracting the first slice of a pie neatly is a challenge for even the most poised and accomplished server. Try this method to increase the chances of getting that first slice as neat as can be. This method also works for cakes.

After making the first two cuts (to form the first slice), make a third cut to form the second slice. This makes it easier to slide out the first piece tidy and intact.

P

Pies | PRESSING CRUMBS INTO PLACE FOR CRUSTS

Pressing graham cracker crumbs into a pie plate can be a messy proposition, especially when the buttered and sugared crumbs stick to your hands.

Keep the crumbs where they belong by sheathing your hand in a plastic sandwich bag and pressing the crumbs firmly but neatly.

Pies | ADDING ICE WATER TO DOUGH

Most pie pastry recipes use ice water to bring the dough together. However, if you add too much water, the dough can become mushy. Instead of sprinkling water, 1 tablespoon at a time, over the dough, try this method, which also guarantees properly chilled water.

1. Fill a spray bottle with about ¼ cup water and store it on its side in the freezer.

2. When you're making pastry, grab the bottle from the freezer and fill it with cold water, which quickly chills on contact with the ice in the bottle. Spray ice water over your pastry mixture as needed. This method ensures that the water is evenly distributed over the flour mixture, making it unlikely that you will add too much.

Pies | MAKESHIFT ROLLING PIN

We find that a tapered wooden pin does the best job of rolling out pie pastry. But here's a way to roll out dough when a pin is nowhere to be found.

An unopened wine bottle has the right weight and shape for rolling out dough. If possible, use white wine and chill the bottle. The cold temperature of the bottle will help keep the butter in the dough chilled.

tip 657

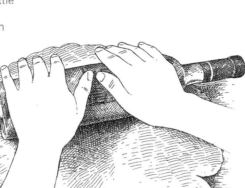

It seems that no matter how much you flour the counter, pie dough often sticks as you roll it out. Adding more flour isn't the solution and can actually make the dough tough.

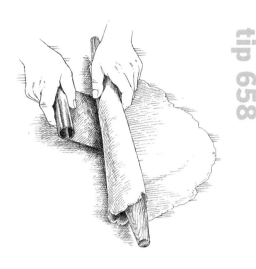

tip 658

Instead, slide a bench scraper (also called a pastry scraper) under the dough every 30 seconds or so. This way the dough never has a chance to stick, and it won't tear when you need to move it. If you don't own a bench scraper, use a metal spatula in the same fashion.

Alternatively, use the metal ruler you've used to measure the diameter of the dough. Its thin edges pry the stubborn dough off just as well as a bench scraper.

tip 659

Pies | MEASURING THE DOUGH

There's nothing worse than transferring the rolled dough to a pie plate only to realize you haven't rolled it large enough. Here's an easy way to measure the dough as you work, if you don't have a ruler handy.

tip 660

Invert the pie plate over the dough. There should be an inch or two of extra dough on all sides of the pie plate.

P

Pies | QUICK DOUGH WRAPPING

Preparing batches of pie dough for the holidays can be a messy venture. Here's a timesaving trick that keeps your hands and the counter clean.

Once the dough is mixed, transfer it directly from the bowl to a large zipper-lock bag. Shape the dough into a disk through the outside of the bag, and chill until ready to use.

tip 661

Pies | NO-CREEP PIE DOUGH

Rather than add more flour, we like to roll out dough between sheets of parchment paper to prevent it from sticking to the rolling pin. But sometimes the dough starts to inch its way across the counter. We keep it in place with this simple trick.

tip 662

Place a nonstick silicone mat underneath the parchment paper, which makes for smooth, stable rolling.

Pies | MOVING THE DOUGH

Once the dough has been rolled out evenly, it must be transferred to the pie plate. This is how we like to accomplish this delicate task.

Work a bench scraper or thin metal spatula under the dough, then roll the dough onto the rolling pin. Move the pin over to the pie plate and gently unroll the dough over the filling.

tip 663

Pies | CUTTING AWAY EXTRA DOUGH

Excess dough must be trimmed so that you can fashion a neat edge for the pie.

We find that kitchen shears make the best tool for slicing away extra dough. Leave about ½ inch of dough hanging over the rim of the pie plate so you have something to flute.

P

tip 664

Pies | FOLDING EXCESS DOUGH UNDER

To create a fluted edge around the exterior of the pie, you need a sturdy, thick piece of dough.

Fold the excess dough back under itself, pressing it firmly to seal. This double-thick edge can be fluted or decorated as desired.

tip 665

Pies | FLUTING THE EDGE

A fluted edge makes a pie especially attractive. It also helps to contain the filling.

Hold the inside of the dough with the thumb and forefinger of one hand and press the outside of the dough with the forefinger of the other hand.

tip 666

Pies | WEIGHTING EFFICIENTLY

Streamline your pie-making efforts by using this all-in-one pie weight storage and lining method.

Store your pie weights in a doubled-up oven-proof cooking bag, which you can simply lift in and out of the pie plate and use over and over, eliminating the extra step of lining the pie crust with parchment or foil.

tip 667

Pies | IMPROVISING PIE WEIGHTS

We prefer ceramic or metal pie weights but if you have neither, try this substitution.

tip 698

Pennies, which conduct heat beautifully, also lie flat and thus make formidable pie weights.

P

Pies | EASY PIE WEIGHT REMOVAL

Pie weights are essential when blind baking a pie shell. Here's an easy way to remove them from the shell when you are finished.

tip 699

Use a large basket-type coffee filter to contain the pie weights. When finished baking, you can simply pull them out all at once.

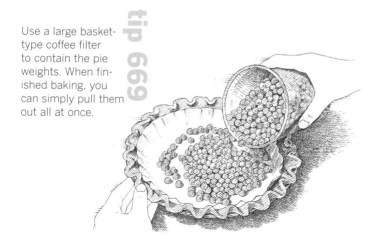

Pies | PROTECTING THE RIM

The fluted edge on a pie can burn in the oven because it's so exposed. Many recipes suggest piecing together strips of foil to fashion a protective cover for the edge. Instead of trying to twist pieces of foil together, we prefer to use a single sheet to cover the pie edge.

1. Lay out a square of foil slightly larger than the pie. Fold the square in half to form a rectangle. Cut an arc that is roughly half the size of the pie.

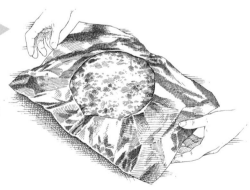

2. When you unfold the foil, you will have cut out a circle from the middle of the sheet. This open circle exposes the filling, while the surrounding foil covers the crust.

A meringue topping that is uneven or has shrunk back around the edges of the pie is disappointing. Here's how to get an even meringue topping that covers the entire surface of the pie.

I. Put dabs of meringue over the filling.

P

2. Once all the meringuc has been placed on the pie, use a rubber spatula to "anchor" the meringue to the edge of the crust. As long as the meringue touches the crust, it won't pull away or shrink in the oven.

Pies | SAFELY TRANSPORTING CREAM PIES

The whipped cream or meringue topping on a pie can be marred easily when covered directly with plastic wrap.

To keep the surface of your pie neat, stand a few strands of uncooked spaghetti or linguine in the pie and suspend a sheet of plastic wrap over the pasta. Don't try this with toothpicks, which are likely to sink down into the pie.

tip 672

Pineapple | PREPARING

A pineapple can seem daunting to peel and core. We find that the following method is easy and reliable.

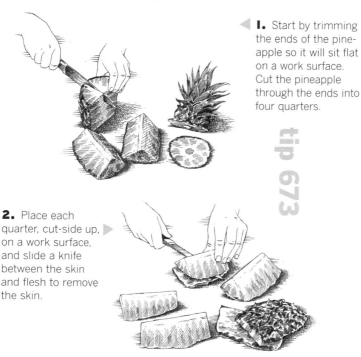

1. Start by trimming the ends of the pineapple so it will sit flat on a work surface. Cut the pineapple through the ends into four quarters.

2. Place each quarter, cut-side up, on a work surface, and slide a knife between the skin and flesh to remove the skin.

3. Stand each peeled quarter on end and slice off the portion of tough, light-colored core attached to the inside of the piece. The peeled and cored pineapple can be sliced as desired.

tip 673

Pine Nuts | TOASTING EVENLY

Pine nuts are difficult to toast evenly on the stovetop. Because of their shape, they tend to rest on one side and are prone to burning.

We find that a hand-cranked stovetop popcorn popper is the perfect vessel for toasting pine nuts. Just heat the popper, add the nuts, and then use the crank to keep the nuts in constant motion until they are evenly toasted.

Pizza | REHEATING

Leftover pizza is a treat that can easily be ruined by a spin in the microwave (it gets soggy), but heating up the oven for a slice of pizza is impractical.

Turn on the stovetop burner instead. Place a nonstick skillet over medium heat and add dried oregano. Place the pizza slice in the skillet and cook, covered, for about 5 minutes. The pizza will come out hot and crisp, with an irresist-ible aroma.

Pizza | KEEPING TOPPINGS ON HAND

Homemade pizza is a blank canvas for the creative use of toppings. The problem is that you don't always have enough topping options on hand. Here's a simple way to create interesting pizzas.

Whenever you are cooking something that would make a good pizza topping, reserve a little bit in a clean, plastic container, label it, and freeze it. When making pizza, sort through the frozen topping options.

Pizza | DRIER TOMATO TOPPING

Don't let juicy tomatoes make your pizza crust soggy.

Place fresh tomato slices in a salad spinner and spin dry.

Pizza | REMOVING FROM A PEEL

Getting sticky pizza dough to slide off a pizza peel can be tricky. We like this method, which relies on parchment paper.

Roll out and sauce the pizza on parchment paper. You can then slide the pizza, paper and all, onto the peel and into and out of the oven with ease. The parchment won't burn, and it easily slides off the peel.

Pizza | DETERMINING DONENESS

It can be hard to tell when a deep-dish pizza is done, especially if cheese and toppings are obscuring the crust. Just because the toppings are sizzling doesn't mean the crust is cooked through.

Use a spatula to lift up the pizza slightly. If the bottom crust is nicely browned, the pizza is done.

Pizza | GETTING TOPPINGS HOT ON THE GRILL

Grilled pizza is delicious, but often the crust starts to burn on the bottom before the toppings are hot. It's imperative to top grilled pizzas very lightly and use ingredients that will cook quickly. Here's a good way to ensure that the toppings get nice and hot.

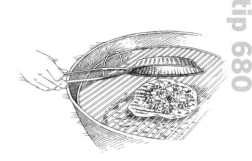

tip 680

Once the toppings have been applied, invert (using tongs) a disposable aluminum pie plate over the pizza. The pie plate traps heat and creates an oven-like effect.

P

Pizza | CUTTING WITH SCISSORS

When cutting pizza, a regular knife can catch and drag the melted cheese, and pizza wheels often dent the pan when you bear down to cut through the crust.

A pair of kitchen shears cuts through pizza easily. Just hold the edge with a folded paper towel to pick up the crust for an easier cutting angle.

tip 681

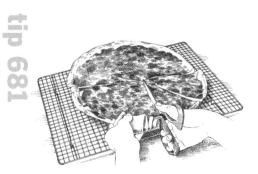

Polenta | PREVENTING LUMPS

Lumpy polenta is not very appealing. Here are a few ways to ensure a smooth porridge.

tip 682

When the water comes to a boil, pour the polenta into the water in a very slow stream from a measuring cup, all the while stirring in a circular motion with a wooden spoon to prevent clumping.

I. After bringing the liquid to a simmer, close off the bottom of a funnel with your finger, then fill it with the polenta meal called for in your recipe.

tip 683

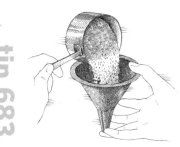

2. With the funnel in one hand and a whisk in the other, open the hole and let the grains slowly pour into the hot boiling liquid, whisking until the funnel is empty and the grains are smoothly mixed.

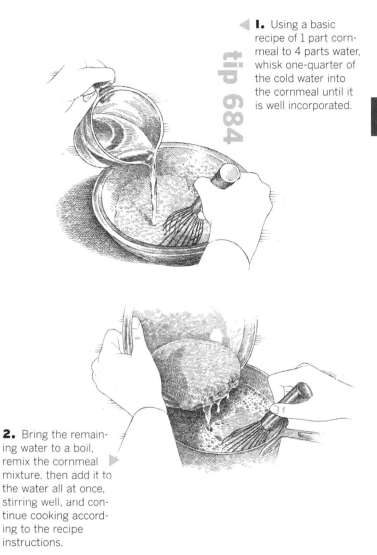

1. Using a basic recipe of 1 part cornmeal to 4 parts water, whisk one-quarter of the cold water into the cornmeal until it is well incorporated.

P

2. Bring the remaining water to a boil, remix the cornmeal mixture, then add it to the water all at once, stirring well, and continue cooking according to the recipe instructions.

Polenta | SMOOTHING OUT THE LUMPS

Even if you add the cornmeal to the water in a slow, steady stream, your polenta might have tiny lumps in it. Here's how to get rid of the lumps and produce perfectly smooth polenta.

Once the polenta has finished cooking, use an immersion blender to smooth out any lumps. The blender can also be used to help incorporate butter, cheese, or herbs just before serving.

tip 685

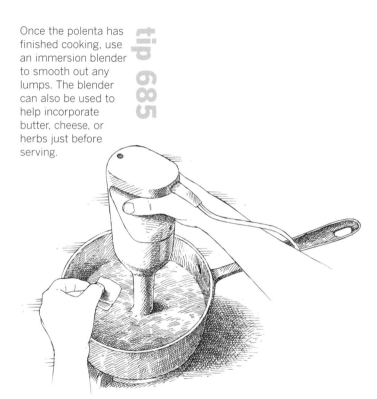

Pomegranates | PREPARING WITHOUT THE MESS

Tart, juicy, bright red pomegranate seeds make a terrific garnish for holiday desserts, fruit salads, and green salads, as well as a refreshing snack. But freeing the seeds from the pith and membrane beneath the leathery skin can be a messy chore.

1. Cut the pomegranate in half and place both halves in a large bowl of cool water. Break apart the halves under water and separate the seeds. The seeds will sink to the bottom of the bowl, and the pith and membrane will float to the top.

tip 686

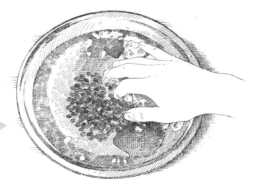

2. When all of the seeds are separated, skim the detritus off the top and drain.

Pork | KEBABS

Pork, especially smaller pieces like those for kebabs, can easily dry out on the grill. This method, using butterflied pieces of boneless center-cut pork chops, guarantees maximum surface area when marinating for moist, tasty meat.

tip 687

Cut the boneless pork chops into 1¼-inch cubes, then cut each cube almost through at the center to butterfly before marinating.

Pork Tenderloin | REMOVING THE SILVER SKIN

The tenderloin is covered with a thin membrane called the silver skin. When heated, the silver skin shrinks and can cause the tenderloin to bow and thus cook unevenly. Here's how to remove the silver skin before cooking.

tip 688

Slip a paring knife between the silver skin and the muscle fibers. Angle the knife slightly upward and use a gentle back-and-forth sawing action.

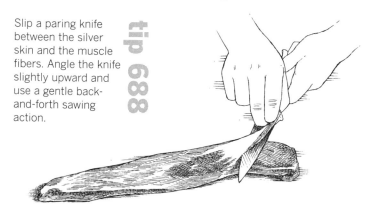

Pork Tenderloin | CUTTING INTO CUTLETS

Rather than buying cutlets, which can be of uneven size, we prefer to make our own from the tenderloin.

tip 689

P

I. After removing the silver skin (see tip at left), cut the tenderloin crosswise into six equal pieces, including the tapered tail end.

2. Standing it on its cut side, sandwich one piece of tenderloin between two sheets of plastic wrap or parchment. Pound gently with a mallet or meat pounder to an even thickness of ½ inch.

3. The thin tail piece of the tenderloin requires extra care to produce a cutlet. Fold the tip of the tail under the cut side before pounding between the sheets of parchment or plastic wrap.

Pork Tenderloin | SLICING FOR STIR-FRIES

Our favorite cut of pork for stir-frying is the tenderloin, which is lean and tender. Here's how we get thin, even strips from this long piece of meat.

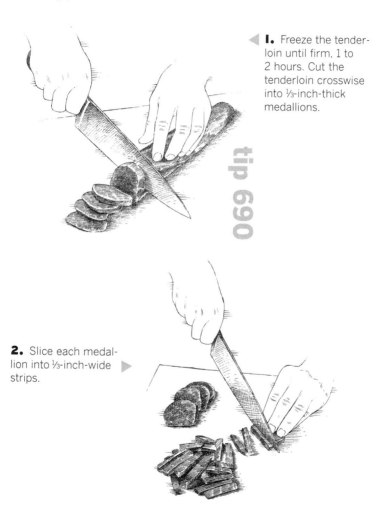

1. Freeze the tenderloin until firm, 1 to 2 hours. Cut the tenderloin crosswise into ⅓-inch-thick medallions.

2. Slice each medallion into ⅓-inch-wide strips.

tip 690

Potatoes | HOLDING MASHED POTATOES

Finishing the mashed potatoes at the same time as the roast, the gravy, and the green beans can become quite a juggling act.

Free up some of those precious few last minutes (and some valuable stovetop space) by making mashed potatoes a couple of hours ahead of time and keeping them warm in a slow cooker on the low setting. All they need is a quick stir before serving.

P

Potatoes | SLICING SUPERTHIN

It can be quite a culinary challenge to thin-slice potatoes for recipes such as scalloped potatoes, pommes Anna, a Spanish potato omelet, and homemade potato chips. For those with neither a razor-sharp mandoline nor superb knife skills, try this alternative.

Use a cheese plane to slice small, peeled potatoes. Just make sure the potatoes are no wider than the blade of your plane (usually about 2 inches).

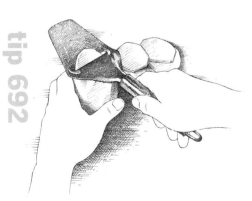

Potatoes | SCRUBBING CLEAN

Recipes in which the potatoes are not peeled usually instruct the cook to "scrub" the potatoes. This same technique is used with other root vegetables that will be cooked with the skin on, such as turnips, carrots, beets, and sweet potatoes. Here's a quick and easy way to get the job done.

Buy a rough-textured bathing or exfoliating bath glove and dedicate it for use in the kitchen. The glove cleans away dirt but is relatively gentle and won't scrub away the potato skin.

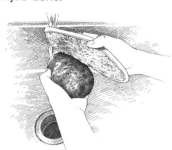

Potatoes | DRYING BOILED POTATOES

Shaking just-boiled potatoes gently in the hot pan after pouring off the water is one way to dry them a little, but it's all too easy to break the potatoes apart. Try this method instead, making sure to set the pan on a cool burner or trivet.

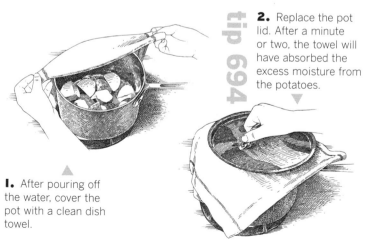

2. Replace the pot lid. After a minute or two, the towel will have absorbed the excess moisture from the potatoes.

I. After pouring off the water, cover the pot with a clean dish towel.

464

Potatoes | EASY PEELING

Peeling the skin from a slippery potato can result in scraped fingers or a dropped potato. Equally frustrating is trying to peel a hot cooked potato held in an oven mitt. Here are two ways (one for raw potatoes, one for cooked) to make this task easier.

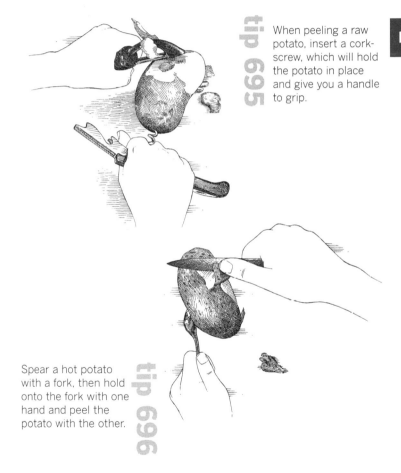

tip 695

When peeling a raw potato, insert a cork-screw, which will hold the potato in place and give you a handle to grip.

P

tip 696

Spear a hot potato with a fork, then hold onto the fork with one hand and peel the potato with the other.

Potatoes | MASHING SHORTCUT

When potatoes are destined for mashing, we prefer to boil them with their skins on to keep them from getting water-logged. There is no doubt, though, that peeling just-boiled potatoes can be a painstaking job. Try this trick to skip a step.

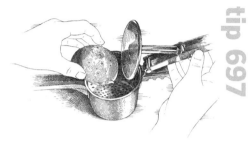

tip 697

Cut each potato in half and place cut-side down in a ricer. The flesh will be forced through the holes while the skin remains in the hopper.

Potatoes | WARMING THE SERVING BOWL

It's always nice to serve food from a warm dish, but it's particularly nice with mashed potatoes, which otherwise cool quickly.

tip 698

Drain the water in which the potatoes have boiled into the serving bowl. While you mash potatoes, the heat from the water will warm the bowl. Be sure the bowl you use is heatproof.

Potatoes | OPENING A BAKED POTATO

For the best results, bake potatoes in a 350-degree oven until tender, about 1 hour and 15 minutes. To ensure that the flesh does not steam and become dense, it's imperative to open up each baked potato as soon as it comes out of the oven. This technique maximizes the amount of steam released and keeps the potato fluffy and light.

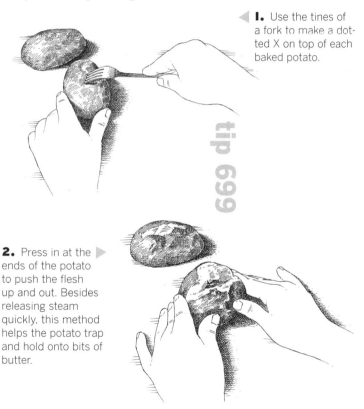

P

1. Use the tines of a fork to make a dotted X on top of each baked potato.

tip 699

2. Press in at the ends of the potato to push the flesh up and out. Besides releasing steam quickly, this method helps the potato trap and hold onto bits of butter.

Potatoes | FOLDING HASH BROWNS

The best hash browns have as much potato crunch as possible. Removing excess water from the grated potatoes before cooking will help them crisp up in the pan. This folding technique ensures that every bite is packed with crunch.

Once the potatoes have been browned on both sides, fold the cake over, omelet style. When cut into wedges, each piece will now have four crisp surfaces— two inside and two outside.

tip 700

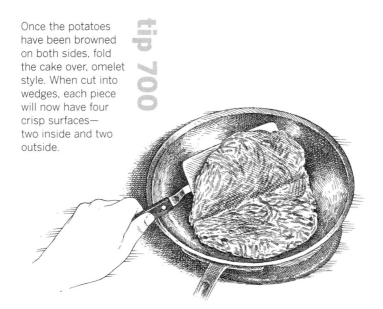

Potatoes | CUTTING FOR STEAK FRIES

The starchy, thick-skinned russet is the potato of choice when it comes to steak fries. The following technique ensures uniform wedges for even cooking.

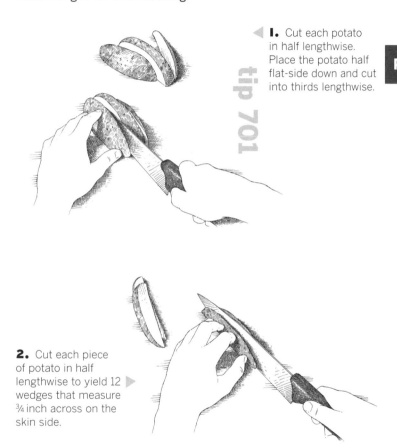

1. Cut each potato in half lengthwise. Place the potato half flat-side down and cut into thirds lengthwise.

2. Cut each piece of potato in half lengthwise to yield 12 wedges that measure ¾ inch across on the skin side.

P

Poultry | RINSING BRINED POULTRY

Brining chicken or turkey produces a moist, well-seasoned bird, but rinsing the excess salt off the surface can make a soggy mess of your countertop. Here's a way to streamline the process.

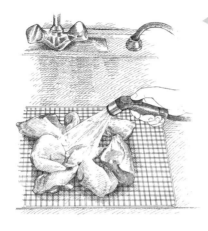

1. Place the chicken or turkey on a wire rack. Set the rack in an empty sink, and use the sink sprayer to wash off the meat. Then blot the meat dry with paper towels.

tip 702

2. If you plan to air-dry the chicken or turkey, simply set the rack with the towel-dried pieces on a rimmed baking sheet or jelly roll pan and place the whole thing in the refrigerator.

Ravioli | IMPROMPTU WRAPPERS

Store-bought wonton wrappers can be used as a substitute for homemade pasta when making ravioli.

R

I. Place one wrapper on a work surface. Spoon some home-made filling on top. Brush the edges of the wrapper with a little water, and then cover with a second wrapper.

2. Use the tines of a fork to seal shut the edges of the ravi-oli. Make sure that the seal is tight so that the filling won't leak out while the ravioli are being cooked.

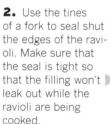

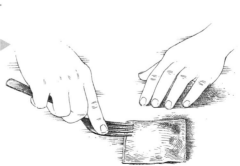

Recipes | PROTECTING IN THE KITCHEN

To protect recipes from the splotches and splatters of usual kitchen duty, many cooks use plastic page protectors, available at office supply stores. Another common household item can also do the job.

tip 704

Place a zipper-lock bag flat on the counter, slide the sheet of paper right into it, and zip shut. Gallon-sized bags work nicely for 8 ½ by 11-inch sheets, while sandwich-sized bags work nicely for newspaper recipes mounted on index cards.

tip 705

Clean, dry glass pot lids also do the job. Place the lid over the sheet of paper, or even over an open cookbook or magazine. The weight of the lid will keep the pages open.

Rhubarb | PEELING

Rhubarb stalks, especially thick ones, are covered with a stringy outside layer that should be removed before cooking. Make sure to cut away and discard the leaves, which are inedible.

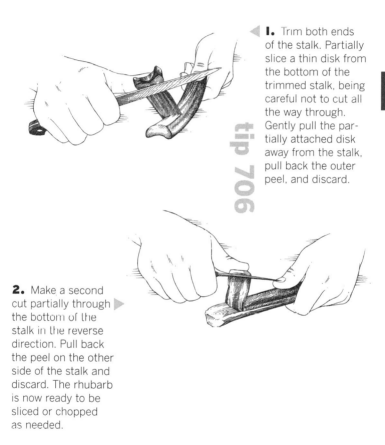

1. Trim both ends of the stalk. Partially slice a thin disk from the bottom of the trimmed stalk, being careful not to cut all the way through. Gently pull the partially attached disk away from the stalk, pull back the outer peel, and discard.

tip 706

R

2. Make a second cut partially through the bottom of the stalk in the reverse direction. Pull back the peel on the other side of the stalk and discard. The rhubarb is now ready to be sliced or chopped as needed.

Rice | EASY RINSING

When rinsing rice prior to cooking, it can be tricky to pour off the water without sending some of the rice down the drain. Here are two different methods that tackle this problem.

tip 707

Place the rice on a splatter screen. Use the sink sprayer to rinse the rice through the screen. This method works best with small amounts of rice.

Pour the rice in a wire mesh strainer or colander, and then set the strainer into a large, water-filled bowl. When you're done soaking, simply lift out the strainer and let the rice drain.

tip 708

Rice | STEAMING FOR FLUFFY TEXTURE

Whether cooking regular rice or making pilaf, we find that a dry, fluffy texture is best.

Once the rice is tender, remove the pan from the heat, place a clean kitchen towel folded in half over the saucepan, replace the lid, and set aside for 10 minutes. Residual heat continues to steam the rice and improves its texture, while the towel absorbs excess moisture.

tip 709

Rice Cooker | IMPROVING AN OLD RICE COOKER

Rice cookers can produce perfect rice, but they can be difficult to clean—especially as they age—whether nonstick or not. Breathe some new life into a sticky old rice cooker with this tip.

tip 710

2. The oil will help keep the rice from sticking once cooked.

I. Spray the bottom and sides of the rice cooker bowl with cooking spray before adding the rice and water.

Roasting | MAKESHIFT ROASTING RACK

If your kitchen lacks a metal roasting rack that fits your roasting pan, make do with aluminum foil.

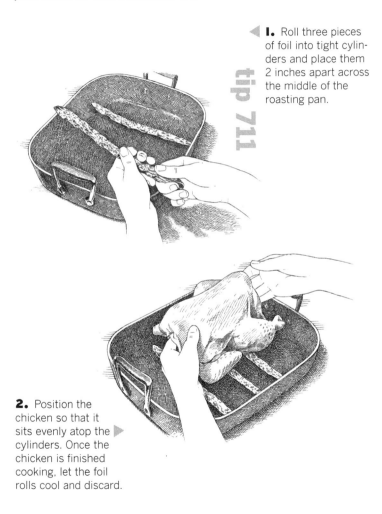

1. Roll three pieces of foil into tight cylinders and place them 2 inches apart across the middle of the roasting pan.

tip 711

2. Position the chicken so that it sits evenly atop the cylinders. Once the chicken is finished cooking, let the foil rolls cool and discard.

Roasting | NEW USE FOR STOVETOP GRATES

When you want to roast a chicken but find yourself without a V-rack, here's what to do. Build your own rack using the grates from a gas stove and aluminum foil.

1. Wrap two light-gauge stovetop grates with foil and use a paring knife or skewer to poke large holes in the foil so that juices can drip down into the pan as the bird roasts.

R

2. Place the grates in the roasting pan, resting them against the sides of the pan so that the bottoms of the grates meet to create a V-shape. Roast the chicken (or turkey) as directed in the recipe.

Roasting | EDIBLE ROASTING RACKS

Not everyone owns a roasting rack, but any cook with celery or onions on hand can improvise one for roasts.

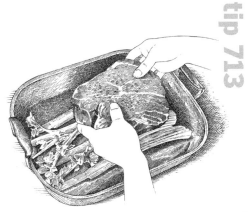

tip 713

Place several stalks of celery across the bottom of a roasting pan, then place the roast on top. Not only does the celery add flavor to the meat, but it also saves on cleanup time.

Place six ½-inch-thick slices of onion on the bottom of a roasting pan to keep the roast just above the bottom of the pan. The onions will become flavorful and sweet after cooking in the pan drippings.

tip 714

Roasts | STANDING (UP) RIB ROASTS

Some standing rib roasts aren't so great at the "standing" part, especially smaller roasts, which have a tendency to tip over during cooking. Avoid this problem by turning a skewer into a support bar.

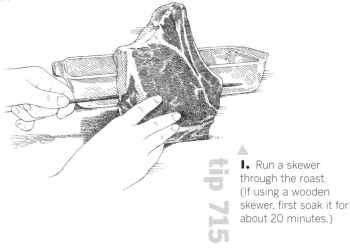

tip 715

1. Run a skewer through the roast. (If using a wooden skewer, first soak it for about 20 minutes.)

2. Rest the ends of the skewer on the sides of the roasting pan and cook the roast. When ready to carve, simply remove the skewer.

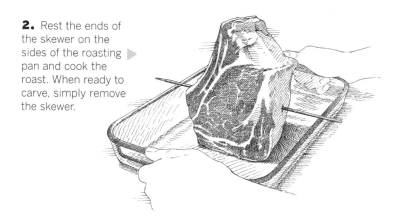

Saffron | CRUMBLING TO RELEASE FLAVOR

Saffron is the world's most expensive spice, so you certainly want to extract every drop of flavor. Here's how to get the most bang for your buck.

tip 716

Before adding saffron to a stew or soup, crumble the threads between your fingers to break up the saffron. Crumbling releases flavorful oils and helps the saffron dissolve in the liquid.

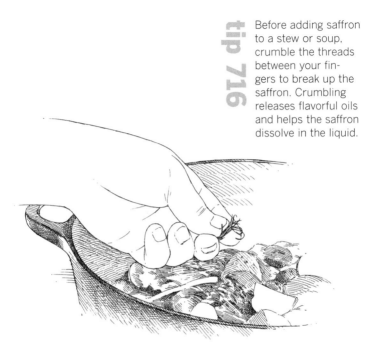

Salad Dressing | NO-WASTE SALAD DRESSING

When putting together a salad, it can be easy to accidentally go overboard and overdress the greens if the container holding the vinaigrette has a large opening. Prepare vinaigrette in a child's "sippy" cup and use the cup as a tool for dressing the salad as well. The small spout releases the dressing slowly, making it nearly impossible to waste vinaigrette or overdress a salad.

1. Add all the dressing ingredients to the cup and secure the lid. While holding one finger securely over the spout, shake the cup vigorously to incorporate.

S

tip 717

2. Remove your finger from the spout and sprinkle the dressing over the salad.

Salad Spinner | GETTING BETTER LEVERAGE

Salad spinners with a top-mounted turn crank can rumble and vibrate during use. Here's how to make the spinning go more smoothly.

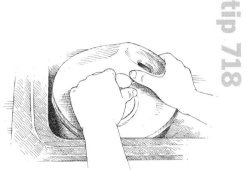

tip 718

Place the salad spinner in the corner of your sink. This increases your leverage by lowering the height of the crank. This extra leverage also acts to push the spinner down to the sink floor and into its walls, stabilizing it.

Salad Spinner | SPINNING GREENS DRIER

Salad spinners go a long way toward drying clean, wet salad greens, yet greens sometimes need a post-spin blot with paper towels before they are tossed into a salad bowl. Try this all-in-one method for drier greens in no time.

Combine the two steps by spinning two or three paper towels in with the greens.

tip 719

Salmon |
REMOVING PINBONES FROM A SIDE OF SALMON

Locating and removing the pinbones from a side of salmon can be tricky. Running your fingers along the flesh is one way to locate them. This way is even better.

Invert a mixing bowl on a work surface and drape the salmon over it, flesh-side up. The curve of the bowl forces the pinbones to stick up and out, so they are easier to spot, grasp with pliers, and remove.

tip 720

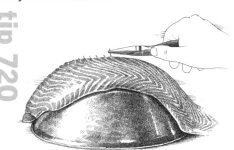

Salmon | REMOVING PINBONES FROM FILLETS

Salmon fillets will occasionally contain a few tiny white pinbones. These bones are smaller and thinner than a toothpick and can be hard to find.

tip 721

2. If you find any bones, use a clean pair of needle-nose pliers or tweezers to pull out the bones.

1. Before cooking, rub the tips of your fingers gently over the surface of each salmon fillet to locate any pinbones. They will feel like small bumps.

Salmon | TURNING A FILLET INTO A STEAK

Many people prefer fillets to steaks because they would rather not deal with the bones. But because they are thinner at the edges, salmon fillets do not cook evenly. Some people may like the gradation from well-done at the edges to rare in the center, but others may not. Steaks have a consistent thickness and cook evenly from edge to edge. Here's a neat way to turn a fillet into a boneless steak.

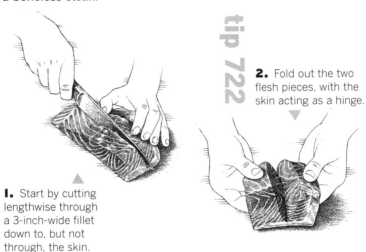

2. Fold out the two flesh pieces, with the skin acting as a hinge.

tip 722

I. Start by cutting lengthwise through a 3-inch-wide fillet down to, but not through, the skin.

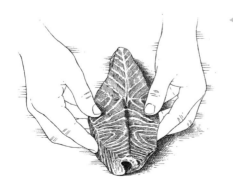

3. A 3-inch-wide fillet will now look like a steak, but without any bones, and have an even thickness of 1½ inches. The cooking time for mock steaks is the same as for regular fillets. The one drawback to this method is that the skin won't crisp because it is sandwiched in the middle of the steak.

Salt | TWO IMPROMPTU SALT CELLARS

Measuring from the pouring spout on a cardboard container of salt can be frustrating when the salt flows out in an uncontrollable rush. And if you pour salt into a bowl for easier measuring, it can easily get contaminated.

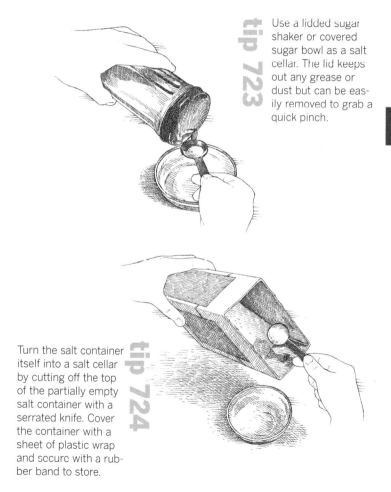

tip 723

Use a lidded sugar shaker or covered sugar bowl as a salt cellar. The lid keeps out any grease or dust but can be easily removed to grab a quick pinch.

tip 724

Turn the salt container itself into a salt cellar by cutting off the top of the partially empty salt container with a serrated knife. Cover the container with a sheet of plastic wrap and secure with a rubber band to store.

Salt | USING SALT TO PREVENT FLARE-UPS

Fat sputtering up from a broiler pan can cause dangerous flare-ups. You can prevent flames with a generous amount of kosher salt on the bottom of the pan.

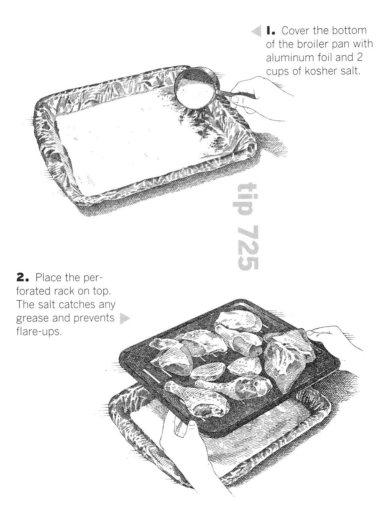

I. Cover the bottom of the broiler pan with aluminum foil and 2 cups of kosher salt.

tip 725

2. Place the perforated rack on top. The salt catches any grease and prevents flare-ups.

Salt | EASY PULL-TABS FOR SALT BOXES

Fiddling with the sharp, pesky metal spouts on boxes of kosher salt (or dishwasher soap powder) to open them can lead to both general irritation and broken or scratched nails. Make the task easier with this trick.

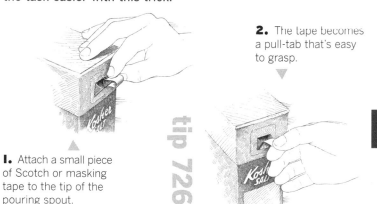

2. The tape becomes a pull-tab that's easy to grasp.

1. Attach a small piece of Scotch or masking tape to the tip of the pouring spout.

Salt | PREVENTING CLUMPS

Cooks who live in hot, humid climates know that salt often clumps in the shaker, making it difficult to sprinkle onto foods at the table.

Add a few grains of uncooked rice to the shaker. The rice will absorb excess moisture and keep the salt crystals from clumping together.

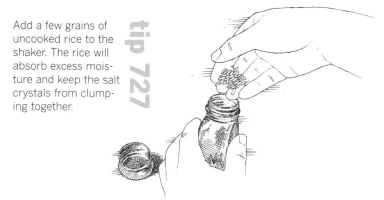

Sandwiches |
STABILIZING OVERSTUFFED SANDWICHES

Overstuffed sub sandwiches (also called hoagies or grinders), can pose a messy problem when the filling spills out every which way.

Remove some of the interior crumb from the top and bottom halves of the bread. This creates a trough in the bottom half for the fillings and a cap on the top for toppings.

Sandwiches | MAKESHIFT SANDWICH PRESS

A toasted, pressed sandwich such as croque monsieur, cubano, or grilled cheese with embellishments like ham or roasted peppers take on a dense, luxurious texture and a deep even crust when weighted in the pan or on the griddle with a heavy, cast-iron sandwich press. If you don't own a press, don't despair.

Fill a teakettle with water and use it to weigh down the sandwiches as they cook. If you prefer, fill a saucepan with water and use it in the same manner. Remember to wipe the kettle or pan bottom before its next use.

Sauces | THICKENING

Here's an easy way to control the amount of thickener added when making a sauce. Use a child's "sippy" cup—a plastic cup with a drinking spout built into the lid.

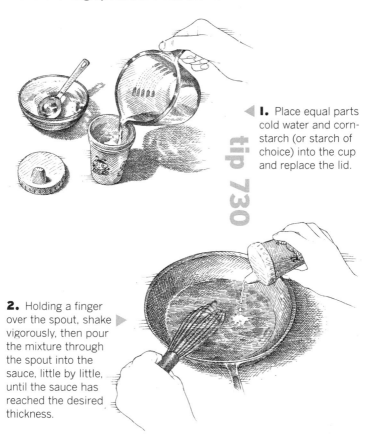

1. Place equal parts cold water and cornstarch (or starch of choice) into the cup and replace the lid.

2. Holding a finger over the spout, shake vigorously, then pour the mixture through the spout into the sauce, little by little, until the sauce has reached the desired thickness.

S

tip 730

Sauces | PREVENTING SCORCHED SAUCES

Pan sauces based on the caramelized drippings of sautéed meat, poultry, or fish (called fond) make simple, flavorful accompaniments to the main course. Many such sauces include aromatics (usually onions or shallots), which must be sautéed in the pan with the fond before liquid is added to deglaze. And that's where you can run into trouble. Occasionally, as the aromatics cook, the fond begins to overbrown, which can lead to a bitter sauce.

If the fond starts to darken too much, spread the aromatics over the area of the pan that's in trouble. The juices released by the aromatics keep the fond from burning.

Sauces | SAUCEPAN SPLASH GUARD

Here's an easy way to prevent simmering sauces from splattering onto the stovetop.

Fashion a splash guard from a round aluminum take-out container by poking at least a dozen holes in it with a skewer. The holes allow the steam—not the splatters—to escape.

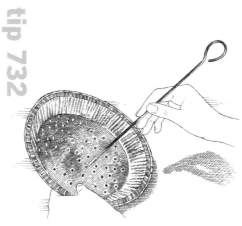

Sauces and Stocks | ACCURATE REDUCTION

When reducing a liquid for a sauce or stock, it can be difficult to accurately determine when the liquid has reduced to the desired amount. This method is a surefire way to get an accurate read.

Before making your sauce, place enough water in a saucepan to equal the volume of the reduced sauce. Place a clean metal ruler into the water and note the mark the water reaches. Empty the pan to prepare the sauce. Periodically dip the ruler into the sauce to see if the sauce has reduced to the right level.

tip 733

S

Sauces and Stocks | DEFATTING

Although overnight refrigeration is the best way to defat a stock or sauce, here is a method that works well for defatting liquids while they're still warm.

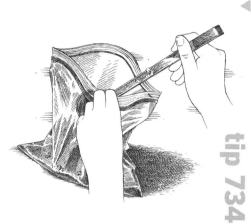

1. Allow the liquid to cool just slightly and then place it in a large, heavy-duty zipper-lock bag. Seal the bag and allow enough time for the fat to rise to the surface of the liquid.

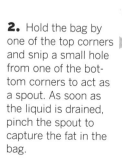

2. Hold the bag by one of the top corners and snip a small hole from one of the bottom corners to act as a spout. As soon as the liquid is drained, pinch the spout to capture the fat in the bag.

Scales | READING KITCHEN SCALES

Bulky containers, large roasts, and the like can obscure the display on a digital scale.

1. Steady a light-weight cake stand on the scale and set the tare at zero.

tip 735

2. The cake stand, which is wide enough to accommodate large pans and big cuts of meat, elevates items so that the display is visible.

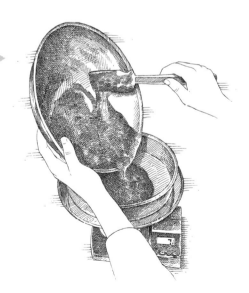

Scales | KEEPING THE DIGITAL SCALE CLEAN

Weighing raw meat directly on the platform of a digital scale is not a great idea in terms of kitchen hygiene. Rather than cover just the platform with a sheet of plastic wrap, try this technique.

tip 736

Slide the entire scale into a large zipper-lock bag. The buttons are usable and the readout is visible through the plastic bag, which can be washed and reused for the same purpose.

Scallions | SLICING WITH SCISSORS

Slicing or chopping scallions with a knife often crushes their natural tube shape and spoils their appearance. Use this method with scallions as well as chives.

Starting at the green end, use scissors to cut neat, intact pieces of scallion.

tip 737

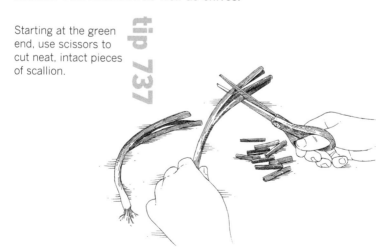

Scallops | REMOVING TENDONS

The small, rough-textured, crescent-shaped muscle that attaches the scallop to the shell often is not removed during processing. It will toughen if heated and should be removed before cooking.

With your fingertips, gently peel away a single tendon from the side of each scallop.

S

Scallops | GRILLING

To promote browning when grilling scallops, skewer them. This will also make it easier to turn many scallops at one time.

Thread the scallops onto doubled skewers so that the flat sides of each scallop will rest on the cooking grate. To turn the skewers, gently hold one scallop with a pair of tongs and flip.

Shallots | MINCING

There are several ways to mince a shallot. We like this technique, which also works with garlic.

1. Place the peeled bulb flat-side down on a work surface and slice crosswise almost to (but not through) the root end.

tip 740

2. Make a number of parallel cuts through the top of the shallot down to the work surface.

3. Finally, make very thin slices perpendicular to the lengthwise cuts made in step 2.

Shortening | MESS-FREE MEASURING CUPS

Many pie bakers have experienced the frustration of trying to clean measuring cups that have contained a solid fat such as shortening or lard. Here's a good way to avoid the mess.

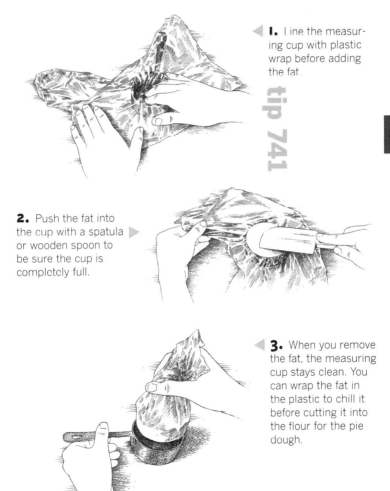

1. Line the measuring cup with plastic wrap before adding the fat.

2. Push the fat into the cup with a spatula or wooden spoon to be sure the cup is completely full.

3. When you remove the fat, the measuring cup stays clean. You can wrap the fat in the plastic to chill it before cutting it into the flour for the pie dough.

S

Shrimp | DEVEINING WITH SHELLS ON

When cooked by dry heat (pan-searing or grilling), shrimp are best left in their shells. The shells hold in moisture and flavor the shrimp as they cook. However, eating shrimp cooked in their shells can be a challenge. Slitting the shells before cooking is a good compromise—the shrimp are easy to peel at the table, but the flesh is protected as they cook.

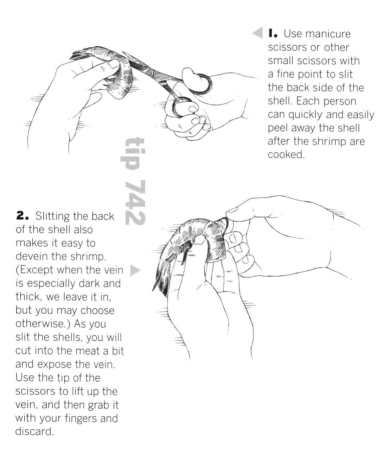

1. Use manicure scissors or other small scissors with a fine point to slit the back side of the shell. Each person can quickly and easily peel away the shell after the shrimp are cooked.

2. Slitting the back of the shell also makes it easy to devein the shrimp. (Except when the vein is especially dark and thick, we leave it in, but you may choose otherwise.) As you slit the shells, you will cut into the meat a bit and expose the vein. Use the tip of the scissors to lift up the vein, and then grab it with your fingers and discard.

Shrimp | GRILLING

Shrimp should be skewered before grilling to keep them from falling through the grate. However, every cook has been frustrated by shrimp that spin around on skewers and are impossible to turn.

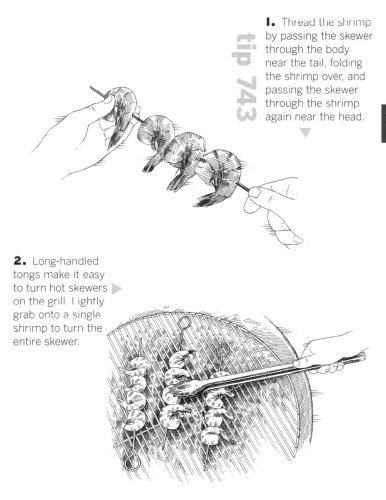

1. Thread the shrimp by passing the skewer through the body near the tail, folding the shrimp over, and passing the skewer through the shrimp again near the head.

2. Long-handled tongs make it easy to turn hot skewers on the grill. Lightly grab onto a single shrimp to turn the entire skewer.

Smoothies | SMOOTHIE POPS

Instead of letting any of the smoothie left behind in the blender melt and go to waste, save the remainder and you'll have a quick snack for another time.

tip 744

Freeze the leftover smoothie in ice pop molds (or 3-ounce waxed paper cups). Let the "pops" freeze partway before placing a popsicle stick in the middle, then freeze them till firm.

Smoothies | BOOSTING FLAVOR

Many recipes for fruit smoothies call for both ice cubes and fruit juice, but some cooks don't care for the dilution introduced by the ice. Here's how to chill your smoothies and add extra flavor.

Trade the ice cubes for chopped frozen juice bars (aka all-natural ice pops) in complementary flavors. Half of a 4-ounce bar will replace three ice cubes in a recipe.

tip 745

Snow Peas | OPENING NEATLY

Stuffed snow peas make tasty and attractive hors d'oeuvres. Neatly opening each pod, however, can be tiresome. This method streamlines the process.

A seam ripper is the perfect tool for opening the pods neatly and quickly.

tip 746

Soups | DRIP-FREE LADLING

Here's an easy way to keep drips and spills to a minimum when ladling soups or stews.

tip 747

Before lifting the filled ladle up and out of the pot, dip the bottom back into the pot, so the liquid comes about halfway up the ladle. The tension on the surface of the soup grabs any drips and pulls them back into the pot.

Soups | QUICK-CHILLING

Soups and stews often taste best the day after they are made. They should be cooled to room temperature before being refrigerated. However, if you cook in the evening, this can mean waiting up until the wee hours just to get the soup in the refrigerator. Here's a quick way to bring down the temperature of a hot pot of soup or stew.

tip 748

Fill a large plastic beverage bottle almost to the top with water, seal it, and freeze it. Use the frozen bottle to stir the soup or stew in the pot; the ice inside the bottle will cool down the soup or stew rapidly without diluting it.

Soups | FREEZING IN SINGLE-SERVING PORTIONS

Homemade soup is a winter treat that's easy to freeze, but most people freeze it in large, multiserving portions that make for a lot of unnecessary defrosting when the need for just one or two servings arises.

1. Set out a number of 10- or 12-ounce paper cups for hot beverages and fill each with a portion of cooled soup (but not all the way to the top). Label, wrap in plastic wrap, and freeze each cup.

S

2. Whenever you want a quick cup of soup, remove as many servings as necessary from the freezer and microwave them until they're hot.

Soups | STRAINING OUT SOLIDS FROM STOCK

Once you have simmered chicken backs or fish heads to make stock, it can be cumbersome to strain out the solids. The solids can splash, and you risk losing a fair amount of liquid in the process.

We use a large pot with a pasta insert to make stock. When the solids have given up their flavor, simply lift the insert and its cargo out of the pot easily and neatly. For clarity, the remaining liquid should be strained, but without any large solids in the pot this job is much easier and neater.

Soups | FREEZING STOCK IN CONVENIENT PORTIONS

Many recipes call for small amounts of stock. Instead of defrosting a large container of homemade stock just to get a cup or two, you can freeze stock in small portions.

I. Ladle the stock into nonstick muffin tins and freeze.

2. When the stock is frozen, twist the muffin tin in the same manner you twist an ice tray, tapping the bottom with a knife to loosen if necessary. Place the frozen blocks in a zipper-lock bag, seal tightly, and use as needed.

Soups | FREEZING STOCK IN PLASTIC POUCHES

Here's another good way to freeze stock in small portions. Stock frozen this way takes up very little room in the freezer.

I. Line a coffee mug with a quart-sized zipper-lock bag. (This keeps the bag open so both hands will be free for pouring.)

2. Fill the bag almost to the top with room temperature stock and seal it. Repeat until all the stock has been placed in bags.

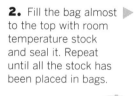

tip 752

3. Stack the bags flat in a large, shallow roasting pan and freeze. Once the stock is solidly frozen, the bags can be removed from the pan and stored in the freezer wherever there's room.

Spaghetti | BREAKING LONG STRANDS NEATLY

Broken spaghetti or linguine is used in some casseroles, such as turkey Tetrazzini. Here's a tidy way to break spaghetti strands in half.

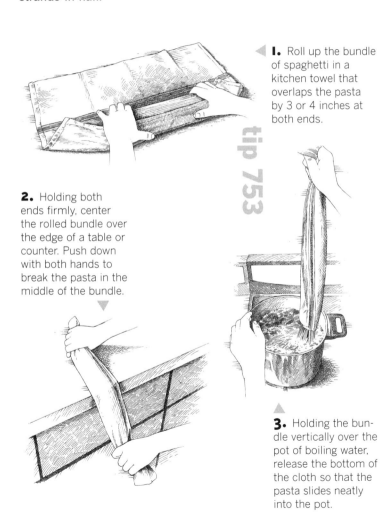

1. Roll up the bundle of spaghetti in a kitchen towel that overlaps the pasta by 3 or 4 inches at both ends.

2. Holding both ends firmly, center the rolled bundle over the edge of a table or counter. Push down with both hands to break the pasta in the middle of the bundle.

3. Holding the bundle vertically over the pot of boiling water, release the bottom of the cloth so that the pasta slides neatly into the pot.

tip 753

Spatula | OFFSET SPATULA SUBSTITUTE

A large offset icing spatula is a great tool, but you can pay a premium price at kitchenware stores.

Head to the hardware store and buy an offset palette knife with a flexible blade, which is normally used for mixing small amounts of paint or Spackle. The knife works almost as well as an icing spatula, and it costs only one quarter to one half as much. Palette knives can also be purchased at art supply stores.

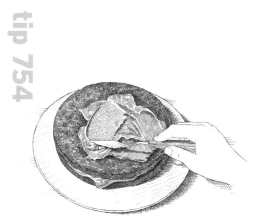

Spices | APPLYING SEASONINGS TO A ROAST

To ensure that meat is well seasoned, it's important to apply seasonings evenly. This is especially important when coating a roast with cracked peppercorns or a spice rub for grilling. Here's how we apply seasonings to beef tenderloin, pork loin, and other large roasts before cooking.

Set the roast on a sheet of plastic wrap and rub it all over with a little oil. Sprinkle with salt, pepper, or other spices, then lift the plastic wrap up and around the meat to press on the excess.

Spices | STORING EFFICIENTLY

It can be frustrating to sort through a drawerful of spice bottles, lifting and replacing each one, to find what you are looking for. Here's a better way to find spices and keep track of their age.

1. Using stick-on dots, write the name and purchase date on the lids of spice jars when you bring them home from the market.

tip 756

2. Now it is easy to locate and extract the spice you want and to know when a spice is past its prime and should be replaced. Dry spices should be discarded after one year.

Spices | MEASURING NEATLY

Measuring spices can be tricky, especially if measuring spoons won't fit into narrow bottles. Also, many cooks measure spices right over the mixing bowl, which can lead to overspicing of foods. Here's how we measure spices, leaveners, and salt in our test kitchen.

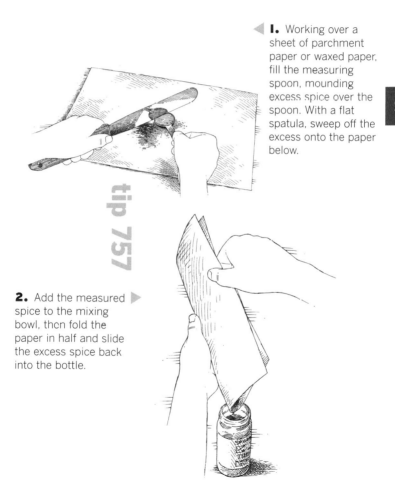

1. Working over a sheet of parchment paper or waxed paper, fill the measuring spoon, mounding excess spice over the spoon. With a flat spatula, sweep off the excess onto the paper below.

2. Add the measured spice to the mixing bowl, then fold the paper in half and slide the excess spice back into the bottle.

tip 757

S

Spices | SHAKER FOR SPICE RUBS

Don't throw away empty store-bought spice jars—give them a second life instead.

1. Gently pry the perforated lid off the jar, refill with your favorite homemade spice rub, and snap the lid back in place.

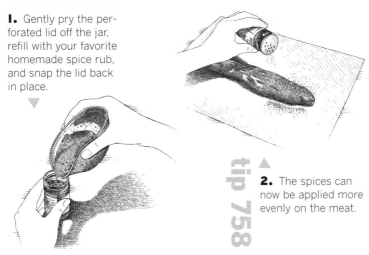

2. The spices can now be applied more evenly on the meat.

tip 758

Fill empty spice jars with flour and different types of sugar (granulated, confectioners', cinnamon). When just a pinch, teaspoon, or tablespoon is needed, there's no need to pull out flour and sugar canisters. Flour-filled jars are also useful for dusting work surfaces, and jars filled with confectioners' sugar can be used to decorate baked goods.

tip 759

Spices | REMOVING SPICES EASILY

Some soup or sauce recipes call for cooking spices and herbs in the liquid and then removing them before serving. Instead of fishing around for black peppercorns, cloves, star anise, bay leaves, or garlic, try this tip.

Place the spices in a mesh tea ball and then drop the closed ball into the pot. Hang the chain over the side of the pot for easy removal.

tip 760

S

Splatter Screen |
IMPROVISING WITH A WIRE-MESH STRAINER

Splatter screens are handy when frying, but if your kitchen doesn't have one, try this substitute.

tip 761

An overturned wire-mesh strainer of the appropriate diameter will work just as well.

Squash | CUTTING WITH A CLEAVER AND MALLET

Winter squash are notoriously difficult to cut. Even the best chef's knives can struggle with their thick skins and odd shapes. We prefer to use a cleaver and mallet when working with large winter squash.

1. Set the squash on a damp kitchen towel to hold it in place. Position the cleaver on the skin of the squash.

tip 762

2. Strike the back of the cleaver with a mallet to drive the cleaver deep into the squash. Continue to hit the cleaver with the mallet until the cleaver cuts through the squash and opens it up.

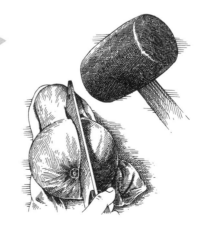

Squash | REMOVING SEEDS

Digging through the cavity of a winter squash to remove seeds and strings can be tedious, even with a large spoon. Here's a better way to ready squash for cooking.

Use an ice cream scoop with a curved bowl to cut out all the seeds and strings without damaging the flesh. Because the edge on this kind of scoop is very sharp, it cuts easily, and because the scoop is larger than a spoon, it can remove more seeds in a single swipe.

tip 763

S

Steaming | PREVENTING SCORCHED PANS

When using just a little bit of water and a steamer basket, it's easy to let the pot run dry, causing a potentially dangerous situation. When steaming foods that take a long time to cook, such as artichokes, here's how to figure out when the pot needs more water.

Before cooking, place a few glass marbles in the bottom of the pan. Add the water and the steamer basket, cover, and cook as usual. When the water level drops too low, the marbles will begin to rattle around, and the racket will remind you to add more water.

tip 764

Stews | CUTTING YOUR OWN MEAT

Packages of "stew meat" sold in supermarkets often contain misshapen scraps of varying sizes. For even cooking, pieces should be 1½-inch cubes.

Buy a boneless roast (from the chuck) for beef stew and cut it into chunks yourself. This way you can also trim excess bits of fat and gristle.

tip 765

Stews | DEFATTING

It's easy enough to remove excess fat from a brothy soup in a flash—use a gravy separator. With a chunky stew, this method just won't work.

Instead, place a large lettuce leaf on the surface of the stew; it will absorb excess fat, and you can then remove and discard the leaf.

tip 766

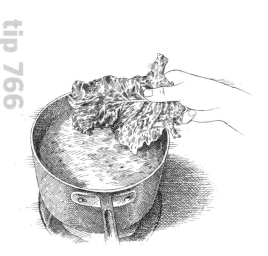

Stir-Frying | ADDING GARLIC AND GINGER

One of the biggest complaints home cooks have about stir-fries is that the garlic and ginger can burn and give the food a burnt, harsh flavor. Instead of adding the garlic and ginger at the start of the cooking process, try this method.

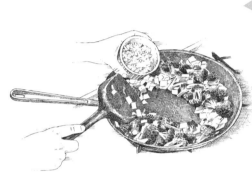

1. Stir-fry the meat, seafood, or poultry and remove it from the pan. Stir-fry the vegetables. Once the vegetables are crisp-tender, clear the center of the pan, add the garlic, ginger, scallions, chiles, or other aromatics, and drizzle with a little oil.

2. Use a wok shovel or spatula to mash the garlic and ginger as they cook. After about 10 seconds, stir the garlic and ginger mixture into the vegetables, add the seared meat, seafood, or poultry along with the sauce, and finish cooking.

Strainer | SMALL STRAINER STAND-IN

If you don't happen to have a small strainer suited for straining the juice of one or two lemons, and would rather not haul out your larger strainer, try this tip.

tip 768

I. Save the leftover mesh bags from small produce items (such as shallots or new potatoes). After cleaning the bag well, drop in a lemon half.

2. Squeeze as much juice as needed. All of the seeds and pith will be trapped in the mesh bag.

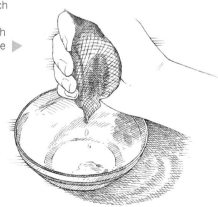

Strawberries | HULLING

Early-season strawberries can have tough, white cores that are best removed. If you don't own a strawberry huller, you can improvise with a plastic drinking straw.

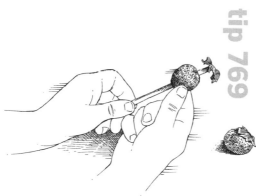

Push the straw through the bottom of the berry and up through the leafy stem end. The straw will remove the core as well as the leafy top.

tip 769

S

Stuffing | TAKING THE TEMPERATURE

When cooking a stuffed chicken or turkey, it's important to measure the temperature of the stuffing as well as the bird. Stuffing is fully cooked and safe to eat at 165 degrees.

Insert an instant-read thermometer into the center of the cavity to measure the internal temperature of the stuffing.

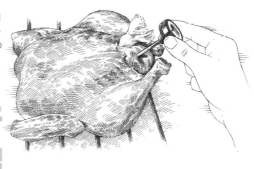

tip 770

Sugars | EASY FLAVORED SUGARS

Cinnamon sugar is commonplace, but sometimes you might want something different on hand for stirring into coffee and tea, sprinkling onto fresh fruit, and decorating cookies, muffins, or homemade doughnuts. Use the food processor to make ginger, vanilla, chocolate, citrus, and cinnamon sugars.

For ginger or vanilla sugar: Process 2 teaspoons minced candied ginger or ¼ fresh vanilla bean with 1 cup sugar in the workbowl of a food processor for 45 seconds to 1 minute.

For chocolate, citrus, or cinnamon sugar: Add 2 teaspoons cocoa powder, 2 teaspoons grated fresh zest from one lemon, lime, grapefruit, or orange, or ½ teaspoon ground cinnamon to 1 cup sugar and pulse 20 times in the workbowl of a food processor.

tip 771

Store the chocolate and cinnamon sugars at room temperature in sealed containers for several months. Store the ginger, vanilla, and citrus sugars in the refrigerator for up to 1 week.

Tacos | QUICK TACOS

Tacos should be an easy weeknight meal, but measuring and mixing the seasonings each time you want to make a batch isn't particularly efficient. To speed up the process, prepare the seasonings in packets ahead of time.

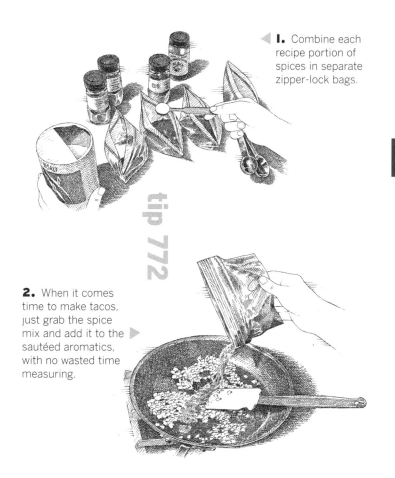

1. Combine each recipe portion of spices in separate zipper-lock bags.

2. When it comes time to make tacos, just grab the spice mix and add it to the sautéed aromatics, with no wasted time measuring.

Tacos | AVOIDING MESSY TACOS

Crisp taco shells are an essential component to any great taco, but stuff them with filling and toppings, and they inevitably shatter. Here's a way to avoid the mess.

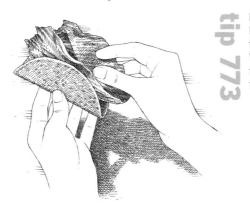

tip 773

Line the shell with a lettuce leaf, then add filling and toppings. When the shell shatters, the lettuce contains the filling.

Tacos | MELTING CHEESE

Grated cheese is a must-have garnish for ground beef tacos. And if grated cheese is good, then melted cheese is even better. Melting the cheese in the individual taco shells is no problem if you use this trick.

tip 774

Arrange the shells on a baking sheet so they can be warmed in the oven before they're filled. Sprinkle a bit of grated cheese onto each shell, and the cheese will melt as the shells warm up.

Tartlets | FILLING INDIVIDUAL SHELLS

Filling individual shells with a custard or other filling can be both messy and tedious. To fill the shells with speed and precision, use a bulb baster.

I. Place the filling in a measuring cup, then fill the bulb baster from the cup.

tip 775

T

2. Move the bulb baster directly over the tartlet shell and squirt out just the right amount of filling. Repeat until all the shells are filled.

Tarts | ROLLING THE DOUGH

Sweet tart pastry, called pâte sucrée, can be sticky, as can regular pie dough. Instead of coating the work surface with a thick layer of flour (which will just make the dough dry and crumbly), use this method for rolling out sticky dough.

1. Place the chilled dough round between two sheets of plastic wrap. Roll the dough outward from the center with even pressure.

tip 776

2. When the dough has reached the desired size, peel off the top sheet of plastic, flip the dough into the tart pan, and then peel off the second sheet of plastic.

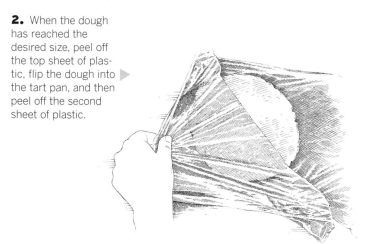

Tarts | LEVELING THE EDGES

The edges of a tart shell should be flush with the rim on the pan. Here's how to remove excess dough.

Once the dough has been fitted into the tart pan, run a rolling pin over the top of the pan to break off any dough that rises above the rim.

Tarts | STORING AN UNBAKED SHELL

Tart dough that has been rolled out and fitted into a tart pan can be refrigerated for a day or two or frozen for several months. Here's how we protect the delicate pastry from picking up off flavors or falling victim to freezer burn.

An 8- or 9-inch unbaked tart shell can be slipped right into a gallon-sized zipper-lock bag. Seal the bag and then refrigerate or freeze as desired.

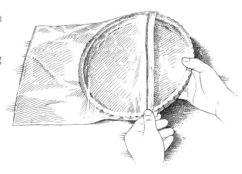

Tarts | PROTECTING THE EDGES FROM BURNING

Sometimes the edges of a tart shell can burn before the bottom is cooked through and nicely browned. Instead of covering the edges of the tart shell with aluminum foil, here's a simple way to protect the crust.

If you notice that the edges are browning too quickly, invert the ring from a second, larger tart pan, place it over the endangered crust, and continue baking.

Tarts | EASY UNMOLDING

Once a tart has baked and cooled, you need to remove the outer ring. Lifting up the removable pan bottom with your hand causes the ring to slide down your arm like a hula hoop. Here's an easy way to remove the ring, without any complicated maneuvers.

Set a wide, stout can, such as a 28-ounce tomato can, on a flat surface. Set the cooled tart and pan on top of the can. Hold the pan ring and gently pull it downward—the can will support the pan base and the tart as you remove the ring.

Tarts | IMPROVISING A COVER

A footed cake stand is probably the best plate for serving a baked tart. But what about the leftovers? A cake stand won't fit in most refrigerators.

Place the tart, still on the removable pan bottom, in the refrigerator. Invert a springform pan and place it over the tart. The tart will be protected and you can stack items on top of the springform pan.

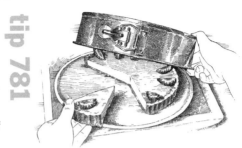

tip 781

Tea | DOUBLE-DUTY FLAVORING

Here's a creative way to add honey to a cup of tea, and add a hint of cinnamon at the same time.

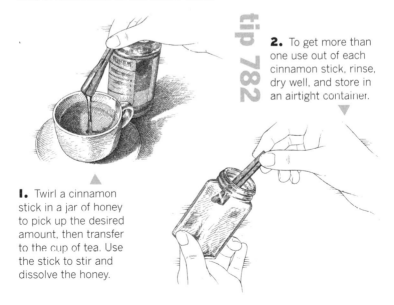

tip 782

2. To get more than one use out of each cinnamon stick, rinse, dry well, and store in an airtight container.

1. Twirl a cinnamon stick in a jar of honey to pick up the desired amount, then transfer to the cup of tea. Use the stick to stir and dissolve the honey.

Tea | TEA-BAG STAND-INS

Here's a way to prepare loose tea without a tea ball or sieve—put a paper coffee filter to use.

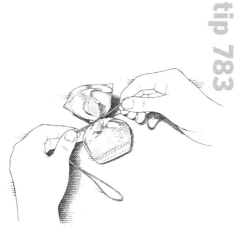

tip 783

When making a pot of tea, place the tea (or an herbal blend—chamomile flowers, mint, and so forth) in the center of the filter, then gather the edges and tie them with cooking twine. When trimming the twine, leave a little extra length to use for pulling the bag out of the cup or teapot when it is done steeping.

tip 784

Use this method for making just one mug of tea: Line the mug with a cone-shaped coffee filter large enough to extend over the rim. Fold the filter over the rim to secure, then fill with loose tea and add hot water. When finished steeping, just pull out the filter and squeeze gently, as you would a regular tea bag.

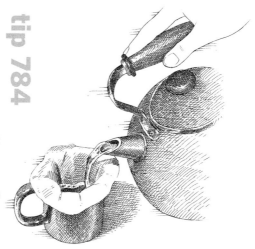

Tea | ADDING SUGAR TO ICED TEA

When sweetening iced tea, there's an easy way to guarantee that there won't be any undissolved granules of sugar left behind. Keep a jar of sugar syrup, known as simple syrup, on hand in the refrigerator.

To make the syrup, combine 1 cup water and 1 cup granulated sugar in a small saucepan. Set the pan over medium heat and whisk frequently, until the sugar dissolves completely. Simmer for 4 minutes, remove from the heat, and cool. For more flavor, simmer one of the following ingredients with the water and sugar:

• ½ scraped fresh vanilla bean and seeds for Vanilla Simple Syrup.

• 3 tablespoons packed mint leaves for Mint Simple Syrup.

• 3 ounces fresh berries (raspberries, blackberries, or blueberries) for Berry Simple Syrup.

• 2-inch piece of ginger cut into 4 coins for Ginger Simple Syrup.

• 2 teaspoons grated citrus zest (lemon, lime, or orange) for Citrus Simple Syrup.

Strain the flavorings out of the syrup once it cools.

Tea | MAKING LARGE BATCHES

Brewing a large batch of tea is efficient, but it can be messy to fish out all those hot tea bags.

Put loose tea bags into a potato ricer and submerge the basket in a 3- to 4-quart pot of just-boiled water. Once the tea has reached full strength, simply lift the ricer out of the pot and discard the tea bags.

Tea | REMOVING TEA BAGS

A pitcher of iced tea requires the use of several tea bags. To keep the tea from tasting bitter, the bags should be removed after steeping for 3 minutes. Here's an easy way to remove the tea bags without having to reach into the hot liquid.

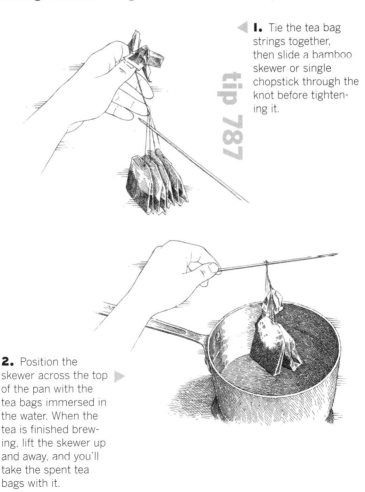

1. Tie the tea bag strings together, then slide a bamboo skewer or single chopstick through the knot before tightening it.

2. Position the skewer across the top of the pan with the tea bags immersed in the water. When the tea is finished brewing, lift the skewer up and away, and you'll take the spent tea bags with it.

tip 787

T

Teakettle | PREVENTING SPUTTERING

To prevent boiling water from sputtering from the spout of a metal teakettle, try this trick.

tip 788

Run the hot metal spout under cold water just before pouring out the contents.

Tomato Paste | EASY SQUEEZING

Squeezing the entire contents out of a tube of tomato (or anchovy) paste can be difficult. A rolling pin or round wooden spoon handle can make the task easier.

Place the opened tube on a piece of parchment or waxed paper. Starting at the far side of the tube and pressing down gently, roll the rolling pin (or round handle) along the length of the tube.

tip 789

Tomatoes | CORING

Tomatoes are almost always cored—that is, the tough stem is removed and discarded. Before chopping or slicing a tomato, we always core it. We also suggest coring before peeling because coring provides a practical place to start when it's time to peel.

Place the tomato on its side on a work surface. Holding the tomato stable with one hand, insert the tip of a paring knife about 1 inch into the tomato at an angle just outside the core. Move the paring knife with a sawing motion, at the same time rotating the tomato toward you until the core is cut free.

tip 790

T

Tomatoes | PEELING

Once you blanch and shock tomatoes (or stone fruits), a knife can still sometimes fail to remove the skin effectively. If that happens, try this easy method to remove the skin.

tip 791

Place stubborn fruits in a kitchen towel and rub lightly.

Tomatoes | QUICKER CORING

Here are a couple of unique ways to core tomatoes.

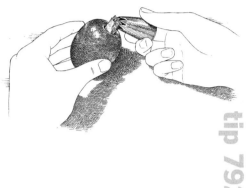

Use the large star tip you normally pull out just once a year when using a pastry bag to make spritz cookies. Pierce the tomato at the stem scar with the pointed end of the tip, give it a twist, and use the tip to cut out and remove the core.

tip 792

You can employ a similar technique with an apple corer by inserting it halfway into the tomato.

tip 793

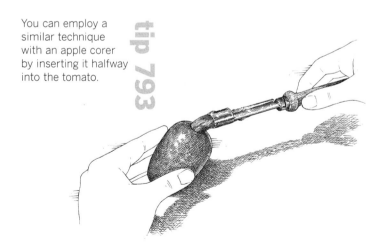

Tomatoes | PEELING

There are many recipes that call for peeling fresh tomatoes. If left on, the peels can separate from the flesh and roll up into hard, unappetizing bits when the tomatoes are cooked. Here's how to get rid of the skins on standard round tomatoes as well as on oblong plum, or Roma, tomatoes.

1. Place cored tomatoes in boiling water, no more than 5 at a time. Boil until skins split and begin to curl around the cored area of the tomato, about 15 seconds for very ripe tomatoes or up to 30 seconds for firmer, underripe ones. Remove the tomatoes from the water with a slotted spoon or mesh skimmer and place them in a bowl of ice water to stop the cooking process and cool them.

2. With a paring knife, peel the skins using the curled edges at the core as your point of departure. (The bowl of ice water serves a helpful second function—the skins will slide right off the blade of the knife if you dip the blade into the water.)

tip 794

Tomatoes | SLICING

Unless you have a very sharp knife, tomato skin can resist the knife edge and the tomato is crushed. Here's a trick that starts with a cored tomato.

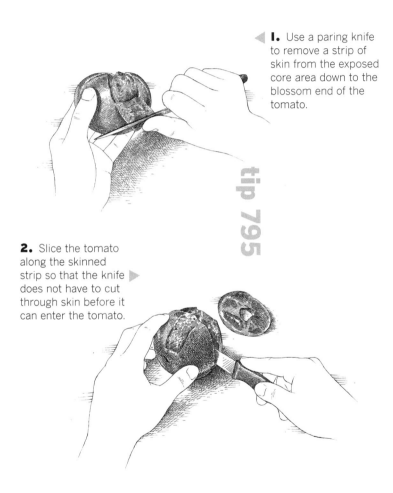

I. Use a paring knife to remove a strip of skin from the exposed core area down to the blossom end of the tomato.

2. Slice the tomato along the skinned strip so that the knife does not have to cut through skin before it can enter the tomato.

tip 795

Tomatoes | SEEDING

The seeds are watery and sometimes bitter and are often removed before chopping a tomato. These techniques work for both peeled and unpeeled tomatoes. Note that because of their different shapes, round and plum (also called Roma) tomatoes are seeded differently.

tip 796

To seed a round tomato, halve the cored tomato along the equator. If the tomato is ripe and juicy, gently give it a squeeze and shake out the seeds and gelatinous material. If not, scoop them out with your finger or a small spoon.

T

tip 797

To seed an oblong plum tomato, halve the cored tomato lengthwise, cutting through the core end. Cut through the inner membrane with a paring knife or break through it with your finger and scoop out the seeds and gelatinous material.

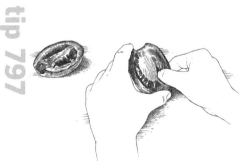

Tomatoes | NEATLY CHOPPING CANNED TOMATOES

Chopping juicy canned tomatoes can be a messy job, but it needn't be if you use one of these tricks.

Pour the canned tomatoes into a bowl and use a pastry blender to "chop" them.

You can also cut them up right in the can with a pair of kitchen scissors.

Tongs | STORING SAFELY

We love spring-loaded tongs for turning foods in skillets and on the grill. But put those tongs in a small drawer with other tools, and they can cause chaos. The tongs can become tangled with other tools and can even prevent the drawer from opening. Here's a safe way to store spring-loaded tongs.

tip 800

Slide the closed tongs into the cardboard tube from a roll of plastic wrap. The tongs can then be stored in the drawer without opening or interfering with other tools.

T

Tongs | CADDY FOR COOKING

The splay of tongs makes them unsuitable for placing on a spoon rest while cooking. We like this space-saving alternative for catching drips and spills.

Place the tongs in a heavy beer mug or coffee mug to keep your stovetop or counter clean.

tip 801

Tortillas | BULK STORAGE

The tortillas sold in bulk packages at warehouse-type supermarkets are much less expensive than those sold in smaller
packages at the grocery store. But if you freeze the whole
package, you'll end up ripping many tortillas as you try to free
just a couple from the frozen block.

tip 802

Before freezing,
separate the tortillas
with sheets of waxed
paper or parchment
paper. Place the stack
of separated tortillas
in freezer bags and
freeze as usual. The
paper dividers make it
easy to pull individual
tortillas from the fro-
zen pile.

Tuna | COOL TUNA

Tuna fish salad sandwiches are quick and easy, but like most people, we prefer tuna salad on the cool side, and waiting for it to chill after opening a new can isn't what we have in mind when hunger strikes.

Store cans of tuna fish in the fridge. (Recommended only for water-packed tuna.)

Turkey | CLEANER TURKEY PREP

Preparing a turkey for stuffing and trussing can be a slippery affair and a difficult mess to contain.

Work on a clean, thick, slightly damp large towel. The towel keeps the bird from slipping and sliding and impedes cross-contamination with the sink, cutting board, or counter. After putting the bird in the oven, simply roll up the towel and toss it in the laundry.

Turkey | BRINING OUT OF THE REFRIGERATOR

For years, we've advocated soaking a turkey in a saltwater bath before roasting. This process, called brining, produces a moist, well-seasoned bird. The problem is where to keep the turkey as it brines. A stockpot or clean bucket large enough to hold a turkey, 2 gallons of cold water, and salt simply won't fit in most refrigerators. A cold basement or garage can be used. When those options are not available, try this method.

tip 805

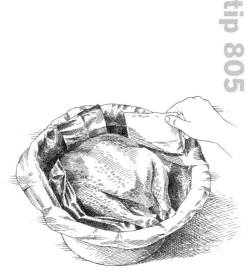

Line a large stockpot or clean bucket with a turkey-sized oven bag. Place several large, clean, frozen ice-gel packs in the brine with the turkey. Tie the bag shut, cover the container, and place in a cool spot for 4 hours. Because of the short brining time, you must use a lot of salt—either 2 cups of table salt or 4 cups of kosher salt. Once the turkey is brined, remember to rinse the bird well under running water and pat it dry with paper towels.

Turkey | REMOVING PART OF THE WINGS

Large turkeys can hang over the sides of even the largest roasting pan and drip fat onto the oven floor. Here's how to keep your kitchen smoke-free and get some extra parts to make gravy.

tip 806

Remove the first two joints of the wing, leaving only the drummette attached to the bird. Reserve the wings for use along with the neck, tail, and giblets when making gravy.

T

Turkey | TRUSSING THE CAVITY SHUT

Once the bird has been stuffed, you must close the cavity to prevent the stuffing from spilling out.

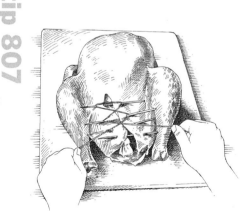

tip 807

Cut wooden skewers into four pieces, each about 5 inches long. Push the skewers through the skin on either side of the cavity. Use a 20-inch piece of heavy kitchen twine to lace the cavity shut, as if lacing a pair of boots.

Turkey | GAUGING DONENESS

For many cooks, the hardest part of preparing Thanksgiving dinner is figuring out when to take the turkey out of the oven. Use an instant-read thermometer properly, and you will never overcook a turkey again.

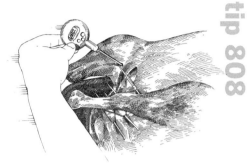

The breast is ready when cooked to an internal temperature of 160 degrees. However, the thighs are not really done until they reach an internal temperature of 175 degrees. For this reason, take the internal temperature of the bird in the thickest part of the thigh, as shown.

tip 808

Turkey | EASY TURNING

Many recipes for roasting turkey call for turning the turkey halfway through cooking. Care must be taken when lifting and turning a hot turkey.

Slip clean plastic produce bags over large oven mitts. The plastic will keep the mitts from getting greasy, and there's no chance of your burning your hands.

tip 809

Turkey | LEVERAGED LIFTING

Transferring a hot turkey from the roasting rack onto the carving board can be a messy, precarious maneuver. We find that two long-handled wooden spoons make this job easier.

tip 810

Insert the bowl ends of the spoons into either end of the bird's cavity so that the handles stick out. Grasp the handles, really choking up on them so your hands are right next to the turkey, and lift the bird off the rack.

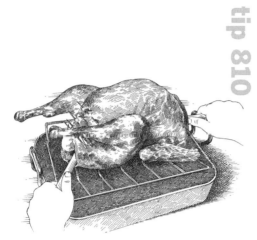

T

Twine | KEEPING IT CLEAN

When tying meat, you want to keep the ball of butcher's twine away from the raw food.

Place the twine on the handle of a meat pounder to prevent contamination of the entire spool.

tip 811

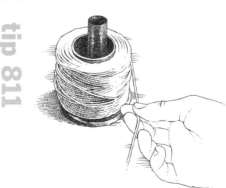

Twine | PRACTICING BUTCHER'S KNOTS

Many cooks have trouble tying roasts properly. Here's a clean way to practice your knotting skills.

tip 812

Tie strands of butcher's twine around a roll of paper towels. Once your have mastered the art of knotting, it's time to move on to food.

V-Rack | SECURING TO ROASTING PAN

If your V-rack and your roasting pan are not well matched in size, or if you have a nonstick roasting pan, the V-rack and its heavy contents can slide around the pan and create a dangerous situation. Here's how to stabilize a slippery rack.

Make four ropes of twisted aluminum foil and twist two onto each end of the V-rack base. Feed the free ends of the ropes through the pan handles and twist to fasten them around the handles.

tip 813

V-Rack | STABILIZING ON THE GRILL

A turkey roasted on the grill can be delicious. But the skin can burn if the turkey is cooked right on the grate. We prefer to elevate the bird in a V-rack. However, the base of some V-racks may slip through the bars on your grill grate.

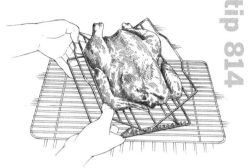

tip 814

Cover the grill grate with a wire cooling rack used for baking so that its bars run perpendicular to the bars on the grill grate. The cooling rack provides a stable surface on which the base of the V-rack can rest.

Vanilla | REJUVENATING DRY BEANS

Vanilla beans are costly, so many cooks are reluctant to throw away beans that have dried out after prolonged storage.

tip 815

Place the dry bean in a closed container overnight (or, better yet, over two nights) with a fresh piece of white bread. The moisture from the bread should soften the bean enough to let you split it and scrape out the seeds.

V

Vanilla | REMOVING SEEDS FROM A BEAN

A vanilla bean adds the truest vanilla flavor to ice cream, custards, and puddings. The seeds inside the bean have the most flavor. Here's how to free the seeds from the pod.

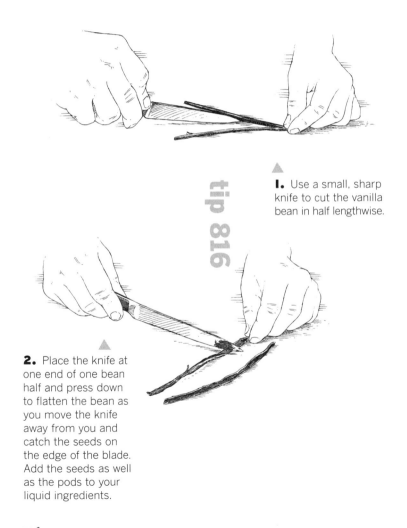

1. Use a small, sharp knife to cut the vanilla bean in half lengthwise.

tip 816

2. Place the knife at one end of one bean half and press down to flatten the bean as you move the knife away from you and catch the seeds on the edge of the blade. Add the seeds as well as the pods to your liquid ingredients.

Vegetables | PUTTING DOWN ROOTS

Ginger, carrots, and beets tend to spoil in the vegetable drawer if not used within a relatively short span of time. Here's a way to keep these root vegetables usable for several months.

1. Fill a plastic container or clay pot with clean, dry sand. Bury ginger, carrots, or beets in the sand, and store the container in a dark, cool cupboard or in the refrigerator.

tip 817

V

2. When you're ready to use a vegetable, just brush off the sand and peel.

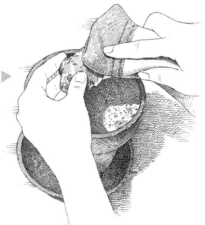

Vegetables | SHOCKING

Vegetables, especially green ones, are often partially cooked in boiling water (a process called blanching) to set their color. The blanched vegetables are then "shocked" in ice water to stop the cooking process.

tip 818

Drain the vegetables into a strainer, then plunge the strainer into a bowl of ice water. When the vegetables have cooled, lift the strainer from the ice water and let the water drain back into the bowl.

tip 819

If you run out of ice to shock vegetables after blanching them, reach for a chilled ice cream maker insert instead. Fill it with cold tap water and after the vegetables are finished cooking, shock them in the cold water in the insert. The water remains cold for at least one batch of vegetables.

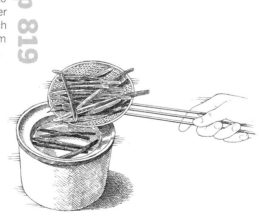

Vegetables | THE ULTIMATE PREP SHORTCUT

While some cooks enjoy the Zen of chopping vegetables for stir-fries or pizza toppings, others consider the task a necessary evil—time-consuming and tedious. Here's what to do if you fall in the latter camp.

Head to the nearest salad bar. Many supermarkets now feature salad bars where cooks can pick out a wide variety of ingredients, cleaned and chopped, in just the quantities they need.

Vegetables | WARMING THE SERVING BOWL

Steamed vegetables can cool off quickly. Here's a way to slow the process.

When steaming vegetables, invert a heatproof serving bowl over the steaming pot so it will heat up while the vegetables cook.

Vegetable Peeler | SHARPENING

A paring knife can be used to restore the edge on a dulled peeler.

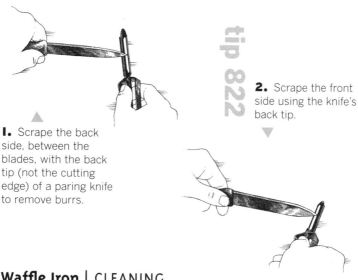

2. Scrape the front side using the knife's back tip.

1. Scrape the back side, between the blades, with the back tip (not the cutting edge) of a paring knife to remove burrs.

Waffle Iron | CLEANING

The nonstick surface of most waffle irons is easy to clean, but getting in between the ridges of the iron can be a challenge.

Cotton swabs are just the right size to wipe away residue in between the iron's ridges.

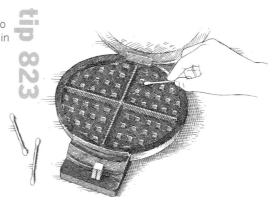

Walnuts | SKINNING

The skins from toasted walnuts can impart a bitter taste to dishes. Here's a simple way to remove these thin skins.

Once the nuts have been toasted, rub them inside a clean kitchen towel. The skins will separate from the nutmeats.

tip 824

Water | PREVENTING BOIL-OVERS

Most cooks with electric stoves who need to quickly cool down a hot pot move it to another burner. Instead of risking a burn while trying to move a large pot of angrily bubbling water, try this safer alternative.

W

tip 825

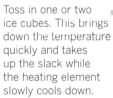

Toss in one or two ice cubes. This brings down the temperature quickly and takes up the slack while the heating element slowly cools down.

Water | QUICK FILTERED-WATER CHILL

Don't wait for filtered water to chill in the refrigerator.

Add ice to the filtration pitcher reservoir before refilling with tap water.

tip 826

Water Bath | MAKESHIFT BASE

Many recipes for baking individual custards recommend lining the water bath pan with a kitchen towel to insulate and cushion the ramekins, but this leaves you with a sopping wet towel.

Instead, line the water bath pan with a nonstick silicone mat (such as a Silpat). The mat will keep the ramekins in place and, unlike a towel, won't need to be wrung out or laundered.

tip 827

Wine | FREEZING LEFTOVER WINE

The next time you're tempted to toss out that last bit of wine from an unfinished bottle, save it for another use instead.

Try freezing leftover wine. The next time you need a little wine to finish a sauce, there is no need to open a fresh bottle. Measure 1 tablespoon of wine into each well of an ice cube tray and freeze. Use a paring knife to remove each wine cube, then store in a zipper-lock bag. Add frozen cubes to sauces as desired.

tip 828

Wine Bottle | FISHING OUT CORK CRUMBS

Few things are more frustrating than fishing out bits of cork that have fallen into a freshly opened bottle of wine. If you're tired of this task, try this ingenious trick.

Insert a plastic drinking straw into the neck of the opened bottle and over the cork crumb, then place a finger over the end of the straw and lift it out. A vacuum is created in the straw that traps the cork crumb along with a little wine.

tip 829

W

Wine Glasses | DRYING ON CHOPSTICKS

With one wrong move or an inadvertent bump, a dish rack filled with drying dishes can wreak havoc on delicate stemware. Here's a good way to dry glasses in a safe corner of the counter, out of harm's way.

tip 830

Set up chopsticks (the square-sided kind are best) parallel to one another and about 1½ to 2 inches apart on the counter. Place the wet glasses on the chopsticks to dry. The slight elevation off the counter allows air to circulate into the glasses and speeds drying.

Yogurt | YOGURT WITH THE FRUIT ON TOP

Here's an attractive way to serve yogurt with the fruit on top instead of hidden at the bottom.

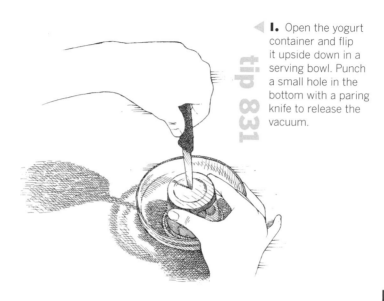

1. Open the yogurt container and flip it upside down in a serving bowl. Punch a small hole in the bottom with a paring knife to release the vacuum.

tip 831

2. Lift the container straight off, leaving the yogurt and fruit behind.

Y

Zest | COLLECTING ZEST NEATLY

If you're tired of watching citrus zest fly off your Microplane zester and all over the work surface, try this simple solution.

tip 832

Invert the whole operation. When you turn the zester upside down, so that the teeth face down and the fruit is under the zester rather than above it, the shavings collect right in the trough of the zester.

Zucchini | DRYING

Many recipes calling for grated zucchini recommend salting it before cooking to rid it of excess water. Drier zucchini browns better and tastes better. However, there's not always time to salt zucchini and wait for an hour or two. Here's a quick way to remove excess water. You can also use this technique for yellow summer squash.

tip 833

I. Shred the zucchini on the large holes of a box grater or in a food processor fitted with the shredding disk.

2. Wrap the shredded zucchini in paper towels and squeeze out as much liquid as possible. When dry, the zucchini is ready to be cooked.

Zucchini | SEEDING

When making stuffed zucchini, it is necessary to scoop out the seeds with a spoon. In fresh zucchini, the seeds and flesh can be very firm, making this job difficult. Here's an easy way to loosen up the seeds. This tip also works with eggplant.

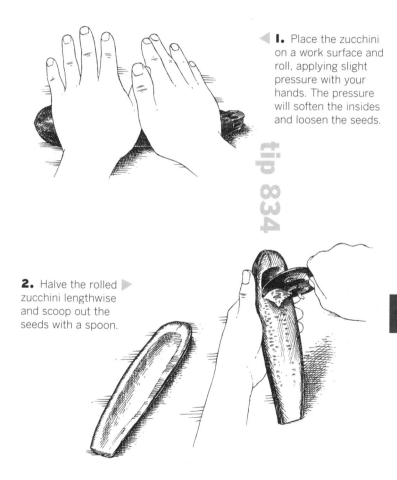

1. Place the zucchini on a work surface and roll, applying slight pressure with your hands. The pressure will soften the insides and loosen the seeds.

2. Halve the rolled zucchini lengthwise and scoop out the seeds with a spoon.

Z

index

A

ACIDULATED WATER, freezing spent lemon shells for, 368

ALMOND PASTE, softening, 2

ALUMINUM FOIL:
capturing bacon grease with, 15
cleaning grill grate with, 278
covering platter with, for use before and after grilling, 288
improvising bread mold from box of, 48
improvising flame tamer with, 228
improvising roasting rack with, 476
making extra-wide sheets of, 3
making wood chip packet with, 276
protecting pie crust edge with circle of, 448
removing brownies from pans with, 62
securing V-rack to roasting pan with, 544
shielding muffin tins from burned batter with, 387
storing boxes of, 355
stuffing cookware handles with, to prevent overheating, 165
taming to fit pan, 4
wrapping stovetop grates with, for roasting rack, 477

ANCHOVIES, mincing, 5

ANCHOVY PASTE, squeezing tube efficiently, 530

APPLE CORER, coring tomatoes with, 532

APPLES:
baking, 6
coring, 6, 7

APRON, substituting large shirt for, 8

ARTICHOKES, steaming, 8

ASH, removing from grill, 289

ASPARAGUS, trimming tough ends of, 9

AVOCADOS:
mashing easily, 291
pitting, 10
slicing and peeling, 11
testing for ripeness, 9

B

BACON:
drippings:
removing from pan, 15
saving for another use, 14
flavoring oven-fried, 12
separating pieces of, 12
storing, 13

BAGELS:
cooking fried egg to fit, 52
shaping dough into rings for, 16–17

BAGS:
improvising small strainer with mesh bag, 516
packing picnic sandwiches in bread bags, 437
securing garbage bags, 244
using pie weights in ovenproof bags, 446
see also Paper bags; Plastic bags; Zipper-lock bags

BAKING POWDER, testing for freshness, 24

BAKING RACKS:
drying breaded cutlets on, 119
improvising drying racks with, 343
protecting meat crust with, 378

BAKING SHEETS:
cooling pastry cream on, 421
fitting aluminum foil to, 4
improvising large trivet with, 346
keeping parchment paper in place on, 20
keeping stovetop clean with, 133
removing kernels from corn on, 175
removing pizza from grill with rimless, 286
storing in vertical file, 356

L

LACE COOKIES, shaping, 156–57

LASAGNA, making small batches of, 361

LATTICE-TOP PIE CRUST, cutting evenly, 437

LAZY SUSAN, frosting cake on, 85

LEEKS, cleaning, 362

LEFTOVERS:

gauging temperature of reheated, 329

marking containers of, 335

LEMON GRASS:

bruising, 368

mincing, 369

LEMON REAMER, improvising, 364

LEMONS:

basting grilling food with, 282

freezing slices for beverages, 363

freezing spent shells, 368

juicing, 364, 367, 516

mashing for lemonade, 365

removing peel from grater, 366

removing tea stains with, 137

seasoning chicken with, 109

see also Citrus fruits

LETTUCE:

basting grilling food with, 282

coring and washing, 370

defatting stews with, 514

lining taco shells with, 520

steaming dumplings on, 198

LIDS:

holding sautéed foods on, 345

inverting on pot to save oven space, 332

lifting hot, 170

protecting recipes with clear, 472

securing chopsticks in dishwasher with plastic, 130

storing, 168–69

see also Jar lids

LIMES:

freezing spent shells of, 368

juicing, 364

LIQUIDS:

capturing from steaming clams, 42

measuring, 23, 316

LOAF PANS:

draft-free rising in, 47

improvising of, 42

making lasagna in mini, 361

releasing breads from, 50

taking temperature of bread in, 49

LOBSTER:

distinguishing hard-shells from soft, 371

draining of water before eating, 371

LUNCH BAG, weighing flour in, 229

M

MAGNETS, keeping parchment paper in place on baking sheet with, 20

MALLET, cutting squash with, 512

MANGOES, peeling and slicing, 372–73

MARBLES, placing in steaming pan, 513

MARSHMALLOWS:

plugging ice cream cone with, 310

protecting cakes with, 95

MARTINI SHAKER, improvising, 140

MASKING TAPE:

creating pull-tabs for boxes with, 487

removing stencils from cake icing with, 93

using for labels, 330, 335

MATS. *See* Cutting mats; Silicone Mats

MAYONNAISE, drizzling oil into, 374

MEASURING:

brown sugar, 59, 60

butter, 66

cake batter, 76

dough, 47, 149

honey, 306

ice water, 313

ingredients, in advance, 21

liquids, 23

spices, 509

water, 328

see also Instant-read thermometer; Scales

MEASURING CUPS:

crushing peppercorns with, 429

hanging from key holder, 341

improvising, 375

reserving pasta water in, 419

using to keep track of dry ingredients added to mixing bowl, 22

VERTICAL FILE, storing wrap boxes in, 356

VISE-GRIP, cracking nuts in, 395

V-RACK:
improvising as rib rack for grill, 281
securing to roasting pan, 544
stabilizing on grill, 545
standing in drawer to control pot lids, 169

W

WAFFLE IRON, cleaning, 550

WAFFLES, keeping warm, 56

WALNUTS, skinning, 551

WASHING MACHINE, keeping beverages chilled in, 214

WATER:
chilling filtered water quickly, 552
preventing boil-overs, 551

WATER BATH:
improvising, 552
removing custards from, 189

WAXED PAPER:
keeping track of dry ingredients on, 22
measuring spices over, 509
placing on grater to catch lemon peel, 366
preserving pages of cookbooks with, 146
storing compound butters in, 67
storing tortillas in, 538

WELDER'S BRUSH, cleaning grill grate with, 278

WHISK:
chilling for whipping cream, 184
making ridges in gnocchi with, 260

WHISK BROOM, testing cakes for doneness with clean, 80

WINDOW CLEANER, using on floor after spilling oil, 134

WINE:
freezing leftover, 535
improvising rolling pin with bottle, 441

WINE CORKS:
cleaning knives with, 138
fishing crumbs out of wine bottles, 535
lifting hot lids with, 170
storing corn holders on, 175
storing sharp knives on, 354

WINE GLASSES:
drying on chopsticks, 536
protecting during washing, 138

WIRE RACKS:
extending counter space with, 340
rinsing brined poultry on, 470

WONTON WRAPPERS, using as ravioli wrappers, 471

WOODEN SPOONS:
lifting turkey with, 543
pressing garlic with, 249
protecting porcelain sinks with, 338
shaping stiff dough into rings with, 16–17

Y

YARDSTICK, affixing to counter to measure dough, 47

YOGURT CONTAINERS:
improvising measuring cups with, 375
improvising mise en place cups with, 326
inverting to get fruit on top, 537
turning into shakers for cookie decoration, 160
see also Plastic containers

Z

ZIPPER-LOCK BAGS:
applying icing with, 313
defatting sauces and stocks with, 492
enclosing digital scale in, 494
filling deviled eggs with, 206
freezing in:
bananas, 24
cookie dough, 152
lemon shells, 368
lemon slices for beverages, 363
small portions, 239
stock, 505